To J.

Enjoy the Memories!

Best

Andy Mele

MW00893412

THE BOYS OF BROOKLYN

THE PARADE GROUNDS: BROOKLYN'S FIELD OF DREAMS

by

ANDREW PAUL MELE

authorHOUSE®

AuthorHouse™
1663 Liberty Drive, Suite 200
Bloomington, IN 47403
www.authorhouse.com
Phone: 1-800-839-8640

First published by AuthorHouse 5/5/2008

ISBN: 978-1-4343-4040-5 (sc)

Printed in the United States of America
Bloomington, Indiana

This book is printed on acid-free paper.

This book is faithfully dedicated to every kid whose spikes touched the skinned fields of the Parade Grounds. If they were not ballplayers when they got there, they were when they left.

Also, to my wife Mildred and all the baseball wives who gave up Saturdays and Sundays so that their men could play a boys game.

And, to my children, especially my grand daughter Alexandra. Hopefully she will read this as history, and know that there once was another time and another place.

Author at Parade Grounds –1958

THE BASEBALL PURISTS PRAYER

"LET THERE BE LONG SLOW SUMMER GAMES;
ON REAL GRASS AND GEORGIA CLAY; WITH
WOODEN BLEACHERS AND NO DAMN DH."
-Anonymous

"IN MY MEMORY BROOKLYN WAS
SIMULTANEOUSLY
NAIVE' AND WONDERFUL
AND ONE HELL OF A PLACE TO GROW UP."
-Roger Kahn

CONTENTS

INTRODUCTION
MARTY MARKOWITZ - BROOKLYN BOROUGH PRESIDENT

There is no question about it; baseball is in every Brooklynite's blood. Ask any Brooklynite about their happiest memory and they'll talk about the day the Brooklyn Dodgers finally got the respect they deserved and beat the dreaded team from "Da Bronx" to win the World Series on October 4th, 1955. And all Brooklynites rue the day when "Dem Bums" pulled up stakes and went west to LaLa Land, aka Los Angeles, California. But the story of baseball in Brooklyn pre-dates the borough's infatuation with the Dodgers. And although the love affair between Brooklyn and America's favorite pastime was stoked in Ebbets Field, it was kindled long before in a patchy scrub of land near Brooklyn's Prospect Park. Set aside by the city for public recreation in 1869, the Parade Grounds teemed with boys and young men hungry for the game of baseball. By the 1930s, the Parade Grounds was one of the premier destinations in the country to scout for talent, and often drew daily crowds of 20,000 or more, in the 50s, many hoped to catch a glimpse of rising stars like Sandy Koufax or Joe Torre.

The Parade Grounds were and are a place where neighbors meet and families gather, where youngsters pick up a baseball and bat for the very first time. So the history of the Parade Grounds - like much of Brooklyn's history - reflects what is best about America: our diversity, our sense of fair play, and our continuing hope of redeeming the American dream.

FORWARD:

DAVE ANDERSON - NEW YORK TIMES

Sandlot baseball is where it all begins, whether in the United States, the Caribbean or Japan, and not only for eventual major-league players but for anybody who grew up fascinated by the game. And of all the areas in the world where sandlot baseball has thrived, the Parade Grounds in Brooklyn has been the game's most famous kindergarten, grammar school, high school, college, and graduate school all rolled into one.

Andy Mele knows this better than anyone and he writes about it better than anyone in "The Boys of Brooklyn," both the boys that made the big leagues and the boys that didn't.

Over the years, whenever I've talked to so many of those Brooklyn boys who made it, such as Sandy Koufax, Joe Torre or Willie Randolph, there is always a softness in their voice when they remember the Parade Grounds or any of their sandlot days. Not long ago I reminded Joe Torre, then the Yankees manager, of a championship sandlot game that was scheduled to be played at Yankee Stadium.

"It got postponed by rain, so we had to play across the street in Macombs Dam Park," he remembered, then his eyes flashed. " I hit a home run to right field."

Joe Torre, who grew up on the Brooklyn sandlots, hit that home run half a century earlier, but he remembered the details the same way that Andy Mele remembers the details of his sandlot years at the Parade Grounds, beginning when he and his teammates sold chances to their friends and neighbors in order to buy uniforms.

I related to that. In the Bay Ridge section of Brooklyn more than a decade before official Little League baseball arrived, I and my 12-year-old pals on a sandlot team known as the Warriors sold chances (3 for 25 cents) for a $5 prize and raised enough money to pay for gray uniforms with a red "W" on the left chest.

We didn't have or need a coach. We just gathered every afternoon and played with old, dirty baseballs, torn gloves and splintered bats on what was literally a sandlot, where Xaverian High School is today. When three real grass diamonds were built between Shore Road and the Belt Parkway, we played there, but the Warriors and my Our Lady of Angels parish team were never good enough to get to the Parade Grounds where Andy Mele and so many others played much more serious sandlot baseball. And where Andy now has written about it so well.

PREFACE

GAME TIME:

Brooklyn's Parade Grounds is a 40-acre tract of amateur playing fields adjacent to Prospect Park and two blocks south of Flatbush Avenue in the heartof New York's most populous borough. It has been a nebula for baseball talent throughout most of the twentieth century. Today when it is referred to, invariably mention is made of the major league stars who had their genesis at *The Park.*

More than sixty of the several hundred players who got their starts at the Brooklyn mecca and went on to professional careers reached the epitome of baseball achievement; the Major Leagues. This does not take into consideration the many more who got there in the late 19th century and the early years of the 20th century. It is not determinable at this point in time how many may have played at the Parade Grounds since its inception in 1869. Some, like Jimmy Wood and Josh Snyder preceded its origin. Undoubtably the vast majority of them didplay some of their early baseball at the Park. Some of the players from earlier years of the century like Waite Hoyt and Tommy Holmes, had long and distinguished major league careers.

During my time there, which was in the post WW II years, beginning in 1948 or '49 and lasting until 1965 when I made the transformation to softball, there were probably upwards of twenty or so to play there. Of those ultimate big leaguers I played against at least a dozen of them. The number of minor leaguers during that period was staggering.

There is a preponderance of memories from the mid-century years. A time when it was possible to be discovered on a sandlot, instead of being categorized and structured by preconceived talent. These differences in society today have created huge commercial enterprises out of athletics and would have undoubtably derailed talents like Phil Rizzuto, Bobby Shantz and possibly even a Whitey Ford because of their size.

Among those who achieved the heights after playing at The Park were the Torre brothers, Frank and Joe; Sandy Koufax; the Aspromontes', Ken and Bobby ; Tommy Davis, Rico Petrocelli, Willie Randolph and John Franco. Some, who made their marks in other fields are also regaled. Chuck Conners, TVs *Rifleman* is one; former governor of New York State Mario Cuomo also played ball at the Park as did a pretty effective left handed pitcher, New York Mets owner Fred Wilpon.

In part the development of young ball players is credited to the managers and coaches, those unerring educators , who taught the game from the ground up to willing and enthusiastic pupils.

Most accounts of Brooklyn baseball mention these names, but in such accounts you seldom read the names of Billy Gates or Wally Edge or George Lopac, yet these names are the heart and the soul of the Parade Grounds. The dreams of youth were born and nurtured there and often terminated with a heartrending finality.

There is a cultural history in the Parade Grounds story as well. As written in the *Brooklyn Daily Eagle* in August of 2006, "For more than a century the Prospect Park Parade Grounds has been the common sporting ground for generations of young athletes from Brooklyn's diverse neighborhoods and cultures."

The historical developments written here of the Grounds are factual as are the vast events and experiences presented in this account. However, there is of necessity a good deal of reliance on the memories and reminiscences of individuals and the years and the mind may render some of them suspect. Yet with that, there has been in many cases an amazing concurrence of events between the accounts of different people who shared the same experience and this in itself lends credence to such tales.

Any dialogue used cannot be accurate to the word since that may be stretching one's memory to the extreme, however, I have used dialogue to further the value of the narrative and the words used, if not exact, do represent the gist of the conversations as I remember them.

If the reader feels that fiction enters into the narrative, perhaps it is notable to recall the words of author Ernest Hemingway in the preface to his auto-biographical account , A Moveable Feast.

"If the reader prefers, this book may be regarded as fiction. But there is always the chance that such a book of fiction may throw some light on what has been written as fact."

-Andrew Paul Mele Staten Island, New York -July 2007

Parade Grounds Diamond # 1
1928 - courtesy Prospect park Alliance

The Clubhouse built in 1905 - c
irca 1917 courtesy Brooklyn Public Library
Brooklyn Collection

I.

A Moment In Time

"Baseball, it is said, is only a game. True. And the Grand Canyon is only a hole in the ground." -George Will

There is a 40-acre site of open land in the heart of a magical place called Brooklyn in the city of New York in the Empire state of the same name .And here men and boys play baseball.

The way it happened was that on the last day of the season there were three teams tied for first place. Now in the Parade Grounds League Open division, this was back in 1958, there were two eight team divisions. The winner of each would then meet in a best two-out-of-three playoff; much like the major league set-up at the time. The problem that arose was that there were only two weekends left in the season. The playoff would start on Sunday of week-end one and then go to game two on the following Saturday, game three, if necessary would be played on that Sunday. Now that left only the first Saturday to settle the three way tie.

So they decided that they would flip a coin and allow one team to draw a bye,   leaving the other two to play each other with the winner playing the bye team in the second game of a doubleheader on the Saturday. Naturally we didn't get the bye. The St. Bernadette club won it and they waited to play the winner of our game. We had to win both games to be the champs while they only had to win one.

Both games were to be played on Diamond # 1. A good crowd of several hundred settled in early. They were mostly regulars who came to the Parade Grounds on Saturday and Sunday afternoons to get some air and watch some good baseball. The league would provide the best of their umpires for games like this and so we had Pete Larkin behind the plate and Stevie Albanese on the bases.

Our club was the Seafarer Virginians and we drew Sacred Heart as our opponent . Their starting pitcher was Billy Litras, a right hander who could throw fairly hard and had a good curve that broke down and away from a right-handed batter. The whole game happened in the top of the first inning and in my mind's eye I can see it all as I have over and over again through the years.

Our lead off hitter was our first baseman Vinnie Marino and Vinnie singled sharply into right center field. Now we had Eddie Mack. Our manager, Fred Weber was coaching at third base and he was gyrating and throwing his hands around. We thought he might bunt so all of us on the bench plus Eddie at the plate kept our eyes on Weber. His hand went to his nose, across his chest, on the side of his leg. The bunt signal was hand on the belt. *"Belt....Bunt...B..B..even you guys can remember it!"* The catch was that there was an indicator. The sign was not a sign unless he flashed the indicator first. Eddie took two pitches without indicating that he might be bunting. Then Fred went to his ear lobe, the indicator, then to the belt. We all got it including Eddie Mack.

He squared off and dropped a beauty toward third. The throw went to first and Vinnie moved on to second on the sacrifice. Weber was taking no chances. With Hottinger pitching, he was expecting a low scoring game and wanted to get off on top. But our number three hitter, DeBarnardo, called *"Putsie"* by the rest of us, popped up to short. Tom Castaldo, our shortstop, hit fourth and was a good hitter with power. With me in the on deck circle, Litras wasn't going to let Tom hurt him. He kept the ball away and walked him on five pitches.

My turn came early. With two on and two out, I had a chance to get us a good start. There's nothing like a run or two in the first inning. Billy started me off with one of those big breaking curve balls that broke over for a called strike. It had me so fooled that I was actually pulling away toward third base. Then a fast ball was high. The next one was high again and I was ahead 2 and 1. I tried not to guess at the plate but just to be ready for anything, but I figured he would come back with that curve expecting me to bale out again.

I caught the spin and in one the proudest moments of my meager career stepped into the pitch and drilled one over the mound and into center field. Marino scored from second and Tommy went around to third. Frank "Chick" Chiarello followed me with a double to the gap in left-center; opposite field for the left handed hitter. Castaldo trotted home from third and I poured it on and scored all the way from first. Then our catcher Vinnie Tiani completed the scoring by driving Chick home with a single to left. Four runs for us in the top of the first inning. It was major because the game wound up with us winning 7-4. Carl Hottenger went all the way for us striking out nine, and he wasn't finished for the day as yet. In the second game we faced St. Bernadette and a good hard throwing right hander named Joe DiGirolomo. We always found him tough to hit. But we had Joe Galetto and it was again anticipated to be a low scoring game. As advertised, we went into the fifth inning trailing by a score of 1-0. Oddly, although we wound up with only four hits in the game, three came in the same inning, actually, back-to-back-to-back.

With one out in the fifth, "Putsie" DiBernardo singled, and Tom Castaldo hit one over the left field screen onto the steps of the refreshment stand. I then singled through the right side, but was stranded. I had walked the first time up and wound up with one hit in two official at-bats for the game. But the pulsating excitement came with two out in the seventh, the final inning in sandlot ball.

Galetto had thrown four strong innings, giving up just that one run, but Weber brought Hottinger back in the fifth inning after having thrown a complete game against Sacred-Heart. It wasn't the first time this had happened. On several occasions, Fred would tell Carl to sit under the huge trees in front of the Clubhouse between games and cool off. If it was a hot day, he might send somebody over there with a towel to fan him and keep him company. He did that this day and called for the skinny righthander to throw three more innings in relief.

We still were clinging to that one run lead. There was a walk after two were out, but it was getting very dark. There were no lights and a late September dusk seemed to descend rapidly. All of a sudden it seemed, I could barely see the hitter. I couldn't catch the sign from Castaldo at short; God only knows how he was able to pick up Taini's signs behind the plate. He flashed me each pitch but I had no idea what he was giving me. Then the ball was hit. I could tell that it was not hit hard and it was up in the air. Instinctively I moved back onto the outfield grass in short right, looked up and held out my arms; I had no inkling where the ball might be.

Then I glanced over toward short and there was Tom , his back to the infield racing into short left. I saw Siracusa coming in from left field, than stopping suddenly with his arms outstretched, having no idea either. It seemed that the only guy on the field who knew where the ball was was the shortstop. With his arms stretched out in front of him and his back to the infield he reached out and caught the ball.

It took a while for the rest of us to realize it, but then I saw Siracusa jump onTom and the others react in a slow, gradual way almost like a slowed up piece of movie film, only then did I realize that we had won. Mr. Staub came running all the way out to short right where I was and grabbed me and held on. We were the champions of the National Division of the Parade Grounds League Open Division and it was a glorious and memorable triumph. There was still a best of three series to be played against the champs of the American division, but we envisioned it to be anti-climatic. How wrong we were.

II.

It Starts With A Dream

"I never feel more at home in America than at a ball game, be it in Park or sandlot ." -Robert Frost

1958 began for me in the early spring when I heard that the Virginians would be holding open tryouts and I decided to give it a shot. My neighborhood team, the Dahills, were finished. At eighteen years old you had reached the end of "kid" ball. The senior division of the Parade Grounds League was for players sixteen to eighteen, and after that it was Open ball; no age limit at all. It saddened me in a way because I was the only one determined to move on. My friends either went to college and didn't have the time or got full time jobs and no longer wanted to devote their limited free time to playing baseball.

We had spent the last seven years as an organized ball club in league play. From the Grasshopper division; ten to twelve years; through senior ball, we laughed and practiced and played together. We were just okay having reached the heights only once. In 1954 our team, then called the Dahills won the Police Athletic League division championship and received gold medals, my first award ever.

I grew up on 35th street in the section called Kensington. It is bordered on the west by Dahill Road and 36th street which means that we just about made the Kensington boundary, abutting on Borough Park. 35 th street is only one city block long between Dahill Road and 14 th Avenue. Historically the section was first settled by Dutch farmers in 1851 and began to proliferate in earnest in the 1920s when Italian and Irish immigrants were attracted to the area.

It was a conglomerate of one and two family brick homes and five and six story apartment buildings which now includes co-ops. In the fifties there were mostly Italian and Jewish residents with some Irish, it has since evolved into an area of multi ethnicities .

Baseball, in one form or another, was always paramount in our neighborhood. We grew up on the streets. We played all the street games; johnny-on-the-pony, ring-o-lievo, kick-the-can. But stickball was king.

On 35th street we played it virtually every day during the spring, summer and fall seasons. Sundays in the summer were very special. On those afternoons the families would gather on the stoops and the porches and the open windows to watch the games. There would be radios tuned to Brooklyn Dodgers baseball and no one missed a pitch of either game. On our block there were two groups of players, the big guys and the little guys. Us little guys were thirteen and fourteen years old while the older group were past high school age and into their twenties. A few, like "Little Vic" were older than that.

There were stickball legends on 35st street also; Eddie Sarlo, "Little Vic" , and Al Burros. One of the best was Billy Nigro. Billy and his parents, Rose and Bill Sr. lived next door to us. On one of those Sundays I was there to witness the longest ball ever hit on 35st street and it was Billy Nigro who hit it. The pink rubber "Spauldeen" ball sailed from home plate, which was a sewer cover about two and a half sewer lengths in from from Dahill Road, across Dahill and over a peaked roof at the corner of Dahill and Avenue C. It landed on C - a good four sewer shot! Stickball was measured by sewer length, three sewers was considered a blast. Billy remembers that the game was against 40th Street and they played for $1 a man.

Billy could hit. He was one of the few of the big guys to play baseball and when he played at the Parade Grounds, often on Diamonds One or Thirteen , my dad and I went to see many of his games. Nigro played first base for three years at St. Francis Prep high school and with a sandlot team at Wingate Field. At a mere 5' 7 ½ inches tall, Billy was an artist around the bag ,he made only one error in those three years and he says it happened because "the webbing on the darn glove broke and the ball went right through". He was a left hander who hit from the right side. Later on when I was playing Open ball, Bill and I played together in the Twi-Light Industrial League. He had good power for a little guy, once hitting two home runs in one game. A headline in the *Brooklyn Eagle* read "Nigro emulates Kiner" referring to the Pittsburgh Pirates slugger.

Nigro had a try-out with the Red Sox, but during the workout an old football injury to a knee cartilage locked up on him and that ended that dream. Billy remembers Brooklynite Steve Lembo , at that time a Dodgers catcher, bringing pitcher Rex Barney to a confraternity meeting at our parish of St. Catherine of Alexandria on Ft.Hamilton Parkway in 1950. Billy loves to talk about the old days

When in his late twenties, Nigro relocated to Tucson, Arizona and hooked up with a team called the Commercials in an all-Mexican League. All the signals and instructions were in Spanish and Bill didn't understand a word. So they worked out a set of "Gringo signs" and it suited perfectly.

But after two seasons, Nigro's career came to an abrupt end at age 34. A severe auto accident cost him the sight in his right eye. At 72 years old, he is ebullient when speaking about the old days and philosophical about growing old. "Do you remember Lefty?" he asks, referring to the old stick ball gang. "Sure," I said. "He's dead," Billy tells me. "Little Vic is gone too." I asked him if he's seen Frankie Guttilla lately. "Yeah, the last time I was in. He was all bald ," he says ,"scared the living hell out of me . We're all getting old," he says although with no loss of enthusiasm in his voice, only surprise, as though he never expected that to happen. His mother Rose passed away years ago, she was the biggest Dodger fan of us all and cried when Bobby Thomson hit the home run in the '51 play-off. Billy says, "I had the rosary beads in my hand." I guess on that day God was a Giants fan. His dad is 96 and still on 35st street. "I call twice a day," Billy tells me. "I worry about him." I speak with Billy Nigro and I find myself back in 1948.

In our day there was no Little League, so we played our baseball all day every day on a lot next to the Thomas Brothers Moving and Storage Company on MacDonald Avenue. There was broken glass and rocks all across the lot and we regularly had to clear it out. There was one small boulder so deeply imbedded into the ground that we couldn't move it at all. Fortunately, we came up with a viable solution. We realigned the field and make the rock first base.

Vacant lots were certainly the *"diamonds of our boyhood dreams."* We played baseball on our own, no scheduled games or practice or meetings or uniforms. Well, we did have uniforms, we felt it was necessary. We each got our newest old sweat shirt and we cut letters out of some black cloth that Jerry Citrano's mom had down in her cellar. Then we asked our mothers to sew them onto the front of our shirts. How proud we were, we were the "Wildcats" and anyone passing the Thomas Brothers lot knew who we were.

We began our season very early, in February, while the remnants of the winter snows were still on the ground. We wore gloves to keep our hands warm under our baseball gloves and we played until it snowed again often in early November. We learned by doing and there were times when I must have gotten twenty-five hits in a single day; of course, I came to bat about three hundred times, but that was the process that led to our development.

Finally, it came together in 1951. It was time to move onward and upward. We had discussed it at length after Christmas and decided that our time had come. On a cold February Saturday morning we gathered on Eddie Mathieson's stoop on Dahill

Road and told him of our plans. We wanted him to manage our team but Eddie already had his hands full. He was a coach with the Open division "Clippers" at the Parade Grounds who were managed by Leo Johnson and Eddie managed the senior division Navajos and helped out with the Clipper Juniors of the Kiwanis League; but he promised to get us a manager and help us get started.

Eddie stood at the open door in a sweatshirt, freezing, and invited us down to his basement. "Okay, what's this all about?" Skelly was our spokesman. "We want to go into a league," he told him. "Wewant to play at Park Circle, on real diamonds, with umpires and everything."

"Well, okay," Eddie said as Mrs. Mathieson came down with chocolate milk and cookies. "Sounds like you fellas have given this a lot of thought." We all nodded vigorously. "I guess you figured the money out, huh."

"Money? What money?"

"Well, you'll need uniforms to get into a regular league. Then there's equipment,bats, balls, catchers gear, stuff like that. And of course, the league fee. Have your parents agreed to give it to you?" We looked at each other. Outside on the sidewalk we sulked, our dreams devastated. But Eddie said he would work things out and we trusted him to do anything he said he would do.

About a week later while me and Joe Skelly were walking past Eddie Mathieson's house, he tapped on the window and beckoned to us. "Everything's all set, " he told us. "Round up the boys and come over here Saturday around 10." We gathered on Eddie's stoop at nine and at nine-thirty Eddie opened the door with a chuckle. "Okay," he began when we were all assembled in his basement. "You'll be called the Dahill Cubs." Eddie and Dee and a couple of the other guys lived on Dahill Road.

"The uniforms will be grey with blue trim. A big English D over here." He placed his hand over his heart. "You'll play in the grasshopper division of the Ice Cream League." Nobody said a word. "Now for the fun part. How are you gonna pay for all this?" It seemed that the dad of one of our boys, Davy Stachel, his dad was Irving, had gone around the neighborhood soliciting in the form of donations. Nat Berger at the print shop on Church Avenue kindly consented to print raffle books. All we had to do was to sell them; to our families, our neighbors, and if each of us would sell his quota, Eddie said it would pay for everything. "I think after this you should all go down the corner and thank Mr. Berger and also Mr. Stachel." Which we did.

"Also, your manager is going to be Al Fortunato. He's a good ballplayer and knows everything you're gonna need to learn. Listen to him." We exhausted our families and inundated the neighborhood until we sold all of our raffles.

I got to be the shortstop, a deference to my idol, Pee Wee Reese.

Then we met the manager. Al Fortunato was nineteen years old, and loved the game. He had a shy, affectionate smile and his soft voice belied his truck driver physique. He was stocky, heavy across the chest with black curly hair. He knew baseball and wanted to impart that knowledge to us completely and in steady doses in the hopes that a goodly portion might take hold.

Al was an outfielder who played his ball at Erasmus Hall high school and Columbia University. He played sandlot ball at the Parade Grounds with a club called the Brooklyn Daytons. Like so many other teams, the Daytons had a history. Teams like this would play year after year, moving up to a higher level of play as the boys grew older. The Daytons played in the Brooklyn Kiwanis League and like so many of the Park clubs would send some members into professional ball.

A 6'5" side arming right hander named Bill Zonner spent some time in the organization of the Boston Red Sox. Zonner came from Flatbush, "30 Linden Boulevard ," he recalls, "just off of Flatbush Avenue, next door to the library." Zonner had those great high school years at Erasmus teaming up with pitcher Dick Miller and with the sandlot Daytons , where he played at the Parade Grounds with high school mates Miller, Al Fortunato and Archie Schwartz. The hard thrower signed with Boston right after high school in 1949 and went the minor league route through Birmingham, Albany, Greensboro and San Jose. He was on two occasions listed on the spring roster of the Red Sox. He says with a laugh, "I thought my full name was 'Well-Bill.' I heard it so many times. 'Well Bill , don't unpack. Well Bill we're leaving you behind. Well Bill you're going to Greensboro!'"

It was at Fenway Park in Boston that Zonner encountered Ted Williams. The club was on the road and the slugger had been injured and was in rehab. Bill was throwing batting practice when the great man came up for some swings. After a few pitches, Williams asked him to throw harder. "Bang- bang, line drives over second base," Bill remembers. "He told me to throw harder. Boom , more line drives . A little faster." Zonner remembers thinking, "hey, I'm here for my speed so let's see if he can touch it. I figured I'd give him everything." Zonner says he did and Williams kept peppering the outfield with line drives. "Can you put a little more on it? " Williams asked..

"There was nothing left," Bill laughs at the memory.

Zonner spent four years in the minors before encountering arm trouble. Years later his son, a doctor of sports medicine, diagnosed the shoulder ailment as rotator cuff .Zonner recalls how his dad attended every game he played at the Parade Grounds,standing behind the screen behind home plate gauging all of his pitches.

In spite of the injury, Bill says his last two years were not good enough and he probably would not have gone all the way anyway. Perhaps not, but Big Bill Zonner, living in the San Francisco bay area now , can relish the memories from Brooklyn toClass A Albany and to Fenway Park. Not a bad bit of recollecting.

The Daytons and Erasmus also produced a speedy outfielder by the name of Arthur Schwartz. Archie had five seasons in pro ball with several clubs beginning with the New York Giants. Another right hander named Dick Miller signed to play in the Braves organization in 1951.

Miller was from Borough Park and he was one of the many Daytons to play at Erasmus Hall HS. He and Zonner pitched virtually all the school games in 1949. It was in that season that the right hander threw two no-hitters. One against Westinghouse, the other in a game played at Ebbets Field against Manual training high. It was fifty years later at a reunion that a teammate pulled a dirty old baseball from the trunk of his car and gave it to Miller, the game ball from that no-hitter.

Miller began classes at Duke University and worked out with the baseball team which was coached by the old major league pitcher Jack Coombs. Coombs had won 31 games in 1910 and 28 in '11, while pitching for the Philadelphia Athletics and Miller figured that it was a good place to play ball. At Duke also was Dick Groat, a shortstop who would go on to a fourteen year career in the big leagues. After only one semester Miller signed with the Boston Braves and played a year in the Georgia-Florida League.

Drafted into the army, the 6'1" 197 pounder played baseball and football in Germany, calling it a great experience, getting to travel and play ball and "better than being out in the field with the infantry. We had a lot of fun." Miller completed his education at Adelphi and pitched for three years there. The fourth year he played shortstop. "It was a lot easier than pitching," he recalls. Dick and his wife are living in Virginia now , outside of Roanoke, and their three daughters are in three different cities.

Even with professional experience , Miller's fondest memory is of a high school game played in 1949. Memories fade but often not without a struggle. Dick Miller still has the " filthy, dirty," treasured baseball from that game.

Fortunato said years later that the Parade Grounds always was "a culture in itself." We all lived and learned within that structure from those early years until the day we quit. And I guess it has proven to stay with us even after that. At Erasmus Al credits coach Austin Dugan for turning him into a hitter. "I used a 36" Johnny Mize model bat, and Dugan made me believe it had some kind of magic or something in it," he now says with a chuckle. " I simply believed that I could hit with that bat."

Fortunato also developed his outfield skills. Taught how to field the ball while moving towards the base you were going to throw to, was just one of the fundamentals that made Al a better ballplayer. Dugan showed him how not to be distracted by players he was in competition with. "The only competition is yourself," he told him. "Just worry about how you do and not the other guy."

It was Fortunato's high school development as an outfielder that resulted in another outfielder turning to pitching. There was no room for Don McMahon in the Erasmus outfield and he ultimately went on to a long and successful major league career as a pitcher following his Erasmus days and his time at the Park with the Flatbush Robins.

Al had broken his leg in his opening game that year which made him very available to us. He spent a good portion of the season hobbling around on crutches and it was heartening to see him bouncing and skipping out to dispute some point with an umpire. He would hit grounders to the infield and fly balls to the outfield while leaning on his crutch. The young manager knew that catching fly balls was not as easy as it looked, especially for kids our age, and he kept peppering the air with fungoes to familiarize us with the ball in the air. He recalls particularly young Eddie Conti chasing down outfield flies. "I remember," Fortunato says now, "the way he got under a fly ball, you could see the Conti kid had talent."

Al had a trial with the Dodgers at Ebbets Field and he stood behind the batting cage awaiting his swings in batting practice against the fire-balling, but wildly erratic right hander, Rex Barney. He held his thin handle bat in his hands when Jackie Robinson approached him. "Here," Robinson said, handing Al one of his own thick handled models, "use my bat. You'll never hit this guy with that bat you're using." Robinson, one of the greatest line drive hitters in baseball, used a thick handle bat with more hitting surface and not such a limited "sweet spot."

Fortunato lost an opportunity to sign with the St. Louis Browns the following year because of another offer he felt compelled to accept. He was drafted into the army. But military baseball was good baseball in those days and at Fort Eustis, Virginia, Al played with and against some top pros. Vern Morgan, a third baseman would spend two seasons in the National League with the Chicago Cubs, and Vernon Law would win 162 games over 16 big league seasons. But at Ft. Eustis Law chose not to pitch and played first base.

Fortunato had always played center field, but with the Ft. Eustis team, he was moved to left in order to allow a kid who spent the '51 season with the New York Giants, a kid named Mays, to take over in center.

Years later one of Al's sons would research the newspaper archives in Newport News and come up with a box score that had his dad in the same lineup as Willie Mays. As teammates Al and Willie actually played a significant role in the contribution to baseball lore of Willie May's signature play, *the basket catch.*

It had been mentioned a number of times over the years that Willie had learned the maneuver from an outfielder in the army. Mays, in fact, referred to it that way. In an April 5, 1966 article published in *Look* magazine, the article (with Charles Einstein, his biographer), says that "a kid in the army taught him a new way to catch a fly."

Willie is quoted, "There was this one boy there who thought the way to catch a routine fly ball was to hold his glove like he was taking out an old railroad watch and looking at it."

At one point during a post game interview with Brooklyn's Happy Felton, Mays responded to the basket catch question by recalling a fellow who played the outfield with him in the army and tried to teach him the basket catch. When asked who the fellow was, Willie said that after the service he lost track of him. The fellow of course , was Al Fortunato.

Years later, Fortunato's son Michael published an article with the title, "My Old Man Taught Willie the Basket Catch."

Here is the way Al Fortunato remembers it today: "I do recall the conversations with Willie while shagging flies during batting practice and particularly the conversation about the basket catch. I was saying that when an outfielder sets himself to catch a fly ball (the standard way), there is a moment when the ball disappears from his sight as it is blocked by his glove, and that's where most dropped flies occur. We started tossing high silo flies to each other to test the theory. At one of these sessions he decided that the basket catch, which he occasionally used ,solved the problem I had posed, and that I should try the basket catch. Soon the whole crew of outfielders were paired off trying the basket catch, ignoring balls hit out to us by the guys taking BP, until Vern Morgan, the team coach and later a major league infielder, came out to remind us that we were out there to shag flies.

Mays went on to make the basket catch one of his signature plays and several people have mentioned that Willie referred to being taught the basket catch by a fellow outfielder on an army team. The truth is that he taught it to me, not the other way." Fortunato never adapted to the basket catch himself, never feeling quite comfortable with it . He felt better being able to set himself for the throw which he couldn't do with the basket catch. Nor was it as easy to deal with as it may have seemed. Mays would put his right hand beneath his glove hand for support. If the ball didn't land squarely in the pocket, there was always the chance that the ball smacking into the fingers would bend the leather back and the ball would drop out.

Mays explained in a 2006 interview that he did drop the ball twice. "I missed two," he said, "one in Pittsburgh, one in New York; ten years apart."

As an aside to Fortunato's memories, he recalls Willie doing something he has never seen anyone else in baseball ever do. Mays would fungo a fly nearly straight up into the air, then move over to where it descended , and hit it again before it dropped to the ground. On occasion, he would repeat the hittings 3 or 4 times. This was the coordination and skill that would product a Hall-Of-Fame ballplayer.

Al obtained the use of a classroom at a local elementary school, PS 230, and one evening each week for the entire winter we went to class. We were taught, lectured, implored about such things as the infield fly rule. He would call on one of us and that one would stand and recite..."the infield fly rule occurs when first and second or first, second and third base are occupied...."

Upon completion of the recitation, the student would take his seat. "Did he leave anything out?" Al would ask. Someone would raise their hand. "He forgot to say that the runners can run at their own risk." Al would nod approvingly. He printed copies of these kind of things for us to study. Also charts telling where each player goes when a sacrifice bunt is executed. First baseman charges, second baseman covers first, shortstop covers second. We learned because we loved the game almost as much as he did. He brought a bat into class and taught us how to square off for a sacrifice bunt. "One... two...three. Simple, three steps. Hold the bat level and loosely. Hey, don't grip it like that, you'll get your fingers busted."

By spring, we were ready and raring to go. But before the league opened we had to get permits from the Parade Grounds in order to practice. Permits were allocated for 2-hour sessions. And now it was my dad's turn to step up. My father was a police officer attached to the 74 precinct. The precinct house was on the grounds of the Parade Grounds adjacent to the clubhouse. It was his job to get the head Parky, Joe Grossman, to issue permits to us each Saturday morning from nine to eleven, and he succeeded brilliantly. Diamond # 11 became our home.

My dad was a player at the Park in his day also. He grew up on Navy Street near the East River and the Brooklyn Navy Yard. Paul Mele played the outfield at Manual Training high school and at the Parade Grounds with a club called the "Little Flower". He didn't play long after high school, but came to softball later on as a police officer. The 74th precinct team played their games at the Park. Growing up I saw him play many times where he continued into his forties.

I was there where his career came to a sudden and ignominious end on Diamond 3. Playing center field , he tried to make a shoestring catch on a sinking line drive. In the resulting fall, he suffered a broken elbow and could never throw well after that. He knew the game and when we went to Ebbets Field or watched the Dodgers on television, the conversation would usually be instructive. "Watch how low Pee Wee is on ground balls, you gotta stay down...." These were my earliest lessons and my first insight into the *inside* game.

I have an old photo of that 1940s 74th precinct team with my dad and his old friends. Some, like Andy Strangio and George Scrivani, I knew well, for they remained close friends for the rest of their lives. In the photo my father has an old glove on his hand, one of those flat ones with no pocket that you had to run your fingers all the way up into the glove in order to control it. He gave me that glove and I used it for a couple of years until he bought me one of my own.

I picked out the one that I wanted. A "Nokona" Bob Milliken model. Milliken was a pitcher who came to the Dodgers in 1953. I had a job delivering groceries for Nat Slater at his store on Church Avenue. My dad told me to save my money if I wanted a new glove. I saved my tips and when I had twenty dollars, he drove me to Friedman's Sporting Goods on Flatbush Avenue. Sam Friedman had the glove boxed and bagged before my father told me to put my money away and he paid for it. I suppose it was his way of teaching me the value of money.

I used that glove until 1957 when I bought a Wilson A2000, a great glove, and I've owned three of them over the next forty-eight years.

Once outdoors we could work on putting our textbook training to practical use. We worked on cutoffs, "hit the cutoff man, don't overthrow him." We practiced covering our respective bases on bunts. Invariably after practices we crossed the street into Prospect Park and lay on the grass or alongside the lake regaling in our good fortune to have Saturday mornings. Then we hit our stride. A column by Jimmy Murphy in the *Brooklyn Eagle.* Murphy was a known and respected columnist of local sports who did some bird-dogging on the side. It was said that he passed along the word on Koufax before Sandy did any real pitching.

The column centered on Ed Mathieson's activities with the Parade Grounds ball clubs and then, "The newcomer to Mathieson's repertoire is the Dahill Cubs, a 10-to-13 year-old Grasshopper aggregation." It went on to state how $105 had been raised to " buy uniforms for the Cubs." We had arrived. We were awed when the new uniforms arrived and we took pictures the first time we wore them.

On some Sundays Eddie took me with him to bat boy for the Clippers. They played double headers each week in the Parade Grounds League Open Division. The manager, Leo Johnson, always let me do it and I enjoyed it very much. There were some good ballplayers on the Clippers. An outfielder named Johnny Powers got as high as triple A ball. Some years later when I was in the army reserve and doing a two week stint at Camp Drum in New York State, me and a buddy took a week-end pass to Syracuse to see a game between the Syracuse Chiefs and the Columbus Jets; this was in 1961. Powers was down in the Columbus bullpen and he remembered me. We had an enjoyable and educational afternoon as John kept us clued in on the workings on the field.

The Clippers had a pitcher named Jerry Casale. We pronounced it Ca-sally. In the majors they called him Ca-sale. He ultimately signed with the Boston Red Sox and along with the Parade Grounds' Ken Aspromonte was considered a key prospect in the organization. Casale pitched for Louisville in the American Association and had a record of 17-11 with a .296

earned run average in 1955. The *Brooklyn Eagle* reported on his progress prior to the '57 season. "As usual," the newspaper wrote," Casale was the workhorse for the Seals (San Francisco in the PCL) last season, winning 19 and losing 11."

Jerry had gone to Manual Training high school and played also with Quaker Maid in the twi-light Industrial League at the Park. He came up with Boston in 1958 and had five seasons in the big time. On April 14,1958 Casale made his major league debut with a 7-3 win over the Washington Senators. He was a good hitter and helped his cause that day with a three run home run over the right field stands at Fenway Park off Russ Kemmerer. Casale could hit even as a kid and old timers at the Park remember the day that as a 15-year-old he pitched a 1-0 game on Diamond # 1 and won his own game with a home run that cleared the center field fence, over the pathway and into Diamond # 13. Jerry teamed up with Boston teammates Don Buddin and Pumpsie Green for three consecutive home runs on September 7, 1959. His best year was 1958 when he had a 13-8 record with Boston. It was in Detroit on June 18, 1961 that Casale tossed up home run number 24 to Roger Maris in his record breaking year.

We didn't win any titles that first year, but we held our heads up. The knowledge that Al had drummed into us all winter paid off. We had little talent, but a great deal of compensation because more than most of our opponents, we *knew how to play the game.* It delighted us to read our revues in the *Eagle.* "Tom Russo pitched a three-hitter and fanned eight, as the Dahill Cubs prevailed over the Ridge Royals 6-1."

We finished in the middle of the standings that year and in 1952, Al Fortunato was drafted into the army. What he taught us kept us abreast until at least the time we hit senior ball , and we won a championship as the Dahills in 1954.

Everyone in Brooklyn began their baseball in similar fashion.

Ray Pecorara is an attorney with a law office in Bensonhurst not far from where he lives and a mere few blocks from the house where he grew up. He started playing baseball in the forties in a program at St. Finbar's, the local parish church. Fr. Donegan ran the program. "He was my mentor," Pecorara said. "Tough, but fair. He used to go around the neighborhood and pull guys out of pool rooms."

Ray began with the Tyros, the youngest group and spiraled upward to the Open division and Ray rode the whole circuit. In 1947, '48' and '49, St. Finbar's qualified for the Journal-American tournament. The one-time daily newspaper sponsored the annual event. In '47 Ray's team was beaten 2-0 by a club in the Queens-Nassau League, the shutout pitched by a youngster named Whitey Ford. The next year it was a 4-3 loss to the same league champs. This time they were beaten by Billy Loes. In 1949 they finally won the tournament by defeating a Bronx team with no future major leaguers on it.

Pecorara attended Lafayette high school before it had such a superlative reputation, and contributed to the schools first championship in 1947. His performance in that game was notable. In the first inning Ray stole home. There is, however, an addendum to his brash exploit. The signal for a steal was right hand in the pocket. The coach slipped his left hand into his pocket which Ray misread for the steal sign.

Trailing by 5 runs, Lafayette tied the score in the ninth inning. In the tenth, with the future major leaguer, Ken Aspromonte on third base, Pecorara drove a hit into the gap in right center and *The Frenchies* were champions over Grover Cleveland high.

In 1948 Ray was a member of the Journal-American All-Stars. After getting a base hit in that game, the ambitious youngster started for second base, was caught in a rundown, and tagged out. The manager of the team was future hall-of-fame player, Rabbitt Maranville. "He bawled the hell out of me," Pecorara remembers. " 'Two runs behind and you gamble like that,' he said.' " The lawyer sat back in his chair, "embarrassed me, but I never made that mistake again." Ray also made the Dodger Rookies team that year. He went on to play at St. John's University, one year ahead of a sub outfielder named Mario Cuomo.

Ray remembers a game at the Parade Grounds in the Senior division against Our Lady Help of Christians in the CYO League. Pecorara belted one and circled the bases, but was out at home plate on a close play. The catcher hit him in the groin and a donnybrook ensued. Not at all an unusual scene at Park Circle.

Ray spoke of the old clubhouse. "I used to take a shower after games, a lot of guys wouldn't go in there, but I did," he laughed at the memory. "The shower pipes were rusted, the place was a mess." Ray Pecorara reflects after sixty years.

"There were a lot of fond memories for all of us at the Parade Grounds."

In the early fifties the trolley cars were still running and they crossed at Church and MacDonald Avenues near my home. The Beverly movie theater on the same corner was a Saturday morning refuge throughout the winter and my father drove a 1947Chevy. It was the end of the *Big Band Era* in music and names like Frankie Laine, Patty Page, Jerry Vale and the Four Aces dominated the pop charts. There was only one *King* then, and Nat "King" Cole was at the height of his reign. The decade would see the emergence of a new genre in music, as the teenagers took over as chief consumers of the recording industry. They called it Rock n' Roll. Elvis Presley would be crowned its King and names like Chuck Berry, Fats Domino and Bill Haley and the Comets would become household words, at least in every house that had a teenager living in it.

The onset of the decade brought the Korean war and in July of 1953 the truce ended it. All that remained throughout the fifties was the detonating of weapons of atomic destruction and the specter of annihilation of the planets' civilizations. But we evaded such mundane concerns with our games and movies and rooting for the Brooklyn Dodgers. The neighborhood was our world and it was self-relying, and autonomous. The candy store was our town hall. At Dahl's luncheonette on Church Avenue, Walter Dahl presided as the empirical wizard of the Chocolate Egg Cream, as well as friend and advisor to the neighborhood population.

Dr. Jonas Salk introduced his polio vaccine and the first open heart surgery was performed. On July 26, 1956 the luxury liner, the Andrea Doria, sank off Nantucket after colliding with the Swedish liner Stockholm. Fifty-one passengers died, more than 1700 were rescued.

On October 4, 1955 every neighborhood in Brooklyn went insane beginning at 4:43 PM when Pee Wee Reese threw out Elston Howard and the Brooklyn Dodgers were *Woild Champs*. Sir Edmund Hillary conquered Mt. Everest and Hoola Hoops were a fad. The great Joe DiMaggio retired and Willie, Mickey, and the Duke took over New York's center fields. At an old-timers game the four appeared together and Roger Kahn called them the *center fielders from Olympus*.

The lexicon of teen lingo went to words like *Cool*, meaning neat; *Hang Loose* said "hey, no sweat," and a guy's car was his *Wheels*. By mid-August of 1951 the Dodgers had taken a 13 ½ game lead in the National League. But you could never tell how a year or a decade would end up.

III.

The Best Of Times

"Those were the best days; the best times we ever had." *-Jack Lang*

By the time we were ready for Open competition, at eighteen years old, most of the guys had already decided to pack it in. Some, like little Davy Stachel figured it was over their heads and were just happy to have had the last seven years. Others, like Tommy Russo and Ed Conti went on to college and there just was no room in their curriculum for sandlot baseball. The rest were caught up in the time-warp. Jobs and girls and Larry Dolan joined the army.

I had no wish to quit playing but I didn't know if I was good enough to play at that level. Assuredly there were weak teams but I didn't know anyone at that point who could place me. Eddie Mathieson had retired to Florida and there was no one else for me to approach. Then I heard that the Seafarer

THE BOYS OF BROOKLYN

Virginians were going to hold tryouts one Saturday morning in the early spring of 1958.

They were one of the top clubs at the Park and I wondered why they were having these tryouts. I certainly didn't want to embarrass myself and in my reluctance I almost didn't show up. But at the last minute I got up my courage. What could they do to me? Would they laugh me off the field? I showed up. I was amazed at the turnout. There were forty or more senior players vying for a spot and now I was sorry I came.

The manager was Fred Weber, a redhead about as wide around as one of the poles that held up the backstop. Fred had been a pitcher and had a short fling in D ball, the bottom of the professional ladder , when he was signed by scout Jack Rossiter of the Washington Senators organization in 1949. Weber followed the path of most of the denizens of the Parade Grounds, having begun with a neighborhood team. He and his friends collected deposit bottles from neighbors and ran errands in order to raise the money for uniforms, which they were eventually able to purchase at *Progressive Sporting Goods* on New Utretch Avenue. In Fred's case, his first team they named the *Talons,* a talon being an Eagle's claw.

Most kid team names were meant to sound tough, like the *Tigers* or the *Lions* and that was the decided aim of Weber and his young teammates. Fred remembers their disappointment when they found out that the *Talon company* made zippers for the flies on mens' pants. The principal team in his area, the Borough Park section, was the *Ty Cobbs,* and in 1943 he joined the *Ty Cobb Jrs.* The organization was run by Jimmy *the Barber ,* a neighborhood legend.

In the mid-forties, the Ty Cobbs sent several players into pro ball. Nick Costello signed with Brooklyn, as did Steve Lembo and Tommy Brown. Brown was a shortstop with "a cannon for an arm" according to Weber. Tommy was in Ebbets Field in 1944 at age 16. He played nine seasons in the major leagues as a reserve infielder and was a Dodger during two world series; in 1947 and '49. Steve Lembo also was signed by the Dodgers , getting to the big club in 1950.He appeared in only seven major league games, but went on to a long and successful career as a Dodgers scout. In the late fifties when I was playing Open ball, Steve was a familiar sight at the Parade Grounds.

Fred Weber started life as a shortstop, but turned to pitching when he found out what he could do with a taped baseball. Taping a baseball was an art indigenous to 12 and 13 year-olds. You used white surgical adhesive tape and wound it tightly about the ball so that each strip barely caressed the strip it covered. There would be two slight bulges on opposite sides of the orb. Fred learned how to use those bulges to deliver sinkers and an assortment of curve balls. But he says,"No one told me not to throw curves every day." He developed chips in his right elbow and turned to throwing *junk* out of necessity.

His short pro career consisted of several weeks at Wellsville, New York in the Class D Pennsylvania-Ontario-New York League; the P.O.N.Y League. He came home to play for the Seafarer Virginians and Pete Cavallo. When *Petey Bull* packed it in after the 1956 season, Fred took over the running of the club. And so it was that I came to play for Fred Weber.

He was energetic and enthusiastic. He was all over the field and acted as though he really was looking for something. We were on Diamond One, the flagship field of the thirteen that made up the Park. It was completely enclosed, one of two like that, and had wooden bleachers running along both foul lines and behind home plate. The fence in center field was about four feet high and spectators would stop out there and drape their coats or shirts over the cyclone fence. A game on Diamond One could attract upwards of 2,000 fans.

There were a number of them on this day who stood around or sat on the bleachers. Some came specifically to watch, others were just passing. It was a relatively comfortable day and neighborhood people often came by to see whatever might catch their interest. They gave their opinions freely. "Hey, Fred, that kid looks pretty good over there. How about that third baseman? I saw him last year. You ought to keep your eye on him. What are you looking for anyway?"

Weber talked to them all, but said nothing, then went back to the field. His friend John Keegan, a catcher, who packed it in after the 1957 season, would coach for Fred this season. Johnny was hitting ground balls to the infielders. I did what I was supposed to do, but still wondered what chance I had. Some of these boys were pretty good and I didn't see myself ranking very high in anyone's expectations.

So it came as a complete surprise when Fred told me that I had made the club. It was very nearly a shock to discover that I was the only every day player to get picked. The other selection was a right handed knuckleball pitcher named Bob Stone. Bob and I would become good friends and he would be best man at my wedding in 1960. It wasn't until later in the summer that Freddy explained why he had chosen me.

The Virginians were a very solid club and Fred felt that they could win the title in 1958. But Tom Castaldo, a top notch shortstop, wanted to quit baseball. He'd been offered a pro contract but he didn't want to go to the low minors and "play for peanuts",so he turned it down. The Virginians played in the Parade Grounds League Open Division which meant a doubleheader every Sunday. They also took part in a Saturday league; another doubleheader; and played in the twi-light or Industrial League , week day evenings. This translated to five or six games a week and Tom decided that it was too much baseball and time to quit.

The main thrust was the Sunday league and Fred convinced Castaldo to stay with the stipulation that he would only play on Sundays. He determined that I was capable of holding down second, third, or short if need be. So he planned on using me at short on the days that Tom wasn't there. It was therefore my presumed versatility and not any exemplary ability that landed me a spot with the Seafarers. In any case I was glad to be there. We were a sponsored club so we had beautiful uniforms; white flannel with royal blue trim, Dodgers style, with raglan sleeves. One day the whole club met at Friedman's Sporting Goods on Flatbush Avenue to select bats. We each got to choose six bats for our own. This was like being a pro and I was flabbergasted by the treatment.

I was thrilled by my luck. I wasn't really that good a ballplayer, just a guy who could hold his own. In spite of this I still had dreams, though I kept them pretty much to myself.

In those days you could dream until you were nineteen or so. There was no draft, so a list of signable players wasn't laid out before you finished high school. There were scouts, and the Parade Grounds was full of them. They hung out watching games and there was always the lingering hope that one would catch you on a good day and flash a fountain pen and a piece of paper.

This inner hope was nurtured through those senior league years with the Dahills. We had dropped the Cubs after Grasshopper ball. The next level was labeled the Freshman division. It was between my time here and in the Senior division that I first heard the name Sandy Koufax. He played for a club called the Parkviews in the Coney Island League, usually playing games at Dyker Park in Bensonhurst., but he also played at the Parade Grounds. I never knew of him until he signed with the Dodgers in December 1954. He was scouted by Arthur Dede and Al Campanis.

A fellow I played with when we were both with the *Cardinals* had the opportunity to hit against Sandy at the Park. Or at least as John Chino tells it, to bat against him, or as it turned out to merely stand in the box. John said that he never saw anything so fast. Actually, he said that he never saw anything, the ball was in the catcher's mitt and he hadn't even seen it. And John Chino was a tough little competitor not given to exaggeration or excuses.

As the story goes Milt Laurie managed the Parkviews and his sons, Larry and Wally played for him. They knew Koufax and brought him over to play for the club and it was Milt who made him a pitcher. It is told this way in Jane Leavy's biography of Sandy and in it she cites a newspaper quote attributed to Koufax as saying, "My sandlot manager, Milt Laurie, was the first to recognize my ability." I knew and played against the Laurie brothers later on but never had any conversation about the pitcher. In any case, Sandy Koufax has been the most dominating ball player to come out of Brooklyn's sandlots. (1)

Koufax was scouted by other teams, notably the Pittsburgh Pirates, but the Dodgers' Al Campanis got the lefty's name on a contract. Sandy signed under the bonus rule of 1954 that made it mandatory for any player getting more than$4,000 to stay with the big club for a minimum of two years. Koufax got a bonus of $14,000 to sign and was relegated to the Dodgers' bench for the 1955 and '56 seasons. He was , however, one of ten Dodgers in franchise history to pitch a shutout in his first major league start. Sandy did in '55 beating the Reds 7-0.

Everyone I knew who had faced him spoke unerringly of his blinding speed and lack of control. The credit for Koufax's turnaround was given to a catcher on the Dodgers named Norm Sherry, the brother of Dodgers' relief pitcher Larry Sherry. In a spring game in 1961 after walking the bases loaded, Sherry told him to take something off the ball and "let 'em hit it." Bob Broeg in the *Sporting News* wrote that it was on a bus ride with Sandy and Norm seated together, that the conversation took place. (2)

He not only began to control his pitches, but it seemed that he didn't lose any of his speed. Along with control came a devastating breaking ball. Tommy Davis, in his book, *Tales from the Dodgers Dugout* ,says that Koufax had a curve that was nastier than his fastball. "It would start way up here, head high, and then Roseboro would catch it just above the plate." (3) Once the pieces were in place, Sandy was not only very nearly unbeatable, but almost unhittable as well. From 1961 to 1966 he won 129 games while losing just 47. Pirate slugger Willie Stargell uttered a most memorable quote when he said that trying to hit Koufax was like "trying to drink coffee with a fork." By the time I got to Senior Ball in 1956, Koufax was in his second year in the major leagues.

It was at the senior level that the competition began to accelerate. It was also here that we developed a rivalry that followed me into Open ball. From the *World Telegram and Sun* in 1956; the *Brooklyn Eagle* had folded early in 1955; "...tightest game was an 11-inning 1-1 deadlock between the Dahills and the Sabres. Tom Morrissey of the Sabers and Art Clemens were the opposing pitchers." Artie Clemens and I had played for the team at Erasmus Hall high school that year and I brought Artie over to the Dahills. With him and Tommy Russo, we had a great one-two mound punch.

Tommy Morrissey was a husky right hander who threw hard. He had a shock of black, curly hair and I cannot remember him without a thick, black mustache. He was six-feet tall and looked very intimidating both on and off the mound. In that regard, he had his physical characteristics working for him, but he did all he could to further the illusion. He liked throwing up and in to a right handed hitter. In the next few years he became tougher to hit and meaner on the mound. Along the way he picked up the sobriquet, "Moose", and it stayed with him to this day. It was not until 1958 that the newspaper accounts of games used the name "Moose."

Some years later, in the '80s, I organized a softball team and asked some of the old guys to play, Moose was one of them. It was arc-ball, where the ball is lobbed on a high arc. One day during a not particularly critical game situation, Moose turned to me at shortstop and beckoned me into the mound. "What's the matter, Tom?" I said. He looked at me a long time. "How the hell can I pitch in this game? I can't knock anybody down with this lollipop." "Do the best you can," I told him and like always ,he did. I once got two hits in three at bats against him. It was the last time I ever faced the Moose and the only two hits I ever got off of him. And this was after five years of facing him. I would be remiss if I failed to mention that the Moose was and is one of the nicest guys you'd want to meet. Perhaps all that meanness on the pitcher's mound wore him out, but I played with him and against him and it was a lot more fun having him on my side.

Years later Tom lost a leg to diabetes. We live near each other and I see him now and again. He limps a bit, his hair and mustache are steel grey, but he still scares the hell out of me.

The Parade Grounds got a good deal of local newspaper coverage. The *Eagle* wrote up games and made frequent mention of Park prospects. After the paper folded in early 1955, columnists like Jimmy Murphy moved to other papers. Murphy went to the *World Telegram*, and continued covering local sports.

Another *Eagle* columnist who had covered the the Brooklyn Dodgers was Dave Anderson. Anderson later achieved a Pulitzer Prize for Distinguished Commentary in 1981 while a sports columnist with the *New York Times*. In the summer of 1955, however, Dave was writing a column called "Brooklyn Sports" for the *New York Journal American*. Anderson came from the Bay Ridge section and played his baseball with Our Lady of Angels in the Brooklyn CYO League. The CYO played in Shore Parkway and Dave never quite got to the Parade Grounds.

He did, however, write about it and its' players in his Brooklyn Sports column. Anderson reported on the progress of Brooklyn boys in the minor leagues, and there were plenty of them during those years, and also on the goings-on at the Park. In one such column during that summer, Anderson reported on the teams due to compete in the New York City Baseball Federation Play-Offs. The Sophomore Sabers as a result of "Butch Gualberti's one-hit, 4-2 win over the Rams," would be competing for that title. The article goes on to mention other Sabers like TommyMorrissey, Pete Vicari, and Sonny Panico. The Cadets are also discussed as Freshman contenders. Managed by Jim McElroy, Anderson alludes to "pitcher-first baseman Joe Torre, kid brother of ex-J-A All Star and Brave farmhand Frank Torre." I played my last high school baseball game for Erasmus that spring of 1956. My high school career was totally undistinguished. I didn't hit well and made far too many errors at shortstop. I can't explain it because I had a pretty fair year on the sandlots with the Dahills. That last game was played on a Wednesday and on Thursday I ran in a track meet. My track coach, Abe Worchaiser , had kindly consented to allow me to run with my teammates in the one-mile relay even though I had not competed in the outdoor season at all because of baseball. My friends had prevailed upon the coach to let me run with them. The meet was held at

Wingate Field and we won gold medals while I ran my fastest 220 yards in high school. So my high school athletic career ended on a high note, just barely.

The reason that I remember the final baseball game was because we were to face Tony Rubilotta, who was an outstanding football and basketball player as well as an excellent pitcher in baseball. I have no recollection of the outcome of the game, only that I was anxious to get the season over with. But at the same time I was excited to face Rubilotta because of his reputation.

The game was played at Erasmus Field on MacDonald Avenue and our opponent was New Utrecht High School. Tony came from the Borough Park section and had played his kid ball with the Calvets in the Shore Parkway league at Dyker Park. But Tony got to the Parade Grounds because New Utrecht played all their home games at the Park. He recalled taking the 13th avenue bus every day for practice. That same year, '55-'56, Utrecht had been division champs in basketball only to lose in the semi-final round to Jefferson high and Tony Jackson, who, of course, went on to the play pro basketball.

In baseball, New Utrecht was beaten out by Boys High that year led by future Los Angeles Dodger and Parade Grounds alumni, Tommy Davis. But I knew Rubilotta as a split end and fullback who had made second team All-City in his junior year. It was during this championship year when they beat out New Dorp high school of Staten Island for the title that Utrecht also snapped a 30-game winning streak compiled by Lafayette high.

Rubilotta's illustrious schoolboy career ended with that game also and though he began Hoftra College with a full scholarship, he did not stay very long. He decided to join the U.S. Army where he spent three years. Married with two young children following his army hitch, Tony was persuaded by his old teammate from New Utrecht, Dom Anile, now football coach at C.W. Post on Long Island, to return to college.

As difficult as it was, he earned a degree and played football for three years, once again excelling. Rubilotta was given a nod from the Green Bay Packers and an offer from a team in the Canadian football league, but with the uncertainty and growing family responsibilities, he passed up both chances. Tony has been enshrined in the C.W. Post Hall-Of-Fame.

Rubilotta spent years playing touch football, including two undefeated seasons with Hong Pan in the Staten Island Touch Tackle League, where he'd moved in 1969. In some ways, he says, the hits in that league were harder than in a tackle league because of the absence of padding. There were plenty of good ball players in that league including Tony's younger brother, Andy.

Andy Rubilotta played in the Parade Grounds League from the earliest. Five years younger than his brother, Andy attended Brooklyn Tech High School where he made All-City in both football and baseball. Rubilotta played the outfield in high school, but the really good ones at that age level could throw and hit, so pitchers played the outfield and fielders pitched. In the semi-final round of the city championships Andy pitched against Rico Petrocelli of Sheepshead Bay high.

Petrocelli, of course, went on to a fine major league career with the Red Sox as a shortstop and third baseman. On this day he pitched and defeated Rubilotta and Brooklyn Tech 1-0, Rico singling in the games' lone run. Rubilotta was signed out of high school by the Cincinnati Reds in 1962 and assigned to Tampa in the Florida State League. In order to draft players from the minor league systems of teams, a payment had to be made by the team doing the drafting, the higher the classification the greater the payment.

In the hopes of protecting Rubilotta, Cincinnati gave him a triple A contract, placing the draft price at $25,000, enough to dissuade some teams. But the Chicago White Sox drafted Andy and paid the price. That spring the young prospect bought a car for the drive to Sarasota, Florida. "I didn't buy a car," Rubilotta said, "I bought a *jaguar*." In addition the club had a rule that there were no cars allowed in spring training. Andy smiles at the memory, "they say youth is wasted on the young. They sent me to Eugene , Oregon and I had to drive cross-country."

It was spring in Sarasota where the Red Sox also trained that Andy established a friendship with Rico Petrocelli, also from the Parade Grounds back home and with Tony Conigliaro whose promising major league career was ended by a devastating injury.

It was in '63 that he began to develop rotator cuff problems and pain in the shoulder and elbow. "When you're a major leaguer and you lose some effectiveness," Rubilotta explains, "you can get by on savvy and experience." In the minors "you're lost because you're still learning and can't reach for that major league experience to get you through." He rehabed in Clinton, Iowa, took cortisone shots,and dealt with the pain for three more seasons. "I was 25," he says, "I wanted to get married, I figured it was time to get a real job."

There is one emotion that Andy shares with so many of the young players whose careers were ended by injury. "No regrets," he says, happy to have had the chance and to have accomplished as much as he did.

The Dahills won one championship in the seven years we were together and that was in 1954 in the Police Athletic League. We were awarded gold medals .We had a new manager named Teddy Feldman and had gotten additional ballplayers from outside the neighborhood. Fellows we knew in school like Harry Margolis and *Nookie* Bernstein. We also picked up a young lefthander named Johnny Lepik. I wouldn't see John again until Open ball, and by then he had grown to over six-foot tall. He was strong and threw the ball very hard. John was another kid from the Parade Grounds who would ultimately play some pro baseball.

Something else I remember about John. A lot of us hung around together, especially the neighborhood kids, and one of our favorite places to be was Coney Island. On one such excursion, several of us were being dared to go for a ride on the treacherous roller coaster , *the Cyclone*. Joe Catalano, from the neighborhood and Johnny Lepik were doing the daring since they were the only ones of us who had ever been brave enough or crazy enough to take the plunge.

Finally we relented. Me, Dee, Joe Skelly and Bobby Marsico. When we stepped up to the ticket window; Joe, Johnny and me first, the others decided to back out, leaving me alone up there with those two smiling daredevils. Over the next 50 years I cringed every time I saw that ride and heard the screams emulating from the riders. I felt that one of them was mine, like the background radiation from the *Big Bang*; a remnant of a perilous and explosive event.

Mike Bodner also joined us that year to play third base. We called him Bogie. He was a good ballplayer, but very volatile. I was caught up in my first on-the-field fight because of him. We were playing a game on diamond eleven and Mike was tossing barbs with an opposing player and when the player got to third base, he calmly called time, stepped off the bag and punched Bogie right in the face.

I had to run over from short to join the melee, with the aim of breaking it up. When I got there Bodner had floored the other kid and was on top of him flaying away at his face. This kind of donnybrook was not at all unusual at the Parade Grounds and this would not be the last time that I would become a reluctant participant. The Dodgers' famed broadcaster Walter "Red" Barber immortalized the baseball melee when he called them *Rhubarbs*. A book published in 1954 in which Barber wrote the text to the photographs of noted photographer Barney Stein,was titled *The Rhubarb Patch*.

We stayed with the Sabres in 1956 for half a season or so and then faded as they went on to win the division title. There was one very embarrassing afternoon that year however. It rated a headline in the *Telegram.* "Sabres' Morrissey No-Hits Dahills" it blared. It said that Moose was ranked as one of the best sandlot pitchers around, "Tom, a fireballer", it said, "fanned 14."

In the spring of 1957 the story of the Brooklyn Dodgers was coming to a head .Dodgers president Walter O'Malley had arranged for seven home games to be played in Jersey City's Roosevelt Stadium in '56 and his bantering with Robert Moses and the city of New York over a proposed site for a new ball park was growing more serious. It was here that Abe Stark, Brooklyn clothier turned politician ,had his say over a suggested site.

Stark had put the well known sign in right center field at Ebbets Field that announced, "Hit Sign, Win Suit." The name recognition that came from the sign over the years had propelled Stark into local politics. In 1957 he was president of the City Council and guest speaker at the opening ceremonies of the Parade Grounds League.

Each spring all the teams paraded in full uniform onto the Park grounds and stood for speeches and the National Anthem to officially open the new season. Stark stood at the microphone and unveiled his plan to keep the Dodgers in Brooklyn. By this time we were wearing buttons that said, *Keep The Dodgers in Brooklyn*, and open to all suggestions.

Stark spoke of the Dodgers and how important they were to Brooklyn. We cheered every time he mentioned them. Then he lowered the blockbuster. The President of the City Council suggested that a new stadium be built right there on the 40-

acre site of the Parade Grounds. At that there were catcalls and boos and a few hundred hats were tossed into the air. We certainly did not want to lose the Dodgers but apparently not at the expense of our own careers. The league director, *Cookie Lorenzo*, took the mike and rebuked us saying we should act like gentlemen and quiet down. Fortunately for us anyway, both O'Malley and Moses rejected the idea. O'Malley also turned down Moses' offer of the site at Flushing Meadows; ultimately the home of the New York Mets; saying it wasn't in Brooklyn. Perhaps he thought that the fact that Los Angeles was not in Brooklyn either would escape our notice.

A similar occurrence took place in 1999. Professional baseball would return toBrooklyn after 42 years as the New York Mets would place an entry in the Class A Short Season New York-Penn league, to be called the *Brooklyn Cyclones*. A new stadium was to be built in Coney Island, but until it was ready the Cyclones needed a place to play. Once again the Parade Grounds loomed as a potential site. This time the objections came from the neighboring citizens and some politicians. It was finally determined that the team would play in the interim at St. John's University in Queens.

But some good came out of the hullaballu. Amid the protests a campaign was initiated to renovate the Park. Approximately 12.5 million dollars was raised and the renovation completed and dedicated with a ribbon cutting ceremony in 2004. The next generation of sandlot athletes would have eleven reconstructed athletic fields. Four baseball diamonds, including one with dugouts and lights; two softball fields, one football field, one soccer field, and three multi-purpose fields. Five of the new fields would contain artificial turf for year-round use. As beautiful as it is , it is nonetheless sad for the old line Parade Grounders to witness the reduction of baseball diamonds from 13 to a mere four.

It was in 1957 also that I got my first personnel thrill in baseball. I was selected to the Parade Grounds League Senior division All-Star team. It was particularly meaningful because the managers made the selections. I wasn't first string, but a reserve shortstop behind Pete Vicari, the little shortstop from the Sabres. He was a good lead-off hitter getting on base a lot and could run. Pete moved around short quickly and effectively and probably could have gotten the nickname *Scooter* if it hadn't already been taken by the veteran in Yankee Stadium. Instead Vicari was called *Peter Rabbit*.

Jimmy Murphy was now writing for the *Telegram* and he wrote a column listing the names of the entire ball club; my first written notice. The club would be managed by Mike Rubino of the Sabres with the aid of coaches Warren Ring of Holy Innocents and Bill Tursellino of the Bonnie Jays. The article then proceeded to name all the players with their batting averages. Next to my name it said, .310.

We were scheduled to open the New York City Baseball Federation All-Star Play-offs against the Coney Island League on Diamond One at the Parade Grounds,"Wednesday night at 5 PM." The announcement came from the "able director,"*Cookie* Lorenzo.

We defeated the Coney Island All-Stars 10-4 to move up to the second round. The *Moose*, Richie Clark of Holy Innocents and Bruce Cramb of the Bonnie Jays shared the pitching chores and gave up just six hits. Morrissey chipped in with an RBI double in the second inning. No doubt we had good pitching and that made our chances considerable.

In game two we eliminated the Shore Parkway group by a score of 7-6 at Dyker Park on Bay Eighth Street. Shore Parkway had been City champs the previous year. We used the same three pitchers plus Shelly Volk of the Tilden Tigers and he got credit for the win. We went back to the Parade Grounds and our beloved Diamond One to beat the Manhattan All-Stars.

I got one at bat in the Manhattan game and grounded out. But in a game thatpitted the All-Stars against the Senior champs, the Sabres, I got to play the whole game at short since *Peter Rabbit* was playing for the Sabres. We beat them and *Moose* Morrissey 5-4. Bruce Cramb got the win for us. Dick Stearns, an outfielder from the Bonnie Jays had three hits, the last knocking in the tying and winning runs.

We went on to win the whole thing and to be declared New York City Senior Division All-Star Champions. I didn't play much but like all the other fellows, I received a postcard in the mail from Mike Rubino instructing me to be at the Park on Sunday September 15 on Diamond One at 1 PM to receive my "All-Star Ring." It was sterling silver with the words "NYC Federation All-Stars" written on it.

The Cadets, Sophomore Division champs defeated the divisions' All-Stars, 4-3. The Cadet pitchers were Al Tennerella, whom I would play with on the Cardinals, two or three years later, and Joe Torre who got the win. Torre also scored the winning run in the seventh inning. Joe Torre was in high school at St. Francis Prep and already a prospect, although he pitched and played first and didn't do much ,if any catching. However, it wouldn't be until the next year that I would see Joe a lot on the field. His Cadets and my Virginians played in a Saturday League. There were two seasons that I would see him before he signed with the Braves in September of 1959.

Another of the Parade Grounds alumni whom I saw but never played against was Joe's brother Frank. Like Koufax, Torre was older than I was, seven years, having been born in 1931, and so we were never on the same field together. I do have an image, however, of a day when I stood on the steps of the refreshment stand which was beyond the left field fence of Diamond One. Standing there waiting to go out and play my game, I saw Frank hit one up on top of the roof of the stand. It was quite a wallop especially since Frank was a left handed hitter.

Frank began his professional career with Hartford in the Eastern League and Denver in the Western in 1951 when he batted .314. After a military stint , he came back in 1954 to play at Atlanta in the Southern Association. One more minor league season at Toledo where he hit .327 proceeded his debut in the National League with the Milwaukee Braves in 1956.

Frank Torre , had two three hundred seasons with the Braves and the Phillies and wound up a seven year career with a .273 average and played in two World Series with Milwaukee in 1957 and 1958.

Another future major leaguer that I had seen play at the Parade Grounds was Ken Aspromonte. Again, being younger, I never played against him. Ken played his first year in pro ball in 1950, one year before our Dahill Cubs got started. He began his career at Oneonta, New York and was thus initiated to the travails of all minor leaguers. It was Kinston the same year and the next Scranton and San Jose. It led Aspromonte to the Pacific Coast League and AAA ball in 1956 and '57 and then to the Boston Red Sox for 24 games in the latter year. Playing in 143 games in the infield at San Francisco that year, Kenny hit a lofty .334. He spent seven seasons in the majors with five clubs and hit .249. Ken and his brother Bob, whom I did get to play against were from the Marine park section of Brooklyn.

By this time I had seen three future major leaguers play at the Park; Frank Torre, Jerry Casale and Ken Aspromonte, in addition to Koufax whom I don't remember ever seeing play at that level. Minor leaguers were almost too numerous to mention, but the next year when I ascended to Open competition, more pro ballplayers would come into my experience than line drives off of Stan Musial's bat.

IV.

The Sparkle In "Brooklyn's Jewel"

"Whoever wants to know the heart and mind of America had better learn baseball....and do it by watching first some small town teams." -Jacques Barzun

It was in the year 1868 that the beautiful Prospect Park was completed. Designed by Frederick Lew Olmsted and Calvert Vaux, the park contained 585 acres with a 60 acre lake. These two gentlemen, as a team and independently, created hundreds of parks across the country including Central Park in Manhattan, but considered the Brooklyn landmark to be the brightest jewel in their crown. The Park contains Brooklyn's only zoo, and a carousel with its 51 animals carved in 1912 by Charles Carmel. The park has been an integral part of Brooklyn and its people and its history spans wars, the onset of the industrial age, and the shift of the population from rural to urban settings.

It was in 1646 that the town of Breuckelen was chartered by the Dutch. The present day Prospect Park region was the site of homesteads of early European settlers. The British took over the Dutch colonies in 1664 under the Duke of York and the agrarian lifestyle continued until the Revolutionary War in America. The Park location and the surrounding area was the setting for the first major battle of that war, now called *The Battle of Brooklyn.*

The largest battle of the Revolution in terms of troops and casualties, it very nearly signaled the beginning of the end for the American colonies. The events of August 21, 1776 in Brooklyn "comprised not only a major event in the War of Independence , but marked an important transition in the history of warfare as well." (1)

The Continental Army and in particular the Maryland Regiment held back the British and Hessian troops long enough for George Washington and his forces to escape by night from Brooklyn Heights to New Jersey. The brave Marylanders fell on the site of the future Washington Park on First and Third streets between Third and Fourth avenues. The Old Stone Building ,originally built in 1699 and restored in 1935 , was Washington's headquarters for a time and later a clubhouse for the Brooklyn ball club. The Maryland troops lost about 400 killed- nearly all of their company. Many are believed to be buried under the streets at that location.

Plaques commemorating the battle are placed just north of the zoo. There is also the Maryland Monument at the foot of Lookout Hill in the Park to honor those Marylanders who gave their lives in this battle. There are reminders of the

American efforts in the revolution throughout the borough. A monument in Fort Greene Park ; the Prison Ship Martyrs Monument, commemorates the 11,500 prisoners who died on British prison ships in Wallabout Bay (the location of the Brooklyn Navy Yard) during the duration of the American Revolution. The next major development in the evolution of a city was the emergence of Robert Fulton's steamboat in 1814, transforming Brooklyn into a commuter suburb bringing the first great transformation of the early towns into hubbubs of urban activity. Brooklyn was chartered in 1834 and soon became the third largest city in the country, behind Manhattan (New York) and Philadelphia.

The waves of European immigration in the latter part of the nineteenth century began to eat up the rural landscape as farms gave way to homes built in rows. Vaux and Olmsted had , in 1858, begun turning 800 acres in Manhattan into the first landscaped public park in the United States. It naturally followed for Brooklyn to begin seeking a tranquil oasis in the turmoil of urbanization. A movement in Brooklyn led by James Stranahan, a business and civic leader, developed, with the idea that a park in Brooklyn would according to Stranahan, "become a favorite resort for all classes of our community."

Stranahan, with considerable real estate interests in Brooklyn also envisioned a park as a way to lure wealthy residents to the town. There were layouts proposed and in 1865 Stranahan was impressed by Calvert Vaux's sketches; so much so, that authorization for the purchase of the necessary land was made, and in 1866,Vauz and Olmsted submitted a comprehensive plan for the design and development of Prospect Park. Olmsted's vision was for a tranquil, rural landscape where people could escape the escalating pace of city life.

"Brooklyn's Jewel" was completed in 1868. The Pavillion was adjacent to the 60-acre lake. There was a Dairy with milking cows and the Concert Grove House so visitors could listen to music while enjoying the pastoral setting. The Boathouse was added at the turn of the century. The small collection of animals in the 1880s opened to the public on July 3, 1935 as the Prospect Park Zoo.

Prospect Park is a cocaphony of memories for me. As kids we would go into the Park after playing on the Grounds and lie on the grass or eat lunch we had brought from home or sit by the lake. There is a family memory routed deeply into my psyche that involved Prospect Park, more specifically, the lake inside the Park On December 4, 1944 two police officers from the nearby 74 precinct witnessed a 5-year-old boy fall through the splintered ice on the lake. The officers rushed to the rescue. My dad, Paul Mele , leaped into the freezing water while his partner, Ephriam Friedman tossed him a rope and helped pull the two of them to safety.

My dad was taken to Caladonian Hospital on Parkside Avenue and for whatever reason had his tonsils removed. I recall him climbing the stairs to our apartment, hat pulled low on his head and his coat buttoned tightly around his chin. He looked gaunt and was severely weakened by the ordeal. But the hero cop received a medal, membership in the Police Honor Legion and a $50 bonus. While he didn't speak of the incident much in later years unless someone else brought the subject up, he did comment to me once that "I never heard from that kid again."

Parade Grounds were traditionally an area of military drills and exercises and considered an essential part of heavily population centers. Originally the Park proposal called for a Parade Ground to be located in what is the East New York section of Brooklyn. But Frederick Law Olmsted and Calvert Vaux chose a large rectangular site just south of the Park. They did not want the area to be in the Park in order to preserve the grass and plants and the pastoral setting. There was initial opposition to the project upon the grounds that "a Parade Ground is not needed at all in this county....(it is) a useless and extravagant expenditure of public funds." (2)

The supporters won out and the Ground was constructed along with a lodge and shelter and completed in 1869. It was used initially for the purpose that it was created for and on June 20, 1872 the 11th Brigade of the National Guard held a review and a parade. Exercises of this type were common. As late as May 29, 1896 Calverymen of Troop C requested permission to use the entire Grounds for Decoration Day drills. They were limited to only a portion of the Grounds so as not to disappoint the "one or two thousand" who would be forced to give up their activities. (3)

As the military use of the site began to decline and recreation use was on the rise, a field sports shelter called Bowling Green Cottage was added. The Parade Grounds were selected for the annual Polo championships in the 1890s until 1901 when the site was moved to Brookline, Massachusetts.

The Capitoline Grounds opened in 1864 at the location of Nostrand and Marcy avenues between Putnam and Halsey and were called by the *Brooklyn Daily Eagle* ,"the finest, most extensive and complete ball grounds in the country." They were used by the Atlantics and the Enterprise ball clubs, and later the Excelsiors. When the Atlantics moved to Union Grounds in 1873, Capitoline was divided into two fields in order to accommodate the growing number of amateur teams in Brooklyn.

By 1870 the newly completed Parade Grounds would rival the Capitoline. With 20 playing fields there would be at least a dozen games in progress at the same time on a Saturday afternoon. *Commercial nines;* teams representing firms sprang up and played for championships of various occupations. Insurance and banking firms; hardware companies, and more.

Baseball was beginning to proliferate at the Parade Grounds well before the turn of the century. A September 29, 1889 article in the *Brooklyn Daily Eagle* reported that "a large crowd surrounded Diamond One at the Parade Grounds Prospect Park yesterday to see the Windsor and Flatbush Nines compete for supremacy in the Flatbush League." Windsor was the victor by a 9-8 score.

Henry Chadwick, *the father of baseball* wrote: "It is a glorious sight to see the hundreds of young men and boys enjoying themselves to their hearts' content as they do on the Prospect Park Parade Ground every fine afternoon during the summer." (4)

Brooklyn native Bill Barnie tried to resurrect the defunct Atlantics in 1879 and began the season at the Grounds but played only a few games before disbanding for good.

Among the Brooklyn landmarks; the Bridge, Coney Island, Prospect Park, Grand Army Plaza and the Parade Grounds is the Brooklyn Dodgers. The borough's National League entry paralleled its early years with those of the Parade Grounds as early as 1883. On May 9 of that year the Brooklyn team, called the *Greys,* were due to commence their first season in the Interstate Association, a professional league. While awaiting completion of their new home, Washington Park, they were left with no ball park in which to open their season, scheduled against Harrisburg. The *Brooklyn Daily Eagle* on May 10, 1883 had this to say.

"The professional team of the Harrisburg Club, of Harrisburg, Pa., were the opponents of the Brooklyn Base Ball Association's team, in one of the series of inter-State championship matches on May 9, the same being played on one of the free fields of the Parade Ground at Prospect Park...." The newspaper article went on to point out the attendance that day. "Had it been known that a true exhibition of professional ball playing in a championship match was to take place at the park, between five and six thousand people would have surrounded the field; as it was, at the short notice given, nearly a thousand spectators watched the contest."

It was further reported that there was "ungentlemanly conduct" on the part of the visiting nine. The *Eagle* went on to say that there have been some pretty rough nines on the park grounds in its history, but a "worse lot of 'kickers', or a more undisciplined and badly managed professional nine has never played in Brooklyn."

It seems that there was constant complaining by the Harrisburg players about balls and strikes and umpires' decisions. Incredibly, over one disputed call involving a runner touching a ball, Shetzline, the Harrisburg team captain, wanted the ump to ask the opinion of the audience. It was pointed out that this sort of action by an umpire was prohibited by the rules. Schappert, the pitcher exclaimed, "you make me sick", to the umpire when balls were called on him instead of strikes. In fact, the paper reported , "they kicked against every decision that was not in their favor, Meyers telling the umpire, 'you're the worst I've ever seen,' and 'you ought to be ashamed of yourself.'"

The Brooklyn nine was "commendable under the circumstances, playing a gentlemanly game throughout," and came away with a 7-1 victory. Brooklyn had eleven base hits and apparently played some good defense. The *Eagle* noted that the catching of Walker at first base was "the best ever seen on the park ground, and the outfield, too, was well attended to." (5)

An ongoing attempt to enlarge the Grounds to extend from Caton to Church avenue extended over a period of several years. The proposed extension was backed by the Brooklyn Cricket Club with the claim that there wasn't enough room for them to fully engage in their sport. In 1901 the local board refused to act on the proposal until accurate costs were ascertained. they called the plan "faulty."(6)

This spring also, the city was readying for the inauguration of the newly completed Brooklyn Bridge, the "eighth wonder of the world." (7) In March of 1889 Brooklyn manager Bill McGunnigle brought his ball club to Diamond #1 at the Parade Grounds for two weeks of spring practice as that field would be in playing condition before Washington Park would be ready for the season.

By 1900 games played on the Parade Grounds included baseball, cricket, lacrosse, polo and football. A May 27, 1883 item in the *Brooklyn Daily Eagle* said that "Brooklyn's great recreation ground was crowded yesterday afternoon not only by the exemplars of the national field game of base ball, but by reckless lacrosse players, and tennis and *raquet* players."

The "Dauntless" and "Star" nines of the Long Island Amateur Association played their game on "field No. 1", while the "Commercial and Bedford nines occupied field No. 3, the Polytechnic and Invincible nines being between them." The "Dauntless" - "Star" game was officiated by umpire" Mr. Griswold" and ran one hour and thirty minutes. (8)

According to the *New York Times*, during 1885 there were approximately 900baseball games played at the Park, 150 cricket matches, 150 football matches, and 35 lacrosse games.

Baseball was played on Saturdays and holidays; Sunday ball had been rejected by the Board of aldermen in 1895, though there were twenty diamonds for use. The *Eagle* on June 10, 1900 reported:

rrr

"*Whenever two clubs of extraordinary merit are playing, two sides of the. diamond are given up to onlookers, who eagerly stand as near the base lines as the rules permit, sometimes a dozen deep. The excitement during a game rivals that of Washington Park when the champions are playing with one of the best league teams.*"

Washington Park was the home of the Brooklyn ball club; winners of the National League pennant in 1899.

The newspaper comments could just as easily have been repeated word-for-word in later years, at least through the fifties and early sixties. The scene had been played out at least once in my memory, on Diamond #5 during a 1958 game between the Virginians and Sacred Heart. With the crowd inching onto the field of play, plate umpire Pete Larkin had to keep stopping the game while he waved the fans back across the foul lines.

An account of the opening of the 1894 Brooklyn amateur base ball league was found in the *Brooklyn Daily Eagle* with what would seem to be a misprint or at least a gross exaggeration. The newspaper said that there were 25,000 expected to be on hand as the defending champs *The Fultons* met *The Sidneys.* Threatening weather dimmed the crowd but apparently not the enthusiasm of the"*ball tossers.*"*The Fultons* defeated *The Sidneys* by an 8-5 score as Fulton's pitcher Brown struck out 13 opponents on a muddy field where sliding was "difficult.

In his study of nineteenth century baseball in Brooklyn, *Long Before the Dodgers,* James L. Terry says, "the Parade

Grounds is perhaps the best living memory to the early days of baseball in the city."

But to all the ball players of 30s, 40s, and 50s, the Parade Grounds was begat in 1905 when the original wood shelter was replaced by the Athletic Building. To us it was *The Clubhouse*, a huge edifice with gigantic Corinthian columns that rose two stories from the platform to the roof. A wide concrete stairway in front led to the double doors. By the 50s the concrete on the stairs and the columns was cracked and peeling in many places.

The inside of the building housed a shower room with rusted pipes, and several locker rooms with bent and twisted metal doors. The warped wooden floors were spike-scarred and creaked as they gave way to the weight of the passers. Outside the sounds of the spiked shoes clattered over the cement porch and down the long flight of stairs. But each time you left the building in uniform you felt like a gladiator must have felt entering the arena, and at times the anticipated game seemed to have the same mortal consequences.

The Parade Grounds was also known as *Park Circle*, or simply, *The Park*. The site is bound by Parkside Avenue, which runs adjacent to Prospect Park, and Caton Avenue. Also by Coney Island Avenue and Parade Place. Where Coney Island Avenue intersects with Parkside, there is a traffic circle called ParkCircle that included a Park entrance, Prospect Park South and Ft. Hamilton Parkway. Abutted against the clubhouse was the 74th police precinct station house where my dad was stationed for fifteen years and helped us get those early permits for the fields. There were always squad cars and police officers around Park Circle. Invariably when we were playing on one of the open diamonds, a squad car would pull up on the grass in foul territory and my dad would catch a couple of innings.

Across Coney Island Avenue there was a diner called *Archie's Diner*, a typical "greasy spoon" where Freddy and me and Johnny Keegan would meet for breakfast often on Saturday mornings before a double header. Next to *Archie's* was the *Caton Inn*, a bar where the guys would stop off sometimes at the end of the day. I seldom went in. I didn't drink and after playing two games in the hot sun without eating, merely the smell of the beer would turn my stomach and spin my head. On one corner was an ESSO gas station and on the other, at Coney Island and Parkside avenues at the Circle was the Riverside Chapel, the funeral home where pitcher Billy Litras went to assist his father after pitching the first game of a double header.

In the early years of the twentieth century the Park proliferated until there were the twenty diamonds referred to in the *Eagle* in 1900 and 21 that Cookie Lorenzo remembers. I never saw it like this. In my time there were 13 diamonds. At the apex of Coney Island and Caton Avenues was Diamond # 1, the flagship of the fleet. It was one of two that were completely fenced in with cyclone fencing about ten feet high, except in center field where the fence rose to about four feet. Right field down the line was about 260 feet from home plate, but it jutted out sharply in right center. Dead center was 363 feet away and the left field line ran to 318 feet from the home plate. There are a written set of ground rules for all Diamonds, slightly different for the enclosed Diamonds #1 and 13.

For instance, "a batted ball bouncing over fences or through holes in fence from fair territory, two bases." Also, overthrows to any base on the enclosed fields, the ball is in play, and runners advance at their own risk. On the open fields, only one base on an overthrow is permitted, except at second base, when ball remains in play. On the open fields, there is a rule specifying, " Batted or thrown ball striking spectator, ball is in play."

There were wooden bleachers behind home plate and up the two lines accommodating several hundred spectators. The only other fenced in field was Diamond # 13.It was opposite Diamond 1 with the center field fences running parallel to each other and a black cinder path about ten feet wide between them.

Diamond 13 faced the west and so after the noon hour the sun was in the hitter's eyes and that made it less than ideal. No doubt # 1 was the class of the Park. When schedules were made , they were planned so that each team would play at least once on Diamond 1 , but the better teams were featured. From 1958 to 1964 I played a lot there. My teams won three championships and the other three years were in contention.

Along Caton avenue were diamonds 2 through 5. Nothing was particularlydistinguishable about them except for the dust, especially Diamond 5. When the wind blew, the game stopped while you covered your face as the dust kicked up. In his autobiography *"Chasing the Dream"*, Joe Torre had similar memories of the Park.

"The Parade Grounds included thirteen diamonds, only two of which had enclosed fences and stands. The rest were very ragged , dusty fields jammed together back-to-back. They had damn near flat mounds and clouds of dust with every step you took."(10) In the 19th century "baseball was in the air," according to Burt Solomon in his study of the original Baltimore Orioles, *Where They Ain't*. From that time until my generation kids began their baseball in the same way, on a local lot. That is, after moving from the street. Hall-Of-Fame player *Wee Willie* Keeler grew up on Pulaski Street and played One O' Cat and Kick the Can in the 1880s before playing baseball with the local team, the *Rivals,* at a field at Greene Avenue and Broadway. Like the rest of us, Willie said, "We were only sandlot kids, but what fun we did have." (11)

This was a time when horse-drawn trolleys traveled along DeKalb Avenue and the city was preparing for the official opening of the "eighth wonder of the world",the *Brooklyn Bridge.*   The site of activities beyond baseball, on June 16, 1927, the largest crowd recorded at the Parade grounds, 200,000, congregated to welcome Charles Lindbergh after his record transatlantic flight. Lindbergh addressed the crowd asking that a great airport be built in Brooklyn.

In addition to the sports proliferating at the Park at the turn of the century, the Brooklyn Lawn Bowling Club built a Bowling Green at the southern most corner of the acreage aiding the evolution of activities replacing military parades and exercises.

Future major leagues born in Brooklyn before the turn of the 20th century include Washington Senators first baseman Joe Judge and Hall-Of-Fame pitcher Waite Hoyt. Judge played for twenty years in the majors with the Senators and the Red Sox and compiled a composite batting average of .298.

Hoyt lived in Borough Park on 51 street and attended Erasmus Hall HS. He played ball at the Parade Grounds and at Marine Park. Hoyt won 237 big league games in a twenty-one year career with several clubs, primarily the New York Yankees. He finalized his career, most fittingly, where it began, in Brooklyn with the Dodgers. It was Hoyt who inspired the Brooklynese newspaper headline that was a result of an injury he had suffered. The headline screamed, "Hert was Hoit."

Going from Erasmus Hall to the Parade Grounds to Cooperstown would seem to be good enough for one baseball lifetime, but Hoyt was a part of additional extraordinary events. During his glory years with the New York Yankees in the 1920s , Hoyt was teammate and friend to both George Herman *Babe* Ruth and Lou Gehrig. He stood with his former teammates at Yankee Stadium the day that the*Iron Horse* proclaimed himself to be the "luckiest man on the face of the Earth." He was there also on June 13,1948 when the Babe said his last goodbyes.

Incredibly Waite Hoyt pitched three complete games in the 1921 World Series against the New York Giants, winning two of them and losing the final game 1-0. He gave up just two runs in 27 innings of pitching, both unearned.

Hoyt authored a 1948 book "Babe Ruth As I Knew Him," which has been oft quoted over the years, most recently in a biography of Ruth by Leigh Montville, *The Big Bam. The*

Brooklyn Schoolboy was the first to say, "It's great to be young and a Yankee." (12)

It was Arthur Dede, born in 1895, that I remember because he became a scout for the Dodgers after his "cup-of-coffee " in the big time. It consisted of one game, one at-bat, no hits for Brooklyn in 1916. Dede's scouting career kept him around the Park for decades. He signed and was in on the signing of dozens of young Dodger hopefuls over the years.

With advancing age memory often grows dimmer, but former Parade Grounds ball players seem to have an immunity against such losses of memory. Ninety-yearold Larry Yaffa has virtual total recall of people and events of sixty and seventy years ago. From Bay Ridge, Larry played his Parade Grounds baseball with the *Catons* beginning in the early thirties, and also played at Erasmus Hall high school. Yaffa recalls encounters with some pretty good ball players along the way. There was George Fallon of the Brooklyn Falcons, whom Larry calls "one of the best".Fallon came up to the Brooklyn Dodgers for four games in 1937, then spent time as a utility infielder with the St. Louis Cardinals in 1943,'44' ,and '45. He appeared in 133 big league ball games and appeared in the 1944 World Series as the Cardinals defeated the Browns , also of St. Louis 4 games to 2.

The *Prospects* had Frank Boemberman who was signed by Connie Mack and the Philadelphia Athletics in the late 1920s . Larry speaks highly of pitcher Bill Lohrman. William Le Roy Lohrman was a right hander who played with the Crestons at the Park from 1929 to 1932 before signing with the Phillies. He came up to Philadelphia in 1934 for just six innings and one loss, but was back in the majors in 1937 with the New York Giants.

Lohrman had his best season in 1942 winning 14 while losing just 5 games. He wound up a nine year big league career with a record of 60 - 59 and nearly 1000 innings pitched. Bill did nothing to ingratiate himself to the local fans when on August 30, 1941 pitching for the Giants at the Polo Grounds, he defeated the Brooklyn Dodgers knocking them out of first place. In 1942, Lohrman was sent to the Cardinals in a trade that brought Big John Mize to New York.

Larry's memory seems as fresh as yesterday. He recalls Joe Madden, a terrific ball player, good enough to play professionally. "He was good enough," Larry says, "but he had too many other distractions." Madden was a bird dog scout for several teams in the twenties and was an umpire at the Park for many years. Yaffa thinks of those times and says sadly, "so many are gone now."

Yaffa retains a great fondness for Chuck Connors, also of Bay Ridge, who lived at 88 street between third and fourth avenues and played his baseball at Park Circle with the Brooklyn Celtics. Larry remembers Connors as an "excellent ball player" and a very "decent guy." The two met first at the Parade Grounds, but actually developed a friendship when they met at the McAlpen hotel in Manhattan on 34 street and Broadway. The AAA International League Montreal Royals stayed there and bussed over to Newark and Jersey City, New Jersey for games against the Bears and the Giants.

Chuck was a member of the 1948 Montreal Royals, winners of the Junior World Series, along with future Dodger ace Don Newcombe, infielder Bobby Morgan, 19 game winner Jack Banta and little Al Gionfriddo, whose heroics in the Major League World Series in 1947 would label him an icon in Brooklyn lore. Connors hit a tenth inning game tying grand-slam home run against the Syracuse Chiefs in the second round of the International League play-offs. It was the fourth grand-slammer that he would hit that season. Connors had attended Seton Hall University in South Orange, New Jersey before joining the Army in 1942. After his discharge in 1946 he also played basketball professionally for the Boston Celtics during the baseball off season.

The 6' 5" left handed hitter came to the Dodgers in 1949 and appeared in just one game. He was with the Chicago Cubs in 1951 for 66 games before drifting back to the minors. Always a wit and a joker, Connors was sent to the Cubs affiliate in the Pacific Coast League, the *Hollywood Stars*. It was here in southern California that Connors' tall, good looks and spiritus personality began to get him roles in the movies. His first was in the Spencer Tracy-Katherine Hepburn film, *Pat and Mike*, in which Connors played a state police captain. He starred in *The Rifleman*, the television Western series from 1958-1963.

Wayne Terwilliger was a teammate of Connors at Hollywood and recalls how Chuck's fun-loving lifestyle helped to propel the big first baseman into show business. Connors' recitation of *Casey at the Bat* always made a hit, and he handed out a business card that read: "Kevin (Chuck) Connors, affiliate Brooklyn Dodgers Baseball Club: recitations, after-dinner speaker, home recordings for any occasion,free- lance writing."(13)

By sheer coincidence Yaffa and Connors ran into each other in Chicago some years later. Larry was on a business trip fulfilling his role as vice-president of sales for the Schenley Corp. And Chuck was a year away from beginning his role as TVs *Rifleman,* the hugely successful series for which he would become a household word, at least to those Americans unfamiliar with the Parade Grounds. In1991, Connors was into the Western Performers Hall-Of-Fame, in Oklahoma City, an honor he cherished, although as he indicated during his lifetime, he would have preferred one in Cooperstown.

Kevin "Chuck" Connors died of lung cancer in 1992 at the age of 71.

So many of the Boys of Brooklyn distinguished themselves in one way or another during their professional careers. Mario Picone did his Parade Grounds apprenticeship during the thirties and forties, playing for a team called the "Chiros". Signed by the New York Giants in 1944, Picone was in the majors by '47. He spent parts of three seasons there with only an 0-2 record, but the right hander had a career highlight while in the minors.

The seventeen-year-old was a prospect at Bristol, Tennessee in the Giants system in 1944 when he hurled his team to a 19 inning win over Johnson City while strikingout an incredible 28 batters.

Don McMahon was born in Brooklyn in 1930 and played his Parade Grounds ball in the middle and late forties. Don played high school ball at Erasmus Hall and was signed by the Milwaukee Braves in 1949. His first pro year was an exceptional one. McMahon won 20 games while losing only 9 at Owensboro in theKITTY League. At 6'2" and 210 pounds , the strong righthander pitched 218 innings that 1950 season.

After two years in the military, Don returned to baseball and the path that would take him to the major leagues. It meandered through such minor league towns as Evansville, Atlanta, Toledo, and Witchita over the next four years until Don landed in Milwaukee with the Braves in 1957. By this time he had switched to the bullpen and stayed in the majors as a relief pitcher for 18 years. In '57 and '58 the Braves went to the World Series and McMahon was teammates with Frank Torre, both gaining rings in the Braves 1957 victory over the Yankees.

In 1968 Don was with Detroit and another World Series championship was on his resume'. He was sold to the San Francisco Giants in August 1969 and helped that club to a play-off berth. The 41 year-old made 61 appearances and won ten games, all in relief. In an article out of San Francisco, writer Pat Frizzell wrote about the success that McMahon was having at such an advanced baseball age. Don was quoted, "I don't even think about age," he explained. "That really doesn't enter into my outlook on baseball." The article went on to say that McMahon still depends on his fast ball and curve. "I've been throwing more breaking balls than I used to," he said. "Maybe that makes my fast ball seem faster."

Don was there through changes that affected the game on the field. "The lowering of the mound, the strike-zone change, and the artificial surfaces have made quite a bit of difference for pitchers." (14) He pitched for three more seasons before retiring, all with the Giants, and finished with a record of 90 wins and 68 loses, all in relief, and 153 saves. Don McMahon passed away in 1987 at 57 years of age; far too soon, but with a career in the big time to make the Parade Grounds proud. Another of Brooklyn's success stories.

V.

The Leagues Of Extraordinary Gentlemen

"You remember what the game of baseball can be like when it is played with innocence instead of greed, love instead of ego."
- H. G. Bissinger

The most dominating factor at the Parade Grounds from the 1930s on was the Parade Grounds League, and the single most dominating force associated within the League was *Cookie* Lorenzo.

Vincent *Cookie* Lorenzo directed the League for over sixty years. Duly proud of his charges he would even into his late eighties, lean forward on his cane, and through failing eyesight, look straight into yours and tell you in no uncertain terms; "an all-star team from the Parade Grounds can beat most of those so-called big-league teams!" And he believed it.

Lorenzo remembered when there were 21 diamonds at the Park; ten each along Caton and Parkside Avenues with a single field placed in the center. The two enclosed fields were at that time numbers one and twenty. He was asked incredulously how ten fields could possibly fit alongside each other. He answered with a chuckle. "The most important man on the field was the third base coach," he said. " There was three feet between first base on one diamond and third base on the other. When a runner rounded second he saw two bases and the coach had to holler and point, 'this one! This is your base!'"

Later they reduced the number to fifteen fields, the ultimate thirteen set-up with two in the center. "It was a terrible arrangement ," Lorenzo said, and so they eliminated the two middle ones and left the familiar thirteen diamond arrangement. This stood until the 2003 renovation which resulted in the currant layout.

Vinnie Lorenzo was born on September 26, 1917 in the Borough Park section of Brooklyn at 1009- 40 street between Ft. Hamilton Parkway and Tenth avenue. He recalled how there was no electricity and the cooking was done on coal stoves. Vinnie would go into the cellar where his sister held a candle while he filled the coal bucket and carried it to the kitchen.

Young Vinnie went to school at St. Catherine of Alexandria parochial school and New Utrecht High school. When faced with the choice to go with the forty-fourth street boys and keep playing punch ball in the street or to hook up with the kids from forty-first street and play baseball, he opted for baseball and thus began his Parade Grounds career with a neighborhood team called the Aristons. It was with the Aristons that Lorenzo came by the nickname that would be with him ever after. His older brother who would catch with him and show him how to play the game was known in the neighborhood as Joey Cook. Lorenzo doesn't know why that particular sobriquet was pinned on him, he speculates it may be because Joe liked to cook.

Two of his brothers' friends came by when young Vinnie was catching in a game without wearing a catchers mask. "Hey, look," they said, "it's Joey Cook's kid brother. Hey, Cookie! What are you, Crazy? Catching without a mask." Vinnie explained that the catcher didn't show up, so he had to catch and the catcher was the only one with a mask. The friends prevailed upon the other team to lend the kid a mask and a legend was born. They went around the neighborhood telling everyone, "Cookie was catching without a mask." Cookie...and Cookie it stayed.

Already a leader, after three years with the Aristons, Lorenzo became playing-manager for the *Victoria Panthers* who represented the Victoria Democratic Club, a neighborhood political organization. An organizer now as well as a leader, Cookie and his team were able to make use of the Victoria club house on Ft. Hamilton Parkway and he planned to run dances to raise money. But a problem arose; none of his boys knew how to dance. Cookie took it upon himself to provide dance lessons.

After only one session he announced that in the future, they would bring sisters, mothers, or girlfriends to dance with. "I'm too darn tired," he told them, "I've had it." Most of the young men of Lorenzo's generation had to put a hold on their lives for the next three or four years following the outbreak of World War II. Lorenzo spent four years in the Army and traversed from Aberdeen, Maryland to Europe and Japan, back to Texas and Miller Field on Staten Island. As a staff sergeant, at one point he had to select a squad from a company of men. "I picked all ballplayers," Cookie recalled. "I knew they could follow orders and be team players." In a sense, the highlight of Lorenzo's military career were the times he came home to Brooklyn on furlough. It was then that he met Lucy, his future wife and teammate for the next sixty years.

Already extremely active in running a ball club he became involved with an American Legion Post and there met another organizer named Arthur Bellone. Lorenzo began working for the Sanitation department after the war and in 1946 reorganized the ball club, the Victoria Panthers, and played in the IntercommunityLeague. That league was going to fold after twenty-one years and so Lorenzo and Bellone decided to take it over. The Panthers were playing at the Parade Grounds and they opted to name their new organization," The Parade Grounds League".

Bellone was a Wall Street worker and he solicited aid in the form of donations from his Wall Street friends and got the league off to a flying start. Ed Bannon was named as the first President; Bellone, vice-president and Lorenzo , secretary-treasurer. Until the day of his passing in 2006 Lorenzo was still listed as the league's secretary-treasurer.

They held their meetings in the Windsor Terrace legion post and Cookie continued to run dances and functions as fund raisers for the league. Lorenzo established himself with Tom Flanagan of the Parks Department and got equipment rooms in the clubhouse, which alleviated the need for Cookie to lug bases and other gear from home each and every Saturday and Sunday. At first there were just senior and open division teams. Other leagues that proliferated at the Grounds in that period were the Kawanis, the American Legion, the Police Athletic League and the Ice Cream League.

I spent my first season in the Ice Cream league, whose president was a gregarious public relations type by the name of Milton Siecol, who called himself, "Pop" Siecol.

It was an organization called the Bonnie Boys Club who first approached Lorenzo with the request to help the younger ballplayers. "Give us your cracked bats and old baseballs," asked Bob Trenthan. Together they arranged for new younger divisions to be a part of the PGL. This resulted in the creation of Freshman, and Junior divisions, which meant that a kid could begin to play PGL ball at age ten, and as Cookie explained, "they can stay with us 'til their wife tells them to quit!"

A further development was the formation of the "League Council". All leagues participated and Lorenzo distributed the diamonds for all games held at the Parade Grounds. Next came the NYC Federation of Baseball which took in all five boroughs and meant city-wide tournaments and for the senior division, a trip to Johnstown, Pennsylvania for the National Finals.

Lorenzo is proud of his Federation whose officers have included attorney Bill Shea, of Shea Stadium renown, and Fred Wilpon, owner of the New York Mets. Wilpon was a Parade Grounds League player and of Shea, Lorenzo says, "a very good man, he was with us all the way." A great many outstanding ball players passed in front of Cookie Lorenzo's eyes over the years. There was Jack Conway of the Victoria Panthers who played pro ball, and Waite Hoyt and Tommy Holmes. Al Cuccinello got to the N.Y. Giants for 54 games in 1935. Al's brother Tony, of course, had a fifteen year major league career and hit .280. The brothers were from Long Island City, but Al played in the Parade Grounds when he was employed by the NYC Sanitation Department. The fields were utilized on mid-week mornings by city agency teams; the Police, fire fighters, sanitation workers, and finance department personnel.

They played in the day time, the Industrial League played in the evenings, and all day Saturday and Sunday was occupied by the rest of the leagues, with the PGL being the largest.

The league proliferated under the vigorous leadership of Lorenzo until it reached 72 teams and forced expansion to Marine Park in order to have available the addition fields needed to accommodate the growing concern. It was at Marine Park that Cookie first came upon the youngster that he is most proud of.

A fourteen year-old Joe Torre was pitching and playing first base in the PGL Freshman division at Marine Park not far from his home in the Marine Park section of Brooklyn. Lorenzo was umpiring games. Working from the pitchers' mound one day when Torre was batting, he made a suggestion to the pitcher.

"I told him to 'Pitch him outside, he likes to pull the ball,' Boom- a double to rightfield." The next time Torre came up, Cookie suggested that he jam him, "Boom", he recalls, "left field, another double." The third time Lorenzo told him to throw whatever he wanted to throw. "Boom-double to left center."

Finally, on the fourth time at bat, Cookie says, "I tapped him on the shoulder, I said, 'walk him - because he don't run so good and won't steal second, so at least it's only a single.'"

While being interviewed by a reporter from the N.Y. Times, Lorenzo was asked to describe Torre. "Built like a Johnny pump!" replied Cookie. The reporter leaned forward. Apparently not from Brooklyn, he inquired, "What's a Johnny pump?" "A fire hydrant, short and stocky, " was the reply, "but can he hit". He was a prominent advocate of the young Torre from the very beginning and no one reveledmore in Joe's future successes than the League head. Being a life-long Yankeesfan made it a whole lot easier for Lorenzo to root for Torre when the latter took over the reins of the Bombers in 1996. Lorenzo had a disagreement with the Little League, who wanted to team up with the NYC Federation with their 12-13 year olds, but Cookie refused. The Little League used shorter mounds and shorter bases and put all-star teams into tournaments. Lorenzo could not abide these Little League rules, believing that under them, the youngsters would be hampered in their development. Especially the all-star teams. His approach was that a team that wins together, stays together and never wavered in that judgement.

It is fairly commonplace for the players to frown upon the Little League program. Baseball veteran Larry DaVita recalls the great lefthander Warren Spahn telling him that "Little League will kill the sport". To many of the old-timers, it has contributed. DaVita says, "I've seen kids come off the field crying- that's not theway it's supposed to be."

Cookie Lorenzo has spanned three generations of ballplayers at the Park. The latest producing the likes of pitcher Sal Campisi, who had some major league time in the late sixties, and John Candelaria. The *Candy Man*, even at fifteen could firethe ball. Playing for Holy Innocents, Lorenzo remembers him launching missiles out on Diamond # 3. "He was too fast for the kids," Cookie said with awe. The left hander spent nineteen years in the big time, winning 177 games including a 20-5 season with Pittsburgh in 1977.

Candelaria was pitching for the Brooklyn Mets in the PGL and was managed by Dan Liotta, who would be a vice president under Bob Trenthan and later succeed him as president of the league. Scouts had seen this young fireballer and the Pittsburgh Pirates sent Danny Murtaugh, who had played in the major leagues for nine years and managed the Pirates for 15 more, to look him over. He'd won pennants in 1960 and '71.

He showed up at the Parade Grounds and asked to see Candelaria pitch. Liotta told him that the young man was not scheduled to pitch that day. "Well," Murtaugh wondered, "can we see him throw a bit." Liotta asked John to throw some but he didn't want to. Apparently, he wasn't prepared to pitch and didn't want to throw at all. Now Murtaugh got a little hot. He complained that he had flown in especially to see Candelaria.

"You don't want to pitch him; the kid don't want to throw; what the hell is going on here," he wanted to know.

Liotta went back to talk to the kid. "Do it for me," he pleaded. He agreed. Murtaugh's saw the kid throw and liked what he saw, and thus began the process that would lead ultimately to the Pirates signing John Candelaria. The years having caught up with Cookie Lorenzo, the old warhorse turned the reins of his beloved Parade Grounds League over to his good friend Bob Trenthan in 1992. "I turned everything over to Bob, and I said, 'Bob, I can't see. It's all yours now.'" Trenthan ran the league until he passed away in 2003. At that point Dan Liotta stepped up and took charge.

Following came a 1967 renovation, at which time the decrepit , rundown , beloved old club house was torn down and replaced with a modern building. The changes should have rejuvenated the old park, but over the next twenty years it gradually slipped into disarray. The diamonds were not properly maintained and there were less and less teams active in the PGL. There were homeless people living in the clubhouse. Neglect and insufficient funding led to the deterioration of the Grounds.

The fields became strewn with rubbish and broken bottles and the area and atmosphere was no longer very conducive to young ballplayers. "The Parade Grounds was in horrible, horrible condition," recalled Prospect Park Alliance administrator Tupper Thomas. The Parade Grounds League had dwindled to no more than eleven teams represented.

Liotta and his league persevered, however, and came all the way back. Through the efforts of Tupper Thomas and the Alliance along with the diligence and cooperation of other league reps; like Jerry Katzke, president of the Bonnie Youth Club and Mel Zitter with the Youth Service League, Dan Liotta and Ross Quattro pulled the PGL back where it had always been.

Working to get and keep the fields in shape, the league was rejuvenated and now has more than 70 teams in all divisions competing. Cookie Lorenzo's dream and hard work would perpetuate in the new administration.

On August 5, 2000 the All American Amateur Baseball Association inducted Vincent "Cookie" Lorenzo into their Hall of Fame at a banquets ceremony at Johnstown, Pennsylvania. Vincent *Cookie* Lorenzo passed away in November 2006, a legacy imbued in sandlot history for as long as kids swing a bat or toss a ball in Brooklyn.

Of all the leagues that played at the Park, the Parade Grounds League was the most prolific and longest running, having picked up on the 21 years of the Inter-community league and added another sixty for more than eighty years of continuous service. But there exists another league that has proven over the years to be quite formidable. In 1932 Ted Meyerstein founded the *Brooklyn Kiwanis League*. Later on into the late forties Bill Dunn was in charge. He would hold court in the clubhouse in his big Stetson hat. Nick Maglio had been director of the Kiwanis in 1972 and 1973. The league folded in the 80s and that would have been the end of it, but for Maglio. Out of respect for the departed Ted

Meyerstein, whom he says, "cared about the kids," Maglio felt that the Kiwanis League should be reinstated. It was in 1997 that Nick did so and the Brooklyn Kiwanis League was back. He started out with one division of six teams and by 2005 had grown to five divisions with a total of 42 teams. The 600 players range in age from 9 through 18 years. Much of their baseball today is played on the seven diamonds at Bay 8 street in Bensonhurst., called Ben Vitale Fields.

Due to the lack of resources and employees, the Kiwanis League has taken on the responsibility of maintaining the fields. This effort includes the preparation for two of the local high schools; New Utrecht and Telecommunication, who play their home games at the Ben Vitale Fields.

Like Lorenzo, Maglio has had his disagreement with Little League Baseball. Observing it he says he, "didn't like what he saw." He doesn't like metal bats or the distancing that is part of the Little League rules. Nick believes that there should be a gradual increase of the distances of the pitchers mound and between the bases. The kids then can grow into it getting stronger as they get older and ultimately reach the full 60' 6" and 90' by the time they are thirteen years old.

He also says that baseball "must be fun" for the kids or it's not worth playing. As a young boy, Nick Maglio played ball until he was about eighteen years old, but as he confesses, was not particularly good. He learned early that his forte' was in coaching and managing teams. This began when Nick was fifteen years old and in high school at New Utrecht. He managed the Ty-Cobbs and St. Bernadette teams and was also assistant coach to Dan Lynch at St. Francis College. Nick was physically a big boy and that helped him get the attention of the kids he was managing. But he was after all, no older than they were and this created somewhat of a problem. Some people didn't take his teams seriously with such a youngster in charge.

At one point he worked around it by having his dad, Tony, who'd played some pro ball, coaching at third. "As a decoy," Nick explains, " and I would coach first and give the signs from there." As in so many cases , the inborn love of baseball was passed on from father to son. Born in 1945 at 84 street and 13 avenue, Nick had never seen his father play ball, as the elder Maglio had concluded his career beforethe boy was old enough to understand, but the younger Maglio revels in the scrap-book and clippings of his dad's performances that he keeps.

Tony Maglio was born in 1913 at 56 street and Ft. Hamilton Parkway and became a right handed pitcher who, according to a newspaper article in 1934, "lives to play ball." He played in Bensonhurst and Bay Ridge at the Bay Ridge Oval as well as the Parade Grounds. Tony developed into quite a pitcher. He relied almost exclusively on a fast ball and excellent control and the knowledge that he developed of the hitters he faced. He knew them well enough to be able to pitch to spots and exploit their individual weaknesses.

In 1932 he opened the " Home Talk Baseball League", and pitching for the Veronas against the Emeralds, Tony struck out 20 batters while walking only one. In his very next games he struck out 16 against the Samosets, setting a local record of 36 strikeouts in two games that has never been equaled. It's no wonder that over the next three years, Maglio became known as the "Pride of Borough Park."

That same season he pitched 16 2/3 innings in a doubleheader against Our Lady of Perpetual Help and the Hopeless AC. His strikeout totals were astronomical. In games against the Laytons , he struck out 14; the Excelsiors, 16; the Beaumonts,14 and in 1933 he turned away 20 once again against the Norwegian Turn Society.

Tony got his chance in 1935 when he was signed by the Detroit Tigers, largely on the recommendation of the Tigers power hitting star , Hank Greenberg. At the same time another Bay Ridge standout , Bobby Lane, was given a shot with the Pittsburgh Pirates and farmed out to Portsmouth, Ohio in the Central League.

Maglio was assigned to a club in the Penn State League where he ran up a 7-1record. But then an injury struck, Tony tore muscles in his throwing arm from which he never fully recovered. The injury effectively ended his professional career, although the "never say die" pitcher came home and developed a knuckle ball and continued to pitch. He proved to be effective enough to get another try, this time with the New York Yankees, but it didn't pan out.

In an era of semi-pro ball, Maglio was hired by the Atlantic & Pacific Tea Co. and played for the company team in the "Home Talk Industrial Baseball League" at the Parade Grounds. A schedule in late August of 1935 listed Bush Terminal vs. Atlantic& Pacific Tea Co. at Diamond 6, Parade Grounds; and Maxwell House Coffee vs. Quaker Maid at

Diamond 10. He was also there for games against the House of David and Cum Posey's Homestead Grays of the Negro Leagues. Tony was not as effective in building up strikeouts but kept hits scattered and continued to win ball games. He defeated American Can Co. 1-0 while scattering eight hits. Through the last of the thirties and into 1940 , Maglio played with the"Powerhouse"; named for columnist Jimmy Powers column in the Daily News; and was player-manager for the Brooklyn Bears. By 1940 the papers were still raving about his strikeout record performances in '32.

The Powerhouse nine played in the Intercommunity league, the forerunner to the Parade Grounds League. The Powerhouse played for the 1938 league championship scheduled at "Diamond No. 2 , Parade Grounds" and were defeated by the Shore Views.

In 1949, while the Loew's Bay Ridge theater was screening "The Three Musketeers" with Angela Lansbury and Gene Kelly, The Chanticleer at 93 Street and Fourth Avenue was proclaiming itself Fort Hamilton's most popular Dining Room. Jimmy Powers in his Powerhouse column in the Daily News was writing that "Tony Maglio, former manager of the Powerhouse baseball team that distinguished itself on the Parade Grounds, is now coaching at St. Bernadette's. Maglio was once the property of the Tigers."

Nick Maglio never was the ballplayer his father was, but love for the game was his inheritance. If not for that, there probably would have been no rebirth of the Brooklyn Kiwanis League or dedication to the 600 youngsters now enjoying the privilege of playing there.

The Parade Grounds have been a blessing for the high school leagues. The Public School Athletic League (PSAL) encompasses all the public high schools in the city of New York, and many who do not have their own facility use the Parade Grounds as a home field. This is equally true of the Catholic High School Athletic Association (CHSAA). One of the latter is Bishop Ford Central High School located at 500 19 Street in the Park Slope section. The school occupies the site of the old Brooklyn trolley barns, the site of which, during the Civil War, stood a Federal prison.

Named for a Maryknoll Bishop, Francis X. Ford, martyred in China in 1952, the school was dedicated in 1962. The school colors, Red and Black, are the colors of the Chinese artistic tradition and the Maryknoll Fathers, and symbolize Bishop Ford's Chinese mission. The athletic program has remained a major part of the school's curriculum since its' founding. Current athletic director Peter Goyco expresses the view that "sports should be used to enhance education," and points out that there are more than 600 of the 1300 students enrolled at Bishop Ford who participate in athletics.

The team calls the Parade Grounds home and its three baseball entities; varsity, junior varsity and freshman teams play about 50 ball games at the historic sandlot facility. Diamonds seven and three are the designated "home" fields for the Falcons, while the school's soccer team also utilizes the Park for home games. While Mr. Goyco revels in the new Parade Grounds facilities and the conditions of the recently renovated fields, he wishes there was more room for baseball. He speaks highly of former players and singles out Ron Merritta , who also played with the Cadets , and went into the pros along with Chad Frontera and John Halama. Halama made it all the way to the big time. After high school he attended St. Francis College and was selected by the Houston Astros in the 23rd round of the free-agent amateur draft in 1994. Traded to the Seattle Mariners as part of the deal that sent Randy Johnson to the Astros , John won 14 games for manager Lou Pinella in 2000. Halama has been in the big leagues for nine seasons going to the post season with Seattle in 2000 and 2001.

Chad Frontera was drafted by the Chicago White Sox, but chose college and enrolled at Seton Hall. In his junior year he was drafted in the ninth round by the San Francisco Giants. Frontera made the trek all the way to AAA ball, but he encountered arm trouble that necessitated an operation. He was never the same and was forced to conclude a promising career. The team has at times in the past journeyed to Florida for spring training and Goyco was an assistant coach under Manny Fernandez in the nineties when the club went to Puerto Rico. Usually, though, winter workouts are conducted at the school hitting out of the cages and working in the gym.

What about the fundamentals, once so academic to a young ballplayer's training? "Kids watch the pros," said Goyco, "and lose the fundamentals." There has been a succession of coaches at Bishop Ford and there are several former ones holding other positions in the school. Forte' Bellino coached the squad from 1981-1984, and again from '89 - '91.

Ray Nash is the president of Bishop Ford high school and holds the same title in the Catholic High School Athletic Association (CHSAA). Ray came from the Bed-Sty area and attended Our Lady of Good Council school, eventually relocating to Queens. "I sleep in Floral Park, " he says, "and live in Brooklyn." A Parade Grounder for many years, Nash played baseball and basketball at St. Francis Prep and St. Francis College. "We used to take the GG train to Smith and Ninth Street," he says, "change there and then walk the rest of the way." He recalls a playoff game against Bishop Loughlin at the Park where the distance from first to second ran about 100 feet. "No measurements," he said, " they just dropped the bag where they thought it should go." He coached both baseball and basketball at Ford and took his hoopsters to the NIT in 1963, that year the Ford gymnasium was dedicated to Ray Nash.

A current controversy concerning aluminum bats involves the high schools , but Mr. Nash maintains that it is not an economic issue, "Most of the kids bring their own bats anyway," he said. The issue is more basic to today's environment ."The ball goes further, " Nash says, "they all want to hit home runs." Ray's son went into his dad's business and coaches basketball at St. Francis college.

Manny Fernandez coached baseball at Bishop Ford from 1989 through '96, handling the junior varsity squad in 1988. He had John Halama for one year, and Chad Frontera for his varsity years. The coaches concur that Chad was the finest prospect they had at Ford, even more in demand than Halama. Fernandez estimates that 20 teams were after him to sign. Frontera threw his fastball in the 92-93 MPH range and had a good curve ball. But injuries take their toll far too often in young ballplayers.

Proudly, Fernandez says that there had never been a pitcher injury while at Ford, but he blames the sandlot clubs for using these youngsters too often, thus creating a potential arm or shoulder problem which may not be revealed until later in their careers. Coaches of boys this young should "look ahead," he said. Pitch counts, he believes, are professional baseball's way of "protecting an investment", and nothing more.

Further, Fernandez says that college has become a necessity. "Why should a kid toil in the low minors for little money," when he can get an education and similar development as a player. " Colleges are replacing minor league development ." High school as well as sandlot programs today are geared to readying young players for college.

Manny Fernandez is from the *old school* of baseball. Bunting, stealing, and setting up runs. He recalls a championship game that was tied in the last inning. After a lead off double by the Falcons # 3 hitter, John Halama, a good hitter, batting in the fourth spot , came to the plate. Surprised to receive the bunt sign, he looked at the coach quizzically and fouled the pitch off. A second sign and a second bunt attempt and the sign was removed. John then hit an outfield fly that moved the runner to third base. With one out, he scored the winning run on a sacrifice fly by the fifth hitter. In response to Halama's question, the coach replied, "that's why I wanted you to bunt."

Lafayette High School in Bensonhurst has been one of the leading schools in the nation sending players into the major leagues, indeed, during the seventies, Lafayette had more professional baseball players in the majors than any other high school in the country. Players like John Franco, the

Aspromonte brothers; Ken and Bob, Sandy Koufax and Larry Yellen are but a few who were students at Lafayette.

On November 13, 1939, upon the formal dedication of the school, enrollment totaled 4,500 boys and girls. In 1949, to celebrate the Tenth Anniversary, an Open House was held with entertainment furnished by singers Alan Dale and Vic Damone, both alumni of the school.

So many of Brooklyn's high schools can boast of famous graduates. Not the least among them is my own alma mater , Erasmus Hall on Flatbush Avenue just off Church Avenue. Erasmus can regale former students like actress Barbara Stanwyck, silent movie star Norma Talmadge and Olympic swimming star Eleanor Holm. Major Leaguers players Waite Hoyt , Don McMahon, and Tony Balsamo, along with football star Sid Luckman and basketball's Bill Cunningham are all alumni of the school. NBA player and coach Doug Moe was a classmate of mine.

The buildings were a set of four, encompassing a campus, the Flatbush and Bedford Avenue wings revealing huge archways, the entire structure emitting the aura of a University. The school began as a private academy in 1787 with an enrollment of twenty-six boys. There were more than eleven hundred in my graduating class in 1956. There is a statue of Desiderius Erasmus, the school's namesake, on campus, posed with an open book. Erasmus was a Dutch scholar born in Rotterdam in 1469. He has been referred to as a "classical scholar of the highest order." His greatest achievement was a Greek version of the New Testament which was the genesis for English and German translations.

On test days, students would flip coins at the figure, those landing on the open book signified a passing grade. On occasion some of the fellows would scale the statue and retrieve a handful of coins, possibly negating the passing grades in the process. The naming of the school after the Dutch master linked the borough of *Breuckelen* with its' Dutch origins.

Our baseball team at Erasmus was not one of the schools that used the Parade Grounds as a home field. We had our own; Erasmus Field, on MacDonald Avenue; later renamed for NFL star Sid Luckman. The track team ran around the campus paths and as a member of the Erasmus' cross-country track team, I worked out at Park Circle, where we did laps to warm-up prior to running the five-mile course thatwas laid out through Prospect Park, the last stretch of which we completed over the Park's bridal path, always giving way to the thunder of hoofs behind us.

My high school baseball career was not very distinguished. Bob Fatta, one of our pitchers wrote in my yearbook, "to old hole-in-the-glove," but I recall names and faces. A catcher named Johnny Greshick, infielders Marty Knee and Artie "Batman" Bocian. And pitchers Artie Clemens, who played with the Dahills, and Danny Gordon. My second base partner was Harvey Cohen. My good friend Richie Malone was a pitcher and a rock' n roller. I went to the Brooklyn Paramount Theater with Richie to see a Rock 'N Roll show. I recall seeing Frankie Lymon and the Teenagers and a group called the Flamingoes perform.

The times have changed drastically in the fifty years since I was at Erasmus, as you would expect. But in remembering, it seems that the mind holds people and places as they once were. A Chase bank is on the corner of Church and Flatbush Avenues where Garfield's Cafeteria used to be a hangout for us kids. The building that housed the Loew's Kings Theater is still standing including the marquee, but it is in disrepair and has been closed for many years.

Ebbets Field is gone and the Bond Bread Company building is now a flea market .Steeplechase Park is no longer in existence in Coney Island and Keyspan Park, home of the NY-Penn League Brooklyn Cyclones has risen in its place. You can no longer find an Ebinger's Bakery anywhere in Brooklyn nor a Jahn's Ice Cream Parlor where six or seven of us used to chip in and share something called a *Kitchen Sink*. The trolley cars had long since ceased humming along the borough's thoroughfares and the Brooklyn Paramount Theater is now an appendage of Long Island University, through strolling on Brooklyn's downtown streets, you may sense the beat of a Chuck Berry song in the air, or it could be the remnants of a Richie Malone bop session.

But some things have not altered at all. The Dutch Reform Church is still opposite Erasmus and Friedman's Sporting Goods, where I purchased my first baseball glove is still in business on Flatbush Avenue. There is still an el train running above MacDonald Avenue and Nathan's still serves up the best hot dog in America. And Erasmus Hall High School still sits on Flatbush Avenue, as regal an edifice as you will find in the old borough.

VI.

The Instructor

"You've never hit a baseball, have you, Skully?"
-Fox Mulder; X-Files-"The Unnatural"

Milton Staub looked like a college professor. He was not tall, about 5'7or5'8" and slight of build. He wore brown horn-rimmed glasses and his hair was a thick mane, streaks of black but decidedly steel gray. He spoke softly and could hardly be heard above the din of the ball field.

Fred Weber never had met him before that spring in 1958, he simply appeared one day and attached himself in an unobtrusive way to the club. He was now a coach, but he was above all a teacher, an instructor. But as far as the Virginians were concerned there was no one to instruct, at least not until me and Bob Stone came along. The youngest of the players were 24 or 25 years old. Those that were good enough already had their shot at pro ball, the others were beyond consideration, again, except for me and Stone.

Mr. Staub was one of those intellectuals with a passion for the game, much like Stephen Jay Gould or George Will. But Mr. Staub's passion was directed ubiquitously toward instructing. So it was only a matter of time before he approached me.

It was out on Diamond Five during a spring workout. He had been watching me closely during batting practice. Finally, I assume that he just couldn't stand it any longer, he asked , "Can I speak to you about your hitting?"

"Sure," I said.

"I don't think you're going to hit too many home runs," he told me.

"I don't either. But I wasn't trying to."

"Then why are you swinging a thin handled bat from the end.?"

That was his ice-breaker. He had made his point and got me to listen. He'd established that I was swinging as though I had some power when in reality all my hits were soft and bouncing. Mr. Staub, we all called him Mr., had a habit of stroking his chin with his thumb and forefinger and he did it now, trying to find a place to begin. " Can you come down on Tuesday night?" he said. I readily agreed,happy at the idea of some one-on-one instruction.

He asked Bobby Stone to join us and so on Tuesday we began the learning process that would ultimately include

Bobby as well. Mr. Staub brought a brand new bat with him; a 35" Jackie Robinson model. It had a thick handle, something I was not at all used to. He told me that if I was willing to go along with him, it would mean altering my entire hitting style. "It'll be like learning to walk again," he said. "I want you to start from the very beginning." Bobby looked at me with his elfish grin and observed, "looks like we're gonna be spending a lot of time here." And then he laughed as he always did following one of his self-satisfying observations.

I had hit with a closed stance and Mr. Staub began by opening me up. That is, to bring my left, or front foot away from the plate and towards third base. "You can use both eyes and see the ball better," he explained. He had me choke up about two inches on the bat and told me that I should concentrate on just making contact. Not to swing too hard. Bobby went to the mound and started throwing to me and I began my education. It was a new and different approach and I was uncertain, but once I said yes, Mr. Staub was in charge and he kept me at it.

We met once or twice each week in addition to team workouts. One night Freddie and Frank Chiarello were there. Chick was an outfielder on the Virginians. A left-hander with a near perfect swing. Chick had signed with the Giants a few years before and released while hitting over .300. There was a certain bitterness that stayed with him that I learned about some years later.

This night they were there solely to help me at Mr. Staub's request. I had hit in the second spot in the order with the Dahills because I had a propensity to hit to right field. This was all well and good but Mr. Staub said that I was swinging late and pulling away from the pitch, thus balls would bounce off the bat and bloop into the opposite field.

He wanted me to be aggressive and go into the pitch and direct those balls to the right side with authority. So Chick worked with me that night and by the end of the session I knew what I had to do and how to do it. It only remained for me to put it into practice.

Now I got some variety in my pitchers. Bobby floated his knuckler up there and Weber his assortment of curves. I was getting a first class education and I was determined to improve myself. We played a number of spring games. Freddie would sometimes book three games in one day. When we complained, his justification was that he had to work his pitchers. He carried five for our five or six games a week. I was getting a lot of playing time because of this, but my hitting wasn't showing any noticeable improvement. I was sometimes depressed over this, but Mr. Staub never stopped encouraging me.

I would hit a come-backer to the mound and come back to the bench cursing under my breath. He would say, "good hitting," or something like that. I would just point out to the pitcher's mound as if to say, "are you kidding?" And he'd say, "yes, but you hit it on the nose , you stepped into it real well. Another inch or two and it would have been in center field."

One day he handed me a book, *Big League Batting Secrets* by Jim Smilgoff and Harvey Kuenn. Kuenn was a perennial .300 hitter with Detroit and in 1959 would win the American league batting title with .353. Smilgoff coached college baseball in Chicago. In the forward the authors stated the axiom that sold me when they said that most batters are not natural hitters and that "we believe that you can improve your hitting if you really apply yourself to the lessons set down in this book." I had every intention of doing so. The book was a treasure trove of hitting covering every aspect you can possibly imagine. I devoured it and then reread it. Fifty years later it still sits on my shelf and I still take a look from time to time. Ted Williams said that hitting a baseball is the toughest thing to do in sports. When you consider that a great hitter realizes success barely thirty percent of the time, you think there just might be something to it.

As the season got under way I was getting some pretty good playing time, but on Sundays in the Parade Grounds League games, I rode the bench. My hitting did start to improve, but I was frustrated at my perceived limited chances to play on Sundays. Mr. Staub never stopped encouraging me, but I saw no chance at all.

Our infield was solid. I detected no flaws at all. At first base we had Vinnie Marino. Vinnie had come up through the ranks of another one of the classic Parade Grounds organizations, the *Bonnies.* He was our lead off man. He could hit, run and field his position. Marino wasn't going anywhere. Second base had another veteran , Eddie *Mack* McDonough. Hitting in the second spot , he could bunt and move a runner up and was a good glove man.

The shortstop, of course, was Tom Castaldo; one of the best I'd seen and the only ballplayer I'd ever known who refused to sign a pro contract. Weber had begged him to stay another year just to play in the Sunday league. At third was Tommy Siracusa, another good solid guy who'd been around for years. I decided that none of these fellows would ever sit the bench and in my frustration I told that to Mr. Staub. "Just keep improving. There may be another way. You never know."

I didn't know what he was talking about but didn't question him further. I played every game of the Saturday doubleheaders however, usually at shortstop in place of Castaldo. This opened up the chance to play against teams from other leagues and face additional competition. Teams like Nathan's had Joe Pepitone, and Jimmy McElroy's Cadets had Joe Torre, Matt Galante and Rico Petrocelli. One club we saw regularly was the Senecas. It was a good club with quality players, Richie *"Rebo"* LuPardo, and Wally Edge among them. In 1958 the Senecas had a pitcher named Tony Balsamo whom I considered one of the toughest I ever faced.

Tony came from Woodruff Avenue near Flatbush Avenue not far from the Williamsburg Saving Bank in downtown Brooklyn and began his baseball life in "Pop" Secol's Ice Cream League. Later he played at the Parade Grounds for the Bonnie Cubs and also at Erasmus Hall high school. Tony was two-thirds of a monumental achievement at Erasmus, the other part of the fraction belonging to a pitcher named Jerry Roush. Three consecutive no-hitters were hurled by the two,games one and three by Balsamo with Roush throwing the gem in between.

Tony attended Fordham University where he pitched and played the outfield, never missing a game in three college seasons. He graduated in 1958 with a bachelors degree and

played with the Senecas at the Parade Grounds. It was in that
'58 season at the Park that I faced Balsamo. Tony had a good
fastball but it was a devastating overhand curve that killed me.
He threw it waist high and it broke "off the table." I had a
teammate, Johnny Doerr, who had just as much trouble trying
to hit that pitch. We devised a scheme. We would discuss ways
to beat it and the next guy up would test out the hypothesis.
For example, we thought that moving up in the batter's box
might allow us to hit the ball before it dipped. Whoever was
the next hitter would try it out and then come back to the
bench and explain why it didn't work. We figured two heads
were better than one, and one at-bat was better than two.
Nothing ever worked. Neither one of us could ever hit him.

Scouted that season by the Phils and the Cubs, Balsamo was
signed by Chicago scout Ralph DeLullo. He began in Paris,
Illinois in D ball and progressed to C and then was assigned
to AA San Antonio in the Texas League. Told by manager
Harry Craft that there would not be a spot for him after all,
he was sent down to B ball at Wenatchee, Washington. This
sort of disappointment was always difficult for these young
ballplayers to deal with and it was the same for Tony, so much
so, that he wanted to quit.

His dad got on the phone from Brooklyn and talked him
out of it. "Stick it out," he said. "Give it some more time and
see what happens." Tony did. He went to Wenatchee and
continued his climb to the majors. One spring his dad saved
up some vacation time and drove his son to Mesa, Arizona and
spent the entire spring training season with him, watching and
encouraging. "What a man he was," Tony says now in loving
memory. It was at Wenatchee that Tony "met my wife. That

year changed my life." The couple were married soon after and had "43 great years " before he sadly lost her to cancer. It was the next spring when the catalyst to the majors was sprung.

Back home in Brooklyn Tony's brother Lou was playing with our Cardinals team. One spring day he informed us that Tony called and said he was "throwing BBs." "I don't know," Balsamo says now, "something just clicked. Experience, mechanics, confidence? Nothing replaces confidence."

At a spring training bar-be-que, a writer friend of Phil Wrigley, the Cubs owner, approached Tony and his bride and offered congratulations. Thinking that he meant on their marriage, the couple thanked him. "Oh," the writer said, "that too. But I was congratulating you on making the club. You're going to the majors." The previous year, playing for manager Dick Cole in AAA, they had discussed relieving. Relief pitching was developing prominence and it offered Balsamo an opportunity to possibly "get there quicker." he pondered over the decision. He had the stamina for a starter, having thrown 14 innings once in D ball, but the changing times made the opportunity it offered too good to pass up. On one occasion in the spring, one of the Cubs' "college of coaches", told him to throw three innings, "if you do good you're on the club. If not, forget it."

" No pressure here," Balsamo thought, and went out and threw three good innings, striking out six and so it was as a relief pitcher that Tony Balsamo made his major league debut.

On April 14,1962 it was 41 degrees in Chicago when Tony was told to warm up.He only got to throw eleven pitches before he was called in to face Ken Boyer of the St. Louis Cardinals, a tough guy to start a major league career against. Boyer was entering his eighth year and hit .329 in 1961 with 24 home runs and 95 RBIs. There was a very small crowd in Wrigley Field in the frigid weather, but they included Tony's family and friends. Someone, his brother or Erasmus teammate , Tony Nunzillo, he doesn't remember which, could be heard in the near empty ballpark."Strike the bum out!"

Balsamo wanted to throw on the inside corner and keep the ball low, figuring it would be tougher to hit on the hands in the cold. He did as instructed. He struck out Boyer. The 1962 season inaugurated for the Cubs an incredibly ridiculous and outlandish plan for which, unfortunately, Tony Balsamo became a victim. As Tony says of the Cubs owner,"Mr. Wrigley was a nice man, but he didn't know baseball." In the winter preceding the '62 season, Wrigley confronted coach Elvin Tappe as to how to improve the team. Wrigley had made three managerial changes in the last year-and-a-half alone and that led to changes in the coaching staff as well. Tappe told him that all the changes hurt the continuity of the club. His suggestion was to hire a regular coaching staff and keep them in place no matter who the manager was. Wrigley liked the idea but took it one step further. He decided that he didn't need a manager at all, but one of the coaches could act as manager on a rotating basis. Although Tappe saw the inherent flaws in the system, he had no choice but to go along with it.

As Balsamo remembers , the Cubs were"the laughing stock of baseball." That season began with Tappe, Charlie Metro, and Lou Klein as the Cubs "College of Coaches." As one critic stated it, "the Cubs have been without players for years, now they're going to try it without a manager."

Under Tappe, Tony did well. He got to pitch on a regular basis and was averaging nearly one strike out per inning. But the scenario changed dramatically when Charlie Metro took over as head coach early in the season. "Metro was my downfall," Balsamo said. "He was a difficult man." Metro would call early morning workouts to practice cut-offs, "something I knew from high school." He would threaten juvenile disciplinary actions. During pepper games he would slam the ball and then demean the players, "what are you, a wimp?" Not too terrible in itself, but taken together, it was enough to disrupt the players' moral.

The real danger was in the on-the-field handling of the players. Balsamo was in a groove, pitching well and regularly under Tappe, but now that changed. Metro did not use him for a week or ten days at a time. This led to inconsistency in his performance. It wouldn't be long before the final showdown. Tony's roomie, pitcher Barney Schultz, came out of a game against the Dodgers with a pulled muscle and Tony replaced him. Maury Wills was on first, the potential trying run. Balsamo had him picked off, but first baseman Ernie Banks, not familiar yet with a new position, dropped the ball.

Wills then stole second, one of a record setting 104 that season. Willie Davis popped up and the hitter was Wally Moon. Metro wanted him to throw curves to the left hander, while both Balsamo and his catcher believed that fastballs would have been more effective. They agreed to follow orders and Moon slapped one through the right side scoring Wills. Metro came out to the mound, "I'm trying to give you an opportunity ," he told Tony. "Opportunity?" Tony ranted, "You call pitching every 10 or 12 days an opportunity?" The next day he was sent down.

The following spring he was asked to stay in AAA and that was the final straw for Balsamo. His career was ended that spring.

Balsamo remembers only three moments when he was intimidated on a ball field.Once , in high school, pitching at Ebbets Field for Erasmus against Manual Training high. It was after all, the home of the Brooklyn Dodgers. The second time was his first time as a pro at Paris, Illinois, and the third time was facing Gil Hodges. The big Dodgers' first baseman was the idol of the kid from Brooklyn and here he stood on the mound facing him in a big-league game. He "was so nervous, he could hardly grip the ball." He walked Hodges on four pitches, non even close.

In retirement, Balsamo has been very generous in giving his time to worthy causes. He has worked for the kids' Special Olympics , and for Autistic and children stricken with MS. Once at such an event he took the mound at Ducks Stadium in Long Island. Former Met Buddy Harrelson said, "can you go one inning?" "Sure," Tony remarked. "I got on the mound," he said,"it was thirty years since I threw a baseball and I couldn't reach home plate."

"Tony," Harrelson said, " maybe you'd better move in a little bit."

Balsamo is actively involved with another cause. There are more than 1000 former major league ballplayers not eligible for a pension, having fallen short of the five years requirement in effect when they played. Some, like the Parade Grounds Jerry Casale, didn't miss by much. Casale fell short by a mere three weeks. While all would benefit, some would more so, having financial difficulties, that a pension would help alleviate.

In a multi billion dollar industry whose players average more than one million dollars in annual salary, it is sadly notable that nothing is done for these former players, who were the forerunners of the multi-millionaires in today's major leagues. Tony points out that only Senator Jim Bunning, former big league pitcher and member of baseball's Hall-Of-Fame has been of help. To date no one in baseball's echelon has made a move.

I received my baptism to the Virginians style of play in one of the early games. It was a Sunday and we were on Diamond One. I was sitting on the bullpen bench down the left field line. As usual Weber was the catalyst for the donnybrook. He had gotten into some sort of a verbal battle with a guy from the other club. From my vantage point I had no idea of what was going down.

I was sharing the bench with a catcher , Vinny Lamatina and two pitchers, Stone and a right hander named Joe Galetta. Suddenly, Weber and his antagonist was grappling on the pitcher's mound and both benches cleared as the gathering on the mound became a mob. The others tore off the bench and ran in toward s the excitement.

I started for the scene also, but was stopped by our left fielder, *Putsie* DeBarnardo. "Hey," he called to me. "Where you goin'?"

I pointed. "There, where do you think."

"Come here," he said. I followed him back to the bench where he sat down and motioned for me to sit beside him. "When those lunatics start throwing punches," he said, "here's where you go." We sat there for the duration of the rhubarb and I knew that it was good advice he had given me. I only wish I could have followed it more closely in the future.

I began to encounter another problem with my playing. We had just completed an evening game and I played second base. We attempted three double plays with me in the middle. I completed one, the other two landed me halfway into left field. There was still some daylight when another one of our "old-timers", an infielder named Louie Schalaba came over to me and said, "you better hang around a while. You're gonna have to learn something before you get killed."

He and Freddie worked with me until after dark. Lou showed me three ways to make the pivot. Straddle the bag , take the toss and throw to first; hit the bag and step back and then throw; the third way was to go across the bag and throw from inside the bag on the mound side. Depending on the situation, the runner, the slide, the toss, you had to utilize all three. Whenever possible I tried to stay with the last one. Because of my weak arm I needed to be moving towards first base to get the most I could on the throw.

It was great of those guys to work with me and it all paid off. Ultimately I could turn the pivot pretty well and I did get a fair share of hits. I was the atypical "Sows' ear", and my improvement allowed me to play seven seasons and hold my own in a very good class of amateur ball.

Through all of this Mr. Staub never left my side. He and I and Bob Stone still came out one evening each week. I worked on my hitting constantly, changing my entire approach and learning something brand new. But I loved the game and wanted desperately to succeed at it. During this period of time, although I would not express it to anyone, not even Bobby, I still harbored those deep inner imaginative meanderings of getting a shot at pro ball.

We also got to working with Stone in those sessions. Mr. Staub set up a strike zone. This was something Branch Rickey used to do with the Dodgers. It consisted of two sticks driven into the ground on either side of home plate and strings tied between them; one at the knees and the other at the armpits to indicate the strike zone. I put on the mitt and Bob threw to me, trying to keep his pitches inside the strings.

He had a tricky knuckleball and catching it helped me a lot as a hitter. Trying to follow it necessitated a good deal of concentration. When he had it working , Bobby could float that pitch so that it drove hitters crazy and made him very effective. He was, however, told by scouts that a 19 year old shouldn't be throwing a knuckler."Come back when you're 35," they told him.

I was improving noticeably and Freddie began to help me by playing hit-and-run. I hit at the bottom of the order, but if Vinnie Marino or Eddie Mack weren't there, hemoved me up to the second slot. I was still a right field hitter although hitting it with more authority and with greater intention. The reason this was such a positive step for me was because getting the hit-and-run sign removed the decision making as to whether to swing or not. All I had to worry about was hitting the ball. I became pretty adapt at hitting behind the runner and Weber took full advantage of it.

The Sunday Parade Grounds League was early on looking like a three way race. Besides us there was St. Bernadette and Sacred Heart- St. Stephen. Both were very good ball clubs, with pretty good pitching. My chance on Sundays finally came and it was unexpected. Mr. Staub came up to me before a game and told me I was in the lineup. "Where?" I asked him as I looked around and saw the whole infield present and accounted for.

Weber decided to bench on outfielder and shifted third baseman Tom Siracusa to left field. He moved Eddie Mack to third base and opened up second base for me. Staub had been right all along, "there may be another way, you never know!"There was and I was excited at the prospect. The first few games I hit seventh, but Mr. Staub kept at Weber with his own idea. He wanted me in the five slot. His rationalization was that with DeBarnardo hitting third and Castaldo fourth, a singles hitter in the fifth spot could keep a rally going. With Chiarello and our catcher hitting behind me the power would be turned on again. It made sense to Fred and there I was, smack in between four top notch hitters.

Of the four, three had played pro ball and the fourth, Castaldo, undoubtably could have. Both *Putsie* DeBarnardo and *Chick* Chiarello had played in the low minors. One with the St. Louis Browns and Chick with the Giants. And then there was Vince Tiani.Vinnie was an excellent defensive catcher. I would cover second base on a steal attempt and hold my glove in front of the bag about six inches off the ground and he would hit it every time.

Tiani had signed with the Cincinnati Reds out of college. While waiting for a minor league assignment, he made a road trip with the big club. They came to Brooklyn and knowing that it was Vince's home, manager Birdie Tebbetts allowed him to catch the first infield during the pre-game workout. I asked him if he made any bad throws. "Just one," he told me, "in the dirt to second, but McMillan scooped it up and you didn't even see it hit the ground." Roy McMillan had one of the greatest pair of hands among infielders.

Tiani reached double AA ball with Savannah in the Southern Association before it began to unravel. He was hit in the head with a fastball. It was fairly serious. Batting helmets were in their infancy. We used a skull cap that went under the hat; and even the full helmets were not very durable. He was out for a while and shortly after being back in the lineup, he was hit again in the head.

This one I couldn't understand. He had been hit while behind the plate catching, while wearing his mask."How could you possibly get hit like that?" I asked him time and again. He would smile and shrug. I never believed him. But I apologized to him one day out on Diamond Five. A foul tip off a batter's bat shot back and missed the top of his mask and slammed him on the exposed portion of his head. He was dazed and had to come out of the game. "You believe me now?" he asked me .

I was in the heat of things at last. A *New York World-Telegram* clipping in early June noted all three contending teams winning doubleheaders leaving us one game behind St. Bernadette and Sacred Heart one behind us. We beat the Flatbush Dodgers7-0 with me being "the chief cannonader, knocking in four runs with two hits."

The shutout was thrown by our ace, Carl Hottinger. All the top clubs had one or two good pitchers and Carl was one of the best in the Park. Weber said that he was "the best pitcher to never sign a contract that he'd ever seen." There was a reason why he didn't sign. Carl was a six-footer who never weighed more than 120pounds. He wore two pair of sanitary hose so that his legs wouldn't look so skinny. It was feared that pitching more than once a week in the pros and likely in some hot southern climate, Carl would wilt away or sweat off needed pounds or worse, come up with some breathing disorder.

Carl grew up in the Sunset Park section and began playing ball with the St. Catherine of Alexandria team managed by a fellow named Anthony Lupo. When Lupo gave up the club after a while, Carl's dad took over the managerial duties. I got to know Carl's family when in the Virginian years his parents would come to see all the games he pitched at the Park.

Carl moved to the Celtics in his middle teen years and then to the Virginians at the Senior level where he played for Petey Cavallo. Carl was a teammate to two players he considered to be among the best he ever saw at the Park, Putsie DeBarnardo and Chick Chiarello. Hottinger played for the PGL City All-Star Champs a couple of years before I did and his squad won the city championship, just as ours did. . Carl had thrown nine consecutive hitless innings in that competition leading up to the final game against the Bronx team at McCoombs Dam Park in the Bronx.

The first hitter he faced got the first hit off of him, a towering home run. The manager came out to the mound, "OK," he said, "the streak is over - now let's win the game." The shortstop on that club was Bob Aspromonte.

Hottinger had a try-out with the Dodgers at Ebbets Field and the Giants invited him to the Polo Grounds for a look. It was the Giants who decided to give the skinny kid a shot. They wanted to assign him to a club in the Texas League, but fearing that Carl may dissipate in the Texas summer, they asked to be resolved of all medical obligations should he suffer heatstroke or disappear completely. The Hottingers, of course, refused.

The Giants didn't know what they missed out on. Hottinger had tremendous stamina. Fred would start him in the first game of a double header. If it was a close game he would stay in, but if we had a lead Carl would come out after four or five innings. He would then start and invariably finish the second game. He had a between games ritual. Hottinger would grab a shower, rub a bottle of liniment on his arm, and rest for the second game. If it was a hot day, Weber would have someone stay with Carl under the gigantic oaks next to the clubhouse and fan him with a wet towel. Invariably it worked wonders, he usually won the second game also. Hottinger threw very hard and had a sharp breaking ball. He also changed up well, not a very common pitch on the sandlots. Tiani, with his experience, never hesitated to call for the change. Sometimes even with two strikes on the hitter and Carl never shook him off. Hottinger didn't have a great deal of trouble with opposing hitters, but considered the Senecas to be most formidable with hitters like Richie "Rebo" Lupardo and Marty Somma. He was also very respectful of Matt Galante, always considering him a tough out.

At one point they began making selections for a Parade Grounds League Hall-Of-Fame. It was particularly significant because the voting was done by the managers and league officials. The first choice was Joe Torre, the second was Carl Hottinger. Like the rest of us, Carl has gathered indelible memories of his playing days. As he advised one of his sons, "it doesn't matter how good you are - if you have as gooda time as I did, then that's all that counts. It was one of the best times of my life!"

We also had with us a hard throwing right hander named Mike Taglifaro. *Mickey* had been away also. *Away*, being Parade Grounds vernacular for going to the pros. It was Mike who put us into first place with a 4-hit shutout over St. Bernadette. Our record of 8-3 left us in a tie with Sacred Heart.

The following week St. Bernadette's ace, a southpaw named Joe DiGirolamo threw a perfect game at a team called Gregnanos. He struck out 13 of the 21 outs; sandlot teams played seven inning games. According to the *Telegram*, it was the first perfecto in the 37-year history of the Parade Grounds League.

Each week I would read the newspaper accounts of the games to see how the other teams did. You didn't have to read the papers to know who the hitters were, since you faced them on the field. Nevertheless, the same names would be there week after week. For Sacred Heart there was a constant trio. Emilio Polazzo, Ted Trance and Frank Yurman invariably were the bats behind a Sacred Heart victory.

Moe Polazzo played shortstop and had a great year in 1958. He was signed after the season with the New York Giants , scouted by the Giants perennial bird dog, Mr. Mathieson, who was known to everyone simply as Matty. Moe played just the one season but like everyone else who played away, he came home with stories. His was of a huge left hander who hit *"the hell out of the ball,* watch for him," he told us. His name was Willie McCovey.

On the last Sunday of June Hottinger threw his second straight shutout striking out 10 and giving just three hits to the Brooklyn Revels. We were now 11-3 and stayed one game up. Over in the American division the Sabres' Moose Morrissey and Franny Jamin pitched a double header victory as the Sabres began to open up their division lead. Jamin was another toughie. He threw a ball so heavy that when you made contact it seemed as though the bat was so neutralized by the weight of the ball that it actually snapped back instead of continuing forward. He also kept the ball below the waist. I found him very tough to hit.

I picked up another bit of advice, this time from Tiani. We were standing in the outfield shagging flies during batting practice and I complained to him about not having anything to chew. The gum would lose its' flavor and become tiring to chew. I tried licorice and hard candy, which I once swallowed whole, and had run out of ideas. Vinnie was always helpful, so he pulled a package of Beech-Nut chewing tobacco from his back pocket.

"Here ya go," he said, "solves all your problems with one chaw." Like a fool I took a couple of fingers full, stuffed it into my mouth and started chewing it, like it was a stick of Wrigleys. I swallowed some juice and started to get sick to my stomach, but I spit it out real quick and was okay. I never learned how to chew tobacco, but I did use it from then on and for about the next six or seven years.

The way that I mastered it was to stick a chaw into my cheek and leave it there, limiting the liquid that came from it. When my mouth got dry, I took a chew and spit. It worked fine but later got us in trouble with Weber. We gave some to Bobby Newman before a game that he was supposed to play. He got so sick, he ran up to the clubhouse and didn't come back for the game.

"Keep that shit away from my players," Weber warned us. "I don't want to see it again, ever." Me and Vinnie kept chewing but we never loaded up in front of Weber. It was about this time that I had the chance to follow Putsie's advice about fighting on the field. Weber was on the verge of another rhubarb, yelling across to the other bench. An inning was about to begin and I was first up. I stood near the line in front of our bench with a couple of bats in my hand. Freddie stood next to me on his way to the third base coaching box when his antagonist tore across the infield between the plate and the mound with two teammates right behind him.

Weber clinched his fists and stood his ground. I looked around for someplace to hide. Our entire team was behind me on the bench. We were on Diamond One with three or four hundred people on the bleachers. No where to run, no place to hide. The two met right alongside of me and Weber threw a punch that clipped the other guy on the left side of his face. They both went down with the other two on top ofthem. Both benches emptied. I had no choice , I jumped on top, but with the certain desire to break it up. Suddenly there was an arm around my neck from behind. I turned slightly and saw Mike DePalma. I knew him as both a teammate and an opponent. "Mike, what're ya doin'?"

"I'm tryin' to stop you from hittin' him." he told me.

"I'm tryin ta break them up," I said.

"Oh, okay," Mike said. "I'll help ya."

Weber was often involved in these donnybrooks and it kept things jumping around out club. Of course he no longer had his guardian angel, the very large Petey Bull, to watch over him. Once when Pete was managing the Virginians and Fred got into a fight with an opponent, Pete , always the peacemaker, came to break it up. He lifted Weber's tormenter off his feet and told him that if he didn't lay off his man he would, "break his jaw." That effectively ended the fray. When it came to breaking up fights , Petey Bull was like a mean Gil Hodges.

Television became a major factor in the lives of America in the early fifties. In 1948 there were 325,000 sets in the United States. By 1954 there were 26 million, and in 1957 the homes with TV had escalated to 41 million. Once turned loose on the public , the new media dominated. From *Uncle Miltie*, to *I Love Lucy, Playhouse90* and the *Honeymooners*, television became a way of life in the fifties.

After a 1947 sighing by a private pilot of nine "saucer-like objects" flying over Yakama, Washington, new terms were injected into the vocabulary; *Flying Saucers* and *UFOs* or unidentified flying objects. The skies were full of them in the fifties. We followed their progress by going to the movies and seeing such films as *"The Thing From Another World,"* and *"Invasion of the Body Snatchers."*

We were reaching upwards and outwards. Roger Bannister ran an incredible four-minute mile, and Rocky Marciano retired in 1956 as the only undefeated heavyweight champion in history; 49 fights, 49 wins,43 by knockout. The Yankee Clipper, Joe DiMaggio retired and Hank Aaron began an incredible quest.

These were the halcyon days of youth, but not always so peaceful and tranquil, especially on our particular legendary playground.

VII.

Brooklyn Against The World

"Baseball was in the air in Brooklyn" -Burt Solomon

Contrary to what was once considered an intrinsic part of baseball lore, the invention of the game by Abner Doubleday in Cooperstown, New York in 1839 has long been relegated to myth. In truth, it seems that baseball was never invented at all, but evolved over a long period of time. Games played with a stick and a ball have been shown to have existed as long ago as the civilizations of ancient Greece and Egypt.

An assortment of articles and studies have placed a game involving a bat and a ball in Egypt four thousand years ago suggesting that it may have been an ancestor to baseball (1). What may render all of these clues as moot is a quote found in Homer's Odyssey, to wit, "toss'd and retoss'd, the ball incessant flies."

In 1937 an Italian professor Corrado Gini while studying the Berber tribesmen in a remote village in Libya observed them playing a game remarkably similar to American baseball. They called it *ta kurt om el mahag*, translated as "the ball of the pilgrim's mother." (2) Gini's conclusion was that the game was a cultural result generated by Europeans who had visited the region in North Africa during the Stone Age, thousands of years before Christ. Professor Gini contends also that *om el mahag* was associated with the ancient spring rain rituals of the Berbers, confirmed, he claimed by the Greek historian Herodotus in the fifth century BC.

A 1251 drawing from Spain shows a person tossing a ball underhand and another holding a bat with a common grip. (3) As it turns out there are numerous references to games played with a bat and a ball since ancient times in many parts of the world. In his book *Baseball Before We Knew It*, David Block makes reference to Persians, Romans, Lydians playing a similar game , in addition to the Greeks and Egyptians, and even the Mayans of the Yucatan. In the 17th and18th centuries, there are references from Germany, England , Poland and Sweden.

There is early documentation of the bat and ball game in the American settlement at Jamestown in 1607, apparently brought by some Polish glass-blowers who made the journey to the New World. In translation, the game was called "bat-ball." The Iroquois Indians in New York State played a game in the 1600s that had some kinship with the bat and ball game, though it may have resembled Rugby more than baseball.

Current evidence is overwhelming that bat and ball games have both ancient origin and roots throughout the world. Perhaps it should not be particularly surprising since a stick and a ball are relatively common play items for kids and young people.

Writing in his journal in APRIL 1779, David Block quotes Revolutionary War officer Henry Dearborn: "We are oblige'd to walk 4 miles to day to find a place leavel enough to play ball"- roughly the same distance many of us walked as kids to get to the Parade Grounds. (4)

In Manhattan the game dates back to at least the 1820s. A newspaper account in 1823 speaks of the *"manly and athletic game of baseball "* being played at what is now Eighth Street and Washington Place in Greenwich Village. (NYC) Baseball historian John Thorn has recently uncovered evidence that indicates that baseball was played in Plymouth, Massachusetts in 1791. An ordinance of that date banned the playing of *baseball* within 80 yards of the big church in the town square.

It is a historical truth that the game developed primarily in the Northeast and New York City and in particular, in the city of Brooklyn, not incorporated into New York until 1898. Teams like the Atlantics, the Excelsiors, the Eckfords and the Putnams played in places like the Union Grounds, the Capitoline Grounds, the Satellite Grounds and Washington Park.

It was in Brooklyn that the man credited with inventing the curve ball, William *Candy* Cummings, lived and played, and was ultimately enshrined in baseball's Hall-Of-Fame because of it. The first paid player and the game's first big star also plied his trade in the City of Churches. Jim Creighton's short -lived career with the Brooklyn Stars and the Brooklyn Excelsiors ended in his tragic death in 1862 at 21 years of age.

Reported to be the first Jewish player in organized ball, Lipman Emanual Pike played in Brooklyn during the early 1860s, and the Excelsiors made the first team road trip, traveling through upstate New York to play at Troy, Buffalo, Albany, Rochester and Newburgh. Incidentally, the great Christy Mathewson made his major league debut in Brooklyn's Washington Park on July 17, 1900. He lasted but five innings as Brooklyn won the game 13-7.

The very first *subway series* , although it might be more accurately termed the *coach and carriage* series, was a three game set between all-star squads from Brooklyn and New York and was actually played at the Fashion Race Course in an area that is now Corona, Queens in 1858. New York won two of the games, but the intensity of interest was undoubtably the forerunner of the intra-city rivalries of later years. (5)

In the 1890s the Brooklyn Bridegrooms invented the cut-off play and practiced lining up infielders to take throws from the outfield. In was in 1941 that Dodger owner Larry MacPhail, following the beaning to two of his stars, Reese and Medwick, created solid inserts for players to wear inside their caps.

During the 1890s Brooklyn was growing rapidly, the population exceeding 800,000, and a new city symbol was introduced. The trolley cars became so numerous that to navigate around the city, one had to be a good *dodger* of trolleys, thus giving the ball club the name by which it would ultimately be known.

Charley Ebbets built his ballpark and opened it in 1913 and the love affair between the team and the borough was flourished every summer at Ebbets Field. If Yankee Stadium was a cathedral on a hill, then Ebbets Field was a chapel in the valley. But before it became a house of worship, there were some rocky moments . In the thirties, the club was dubbed the *Daffiness Boys* by columnist Westbrook Pegler because of their propensity to finish in the second division. Hearing a fan debunking a Brooklyn player with the cry of, "ya bum, ya,"sportswriter Sid Mercer wrote a column and a new lexical entered the vernacular of the Brooklyn fan. The degrading sobriquet would turn to one of affection in later years when the Dodgers became the challenging, hard-fighting, winning ball club of the forties and fifties. Illustrator Willard Mullin created a caracature of a bum decked out in tattered rags and chomping on the butt of a cigar. This became the team's trademark and the cover illustration of the Dodgers yearbooks beginning in 1951. The bum didn't go west with the team, however, presumably not classy enough for southern California.

But the greatest claim of this team was the relationship that had developed with the fans of Brooklyn, the *Flatbush Faithful.* In his book, *Brooklyn's Dodgers: TheBums, The Borough, and the Best of Baseball,* Carl Prince notes "For many if not most Brooklynites, baseball was a central focus in their lives." The fan wasbest represented by Hilda Chester, the cowbell ringing, baritone-voiced lady bellowing "Eatcha heart out, ya bum ya!" The *Brooklyn Dodgers Sym-phony Band* began to inhabit Ebbets Field in the late thirties when a group of musically disinclined fans snuck instruments into the park and serenaded the crowds. Ultimately they were given seats for all games in section 8, behind first base. All of this was spontaneous, there were no orders from the scoreboard to sing, or to applaud. The Dodgers belonged to the people of Brooklyn. Stephen Jay Gould, professor, paleontologist, teacher of sciences at Harvard University, author and passionate baseball fan wrote, *"....Ebbets Field, home of the Brooklyn Dodgers, was the greatest ballpark I ever knew - an admission remember, that comes from a Yankee fan."* (6)

Of course the Dodgers' aim was to sell tickets and to this end they bonded with the populous in a number of ways. Free passes were offered to the youth through the Dodgers' "Knot-Hole Club" and the Police Athletic League.

Prior to every Dodgers home game was a telecast of the "Happy Felton Knot Hole Gang" show. Felton was a professional entertainer who presided over the program that brought three local young ballplayers to compete on the show. The judge was a Dodger player whose job it was to select the best of the three. The winner would be invited back the next day to visit in the Brooklyn dugout with a player of his choosing. All three contestants were feted with gifts in the form of baseball equipment. The show took place in the right-field bullpen thirty minutes before the game, while Gladys Gooding would be heard in the background playing the organ.

It was a never to be forgotten experience for the youngsters. Fifty years later Fred Weber can still recall every detail of his appearance as a sixteen year old contestant in 1948. He went up against two other pitchers from the Parade Grounds. Fred's club was the "Robins", Johnny Perrine played for the "Comets", and Lou Iazzino represented the "Pawnee Indians". The boys were judged by Dodgers' catcher Bruce Edwards.

Weber was elated to be selected as the winner. He was given a Rawlings "Mort Cooper" model glove, "top of the line," as he recalls, and a "Sam Mele" model Louisville Slugger bat. But that was only the tip of the iceberg. Fred was a hero in his neighborhood; everybody watched the show. The next day, Happy Felton walked him to the Dodgers' dugout where he met with Preacher Roe, the player of his choice. The young pitcher had a question for the star lefty that Preach said was a very good one. He wanted to know how many pitches it took Roe to warm up before a game, and how he broke down the warmup. Roe very patiently explained that he threw about 100 pitches, how he progressively threw harder, and how many curves and fastballs he threw until he was ready. The excitement that Fred Weber felt that day was, of course, the objective of the program, and it helped to lock in Dodgers' fans for years to come. There were often try-outs held, some open and some by invitation only. The latter were usually held at Ebbets Field, while there were open trials often conducted at the Parade Grounds. Scouts Arthur Dede and Steve Lembo were fixtures at the Park seeking young prospects. The program *Brooklyn against the World*, later simply known as the *Dodger Rookies* was initiated in the thirties and was an offshoot of these tryouts often leading to the signing of local boys.

These were by invitation only, extended to the best teen-age players as judged by the scouts. The team that was formed would play a schedule of games in the tri-state area, and sometimes would travel further away than that. Several boys would be signed each year out of the program;   Dodgers' catcher and Mets coach Joe Pignatano was signed from the 1948 club.

So many of the Boys of Brooklyn settled in other areas of the country. Places where they played or met their future wives, or established businesses when their playing days were over. The Aspromontes stayed in Houston, Mike Napoli in a Texas town outside of Ft. Worth, Rico Petrocelli in Massachusetts. But nearly eighty years after he was born in Bay Ridge, Joe Pignatano is once more a resident of his native borough. Playing at the Parade Grounds, Joe was selected for the Brooklyn Against the World squad and under the watchful eyes of Dodgers scouts signed with Brooklyn in 1948.

A solid catcher with a strong throwing arm, Pignatano began his trek with Cairo in the KITTY League. After three minor league seasons, Joe entered military service and missed two seasons. When he returned in 1953, he was assigned to Asheville, North Carolina where he had his best season. Pignatano appeared in 121games, and led the Tri-State League in triples with 13 and put-outs with 580, while hitting .316. Moving upward through the system to AAA at St. Paul, Joe played in 8 games with the Dodgers in 1957 before being sent back to Montreal in the International League. He came back to the big time with the now transplanted Dodgers in Los Angeles and put in six seasons of major league play before finishing up with the Mets in 1962.

Joe then embarked on a long and successful coaching career that included the 1969 "Miracle Mets" , World Series champions. It ought to be noted that those tomato plants peeking up over the fence in the Mets bullpen were Joe's doing. His world series appearances came as a player in 1959, and then as a Mets' coach.

On that mournful day in Brooklyn, September 24, 1957, the Dodgers played their last game at Ebbets Field. Danny McDevitt pitched a shutout as Brooklyn defeated Pittsburgh 2-0. Behind the plate for the final four innings was Joe Pignatano. Holding on to a last thread of hope like all Brooklyn fans, Joe remembered that game. "We were hoping it wasn't true," he said. "We sort of knew it, but it wasn't announced until three weeks later. We knew, but we hoped."Pignatano still feels that the real villain was Parks Commissioner Robert Moses. "He forced O'Malley out by blocking the attempt at the Atlantic Avenue site. He said 'O'Malley's bluffing.' He wasn't." Be that as it may, Joe had to feel it more than the rest of us. A Brooklyn native, the catcher was wearing the Dodgers white and blue uniform while catching the last pitches throw at Ebbets Field by a Brooklyn Dodgers pitcher.

Nick Costello recalls Dodgers' scouts Arthur Dede and Hall-Of-Fame great George Sisler conducting the try-outs at Ebbets Field in 1950. Costello came from the Borough Park section and played his early Parade Grounds baseball with the Ty Cobbs. Nick said that the one thing he had going for him was a major league arm. This awareness prompted him to make himself a pitcher, figuring that pitching would give him a shot at the pros. He was impressive enough to earn a spot on the squad. They played against similar clubs including one made up of players from Montreal, a Dodgers AAA affiliate.

These were the best amateur ball players at the high school level. Following his tenure with the Ty Cobbs, Nick played his senior ball with Jim McElroy's Cadets, eventually signing to play in the Brooklyn Dodgers organization. Costello had a spring at Vero Beach and was then assigned to Sheboygan in the Wisconsin State League, a Class D aggregation. After two seasons Nick's dreams were done, but as one more Parade Grounder who got a chance, Costello is grateful, has no regrets, and says ,"The lifetime of memories was worth it."

Brother acts were not uncommon at the Park and Nick's brother Charlie spent a season in the Evangeline League in Louisiana as an infielder. There were also Bensonhurst's Aspromonte brothers. Oldest brother Charlie put in five seasons in the minor leagues. Ken and Bobby had full-blown major league careers, Ken spending seven seasons in the big time while Bob had thirteen.

Ken bridged the gap from Park Circle to the Boston Red Sox by way of minor league towns like Oneonta, Kinston, and Scranton. There were several more on the way up to the big time climaxing with a .334 season in 143 games at San Francisco in the AAA Pacific Coast League in 1957 before landing in Boston. Traded to the Washington Senators on May 1, 1958 and then to Cleveland in 1960, Aspromonte was selected by the Los Angeles Angels in the 1960 expansion draft. He wound up his career with the Cubs in 1963. Ken's best year was a .288 season in 1960.

In the winter of 1971 it was announced that Ken Aspromonte was signed to manage the Cleveland Indians for the '72 season. Ken indicated that his approach would be that of a tough taskmaster. "If I see something I don't like," he said, "I'm going to let the man know I don't like it." Aspromonte took over a club that had lost 102 games the previous season. He managed for three years pulling the club to a fourth place finish in 1974.

Brother Bob remembers being a skinny kid at Lafayette High School, though he did have "good hands and a quick bat." Lafayette, incidentally, ranks very high in the country in sending boys to the major leagues, having 20 or so of their alumni in the big time. Bobby began at the Parade Grounds with the Calverts and then played with the Brooklyn Royals, the same Royals of Red Verde, who produced a number of pro ball players like Mike Napoli , who reached the top with the Brooklyn Dodgers. The young Aspromonte also played for the "legendary" Nathans Famous team and got an opportunity to join the Brooklyn Dodgers Rookies aggregation.

I remember Bobby from a game on Diamond 1 as a rangy shortstop. He was one of those kids that just looked so good that one had to marvel at the way he moved around his position. So did the Dodgers. Aspromonte was signed by scout Al Campanis. Young prospects and their families were often courted by scouts and many times the signing was the result of the persistence and friendliness of the scout. Campanis came to the Aspromonte's Italian household armed with cannoli,the all-star of Italian pastries. That may not have been the turning point but it couldn't have hurt; Bobby signed with the Dodgers.

The seventeen-year-old went immediately to the big club following his high school graduation in June of 1956 and had one at-bat. This made him the answer to a trivia question. Who was the last Brooklyn Dodger to retire? -not Koufax or Drysdale, but Bob Aspromonte, before being farmed out. That fact was noted in the November 6, 1971 issue of *The Sporting News*: "*With the release of Bob Aspromonte by the Mets, the last of the old Brooklyn Dodgers has passed from the major league scene.*" Aspromonte began the minor league climb at Macon in the Sally League, spending part of the 1957 season in the military under the government's program that called for six months of active duty and five and one half years of active reserve time. Aspromonte did his active duty with Peter O'Malley, the son of the Dodgers' owner.

The Dodger influence stayed with the young man who still recalls how "good Walter O'Malley was to me." He also came under the positive wing of the Dodgers' Gil Hodges, Aspromonte's idol. Thereafter he always wore number 14 on his jersey in honor of the big first baseman whom he so greatly admired. Although she admitted to not being much of a baseball fan, Laura Aspromonte, Bob's mother proudly proclaimed, "You know Bobby rooms with Gil Hodges." In '58 Bobby had his most significant season : "I learned a lot at Des Moines", he said, where he played 130 games at shortstop.

A promotion to the Dodgers top affiliate followed, AAA Montreal in the Inter-national League and his first stop at Los Angeles in 1960 where he appeared in twenty-one games. Returned to St. Paul, Aspromonte hit .329 in 102 games at third base and then went back to the majors to stay.

It was in 1960 with the LA Dodgers that Bobby had one of those never-to-be-forgotten nights. "A home run off Lew Burdette," his brother Charlie said. "Four hits. Knocked in the winning run with a single in the 10th."

On October 10, 1961 Aspromonte was selected as a first round choice in the major league expansion draft that put the New York Mets and the Houston Colt 45s into the National League. Sorry to leave the Dodgers organization and disappointed at not having been chosen by the Mets, which would have brought him home to New York, Bobby went to Houston. As it turned out not only were there no regrets, but as Aspromonte called it ,"it was a blessing in disguise." He got a wonderful opportunity in Houston, one that might not have come in New York. "God bless Paul Richards," he says of the man who made the selection.

The Mets had chosen to select veteran players in the hopes of attracting crowds, while the Colt 45s went with young players with the idea of building from the ground up. Aspromonte played in 149 games and in 1964 hit .280 in 157 games.

"Somehow," he said, " I got to be a clutch hitter, and it helped a lot." Bob led the league in game-winning hits. This was before the watered down statistics of the eighties and nineties. Game-winning hits meant hits in the eighth or ninth innings, as opposed to today's stats allowing a first inning RBI to be called a game- winning hit. Bobby came back home when he was traded to the Mets in 1971,and for a time the last hurrah was a memorable one. "Bobby has done a remarkable job for us,"manager Gil Hodges said. Bobby played in 104 games in his last season in the majors and briefly fantasized about his career had he been in New York ."I often think about what it might have been like to play my career in New York, " he mused. " it's kind of nice now, coming back here in order to finish my career, but I still wonder what the sixteen years in between might have been like."

During his Houston career, Aspromonte established National League records for the most consecutive errorless games by a third baseman - 57; and the least amount of errors by a third baseman - 11 in 150 games. In retirement Bob has given his time and energy to charitable institutions and is Past President of the Arthritis Foundation for Special Events. As a Vice President of the Lions Eye Bank of Texas, he has been involved in a project to raise 3 million dollars for the Lions Eye Bank Foundation.

Both Ken and Bob Aspromonte are typical of the youth at the Parade Grounds in that they loved the game and learned the game with the aid of some of the best baseball men around. While reminiscing about those early days at Park Circle with the Brooklyn Royals, names from that organization came back to the major leaguer, names like Bobby Honor, Billy DeBenedetto, and Mike Napoli. The comment from the veteran was simply, "My God - what memories!"

The Malone brothers, Joey, John, and Richie all played at the Parade Grounds, good ball players all. John signed with the Giants in 1954. Richie, whose other interest was music had a career in the opera.

Then there were the Lembos, Steve and Anthony. Born in 1926, Steve was the senior brother by seven years, having played his early baseball at the Park was with the Ty Cobbs. He went to New Utrecht high school and was signed by the Dodgers in 1944 and sent to Youngstown in the Ohio State League . Like so many others, Lembo's career was halted by wartime military service; Steve served in the Navy. Fortunately, his skills were not eroded by his time away, and he was able to pick up his career. He hit .291 at Montreal in 1949 while appearing in ninety games, ultimately earning a spot with the Brooklyn Dodgers in 1950 and 1951.

He appeared in just seven major league games, but was part of a historical, though dubious moment for Dodgers fans. Lembo was in the Dodgers bullpen at the Polo Grounds on October 3, 1951 when the Giants' Bobby Thomson hit Ralph Branca's second pitch into the left field seats to win the National League pennant for New York.

Steve's brother Anthony recalls that Steve was warming up Branca in that ninth inning, but Carl Erskine, also throwing in the bullpen doesn't remember the catching alignment that day. He recalls that both Lembo and Clyde Sukeforth were there but does not remember who was catching whom. "You'd throw to one catcher," the Dodgers right hander said, " and then sit down and when you got up again, you'd throw to the other." Undoubtedly, Lembo caught both Branca and Erskine and probably Clem Labine, who got up to throw after Branca went into the game.

Steve suffered a back injury in 1953 and was forced into retirement, but working with young players at Vero Beach was the catalyst that got him started in scouting He began as a Bird Dog , scouting the local high schools and colleges and soon became a fixture at the Parade Grounds. He worked for the Abraham and Strauss Department Store , the old A & S, on Fulton Street in downtown Brooklyn, retiring from the fabled shopping mecca and eventually working full time as a Dodgers scout.

The Lembo brothers grew up in the Borough Park section and Anthony, a first baseman, also played with the Ty Cobbs. He remembers Bill Dunne with his ever-present Stetson hat and scorecard saying, "you guys want a team? Well, get together and I'll be your manager." Anthony attended New Utrecht high school and for a time New York University. He was selected to play in the "Brooklyn Against the World" games. The younger Lembo was also drafted into the military and did not anticipate playing any more baseball. But while still in the army and following the Korean armistice in 1953, he started playing some service ball and he was once again bitten.

On the advice of his brother, Anthony went to Vero Beach as an unsigned free agent and the Dodgers signed him for a bonus of $500. Lembo then played in the pros from 1956 through 1960. He started with Shawnee in the Sooner State League of Oklahoma, played in the Three-I League, and made it to the roster of the St. Paul Saints in the American Association.

There is a classic piece of baseball journalism; arguably the best of its kind ever written; by W. C. Heinz called *"The Rocky Road of Pistol Pete".* It refers to the ill-fated Dodgers star , Pete

Reiser. Heinz caught up with Reiser in the late fiftieswhen he was managing the Dodgers Class D affiliate at Kokomo, Indiana. Pete was having heart problems and Heinz drove him to St. Louis for medical attention. (7)

Anthony Lembo was with the Kokomo club that year. He remembers Reiser as having a "heck of a temper" and that he once "busted down a clubhouse door." Pete was also very active, hitting fungoes and moving quickly around the field. Lembo had gotten the impression that Reiser was not well and recalls that he was gone from the club for a couple of weeks.

The Dodgers minor league head was Fresco Thompson, a hard nose, according to Anthony, "very tough on the players." He would tell some that they will never make it and others that they should , but wouldn't because they were "carousing."Following his pro career, Lembo was reactivated by the reserves in 1966 and served in Vietnam.

To truly appreciate the circumstances that young ballplayers of this era found themselves in, it is necessary to be aware of the mechanisms of the sandlot to pro ball experience as it applied in the forties and fifties. It was a most prolific time for minor league baseball, having classifications from D up to AAA. There were , therefore, several thousand minor league jobs available. Of course, the funnel was inverted in that there were only 400 major league jobs open.

Of necessity, rosters had to be filled out at all levels, so ball clubs would sign any worthwhile prospect. The pay was minimal, especially at the lowest levels of minor league play. C and D contracts ranged from $150 to $250 a month through the forties and fifties. Clubs had little to lose by signing a young player, since their financial investment was so small. If a player moved up the ladder, so much the better.

These ball players also had to face the fact that should they suffer an injury, little or nothing was done for them; they healed or they quit. And so advancing after signing was a precarious proposition at best and a good many young players found that at some point in their career, it became more sensible to quit than to continue.

Joe Torre remembers, how "competition for jobs was fierce, nothing like what you have today, where guys can easily hang on. Back then you had fewer major league teams and more levels of minor league clubs." (8)

Such was the circumstance that Richie Lupardo found himself in while in the low minors. Richie lived in Borough Park and dutifully began with the neighborhood team, the Ty Cobbs. In Brooklyn Tech High School, he captained the baseball team. Nicknames were a way of life in Brooklyn neighborhoods and Richie got one of his own as a young boy. He doesn't remember how he came to be called *Rebo*, but the name is still with him.

As a high school senior, Rebo got the opportunity to attend try-outs for the *Brooklyn against the World* program, though by now, 1952, it had been renamed. They were the *Dodger Rookies* and the top high school and sandlot players from all over the city were invited to try out. There were massive workouts and cuts, and more cuts. The trials were held daily at Ebbets Field on days that the Dodgers were on the road. Lupardo remembers how they took batting practice from the centerfield fence, to avoid chewing up the infield. Cuts reduced the field to a twenty-five man squad. Players were given Brooklyn Dodgers uniforms and began a regiment of road games. They traveled to York and Lancaster in Pennsylvania; to Watertown, New York, and to Pittsfield, Massachusetts. Though players were usually New Yorkers, occasionally exceptions were made.In 1952 the Dodgers recruited a pair of twins from South Amboy, New Jersey - Eddie and Johnny O'Brien, in the hopes that they would sign with Brooklyn. Unable to come to terms, the twins ultimately signed contracts with the Pittsburgh Pirates. Both boys were in the major leagues by 1953; Johnny played second base over a six year stay, and Eddie was in the majors for five seasons playing three infield positions.

Lupardo was signed by Dodgers scout Al Campanis late in the '52 season and would not be assigned until the following season. The Parade Grounds League had a rule against pros playing in the league, but Richie had been assured by Campanis that his amateur status would stay intact until the next year, so he hooked up with the Cadets at the Park. But Cadets' manager Jim McElroy and League president Cookie Lorenzo determined otherwise and so Rebo had to sit out the remainder of the season. The Dodgers had indicated , indicative of his strong throwing arm , that they wanted him to try pitch. Forced to sit out the rest of the year, Rebo used his time throwing to a friend, Fred Weber. Weber recalls that Rebo threw extremely hard and his fastball came from "a foot off the ground and rose to my shoulder."

For the 1953 season, Lupardo was assigned to the Harlan, Kentucky Smokies in the Class D Mountain State League. Adversity began to creep in as the pitching idea was floated. But Rebo had success as a pinch hitter and the club's center fielder, whom Richie says "couldn't hit a bull's ass with a spade," was relegated to the bench. As a center fielder, Lupardo ,after starting 0 for 12, wound up the season hitting .330 and batting third in the order.

What should have been the onset of a potentially successful career wound up by bringing Lupardo back to the Parade Grounds. In spring training of 1954, the Dodgers were loaded with outfielders, the result of Branch Rickey 's having signed every good prospect his scouts came across. There were highly touted players like GinoCimoli, Walt Moyrn, and Sandy Amoros. Others, like Dick Williams, George Shuba and Bill Antonello were in camp. With that crowd at Vero Beach, it was once again suggested to Lupardo that he become a pitcher. He decided against it. He was planning to get married and wanted to complete his education, which he did.

At Brooklyn College Lupardo earned his Bachelors and Masters degrees and later, an MBA, and spent seven years of his vocational career as an English teacher in a Long Island high school, and twenty-five more years in corporate management. Lupardo is a Renaissance Man. Athlete and scholar, he is fluent in three languages, French, German and Italian. Although very confident in his ability, " I feel I could have hit .300 in any league," Richie nonetheless made that difficult decision. He remembers a couple of tough minor league pitchers. Ned Jilton at Kingsport was a veteran minor league lefty and Jim Turgeson, was a right hander in the Mountain State League.

Tugeson had good speed, good command and good control, but Rebo maintains with honesty, and not a hint of braggadocio "I never faced anybody I couldn't hit."

Upon his return to Brooklyn, Richie played for the Windsor Cubs, and belted four home runs in five games at historic Dexter Park. The Giants bird dog scout , Matty Mathieson, wanted to sign him to a Giant contract with the stipulation that it would strictly be as an outfielder. But Rebo had had enough and turned him down. "I'm sorry in a way that I gave it up," he says now." It doesn't really bother me, but I think about it once in a while - God, I loved to play!"

Lupardo played for fifteen more seasons at the Parade Grounds with clubs like the Senecas, the Cardinals, and the Eagles. He won a batting crown in 1958 by hitting .431 in the semi-pro Tri-County League. "Of course," Rebo said, "at that level you get some hanging curves and a lot of first pitch fast balls." He says that his favorite memory occurred on the perennial *Field of Dreams*, Diamond 1. In a 1964 game the Cardinals beat Nathan's by a score of 5-3. With the bases loaded in the last inning, one of Park Circle's outstanding hitters, Neal Baskin, was at the plate for Nathan's. On the mound was Sal Apria, another former minor leaguer. Although Apria no longer had the good fastball, Rebo says, "he still knew how to pitch, and had an assortment of breaking balls." Baskin grounded to third. Jordan Gatti stepped on the bag and threw across the diamond to his brother Lou, playing first, for the game ending double play.

Richie Lupardo finally called it quits after the '69 season at 35 years of age. That year he hit .484 and in 211 at-bats, struck out only five times in a pretty good semi-pro league. "I never really knew how good I was until I gave it up," he said, as he thinks back over what might have been. "But," he said, "no regrets; we accepted things as they were."

Rebo is the subject of a story that his teammates never tire of telling. It was a game against a club called the Bronx Yankees in Pelham, New York. The game was meaningless to Rebo's club, The Senecas, as they had already clinched a league play-off berth, but the Bronx team needed the win or their season would end that day. The Senecas players were somewhat lackadaisical in their approach to the game and went into the last inning trailing 7-0. As Richie remembers, "We couldn't do anything right." He made the last out in the previous inning and so, not expecting to hit again, he began to unlace his spiked shoes. Either not aware of the adage, "Let sleeping dogs lie," or intentionally disregarding it, the Bronx players took notice of Lupardo's action and chose not to ignore it. "Hey, look," they chided, " the great man is giving up, he's changing his shoes. It must be all over." They chanted, "Reee-Bo, Reee-Bo."

Lupardo stood up in his street shoes and issued a warning. "If I have to put these spikes back on, you guys will pay." Rebo swears that he simply meant that if he had to come up again, it meant that the Senecas had batted around. But as fate would have it, the powerful offense exploded and the Senecas scored four times, and loaded the bases for Rebo. The other club took notice and began riding him. "Time to go home," they taunted.

Harry Trimmer, the Senecas manager, told him to take a strike. He did - first pitch fastball, waist high, in the middle of the plate. The second pitch was a curve, almost in the same spot. Richie was guessing curve since with bases loaded they would be looking for the ground ball double play. The ball park was enclosed, the right field fence 315 feet from home plate and twenty feet high. Beyond the fence was a hill and at the top of the hill was a second barrier. Rebo's drive cleared both fences. The Seneca bench was in an uproar. As Lupardo rounded third, he was yelling at the Bronx bench, " I told you what would happen if I had to put these shoes on again. I told you." To the Boys of Brooklyn in the fifties and the sixties, Rebo is a classic.

Bill Antonello was another Brooklyn native to be scouted at the Parade Grounds and ultimately earn a spot on a Dodgers roster. Antonello was a promising outfielder throughout an eight year minor league career after being signed in 1946 by his Brooklyn neighbor, Arthur Dede. Seen as a long ball threat wherever he played, Antonello was the first player to hit a ball out of Miami Stadium, which he did during the spring of 1950.

He earned his promotion to Brooklyn with a fine season at Mobile in 1952, where he hit .290 with 28 home runs and 130 runs batted in. Used mostly as a pinch hitter against left handers , and with the prospect laden rookies on the Dodgers, Bill didn't get much of a chance and 43 major league at-bats was all he was to have.

A Dodgers outfielder of the late forties and early fifties, Cal Abrams had his start in his native Brooklyn. As a member of the Dodger Rookies in 1941, he signed and spent the '42 season in Olean in the PONY League. After three years in the military, Abrams continued his minor league apprenticeship which led to the Dodgers in 1949. Cal never hit less than .327 in the minors, but his major league stay was less distinguished; he did complete eight big league seasons and hit .269. Abrams was with Brooklyn until June, 1952 when he was traded to the Cincinnati Reds Unfortunately, Abrams is best remembered in Brooklyn for his failure to score the run on the last day of the 1950 season, a run which would have put the Dodgers in a pennant play-off with the Phils, somewhat unfairly, however, since with no one out, it would have seemed wiser to have held Abrams at third base. Apparently, the Dodgers' front office felt that way also. Third base coach Milton Stock was fired after the season.

On occasion, as with the O'Brien twins, players who were not from Brooklyn got to play with the Rookies and at the Parade Grounds. If there is one day of infamy in Brooklyn baseball history, that day is October 3, 1951. The play-off series between the New York Giants and the Brooklyn Dodgers was the first sports event to be telecast coast-to-coast. It was as though the coaxial cable installed just a few months before was done so in anticipation of some historical consequence.

The twenty-seven year old Giants third baseman left his home in New Dorp, Staten Island and drove to the ferry terminal in St. George on that Wednesday morning. He took the boat across the bay and drove north on the West Side Highway to his workplace at 155th street in Manhattan in the shadow of Coogan's Bluff. The trip took an hour and a half. "A long ride," he would say, "but Staten Island was worth it."

By the time he sat down to dinner that evening at the Island's *Tavern On The Green* restaurant, Bobby Thomson had gained an indelible place in the history of baseball, and indeed, in the city of New York.

Thomson's electric three-run home run in the bottom of the ninth inning that afternoon had won the pennant for the persistent Giants. Dodger fans bemoaned the fate of their beloved bums. If only it could have been avoided - a split second later on the swing, a breaking ball away, or if Bobby Thomson, *The Flying Scot*,had never signed to play with the Giants. Ridiculous! A stretch to far to be taken seriously. And yet....and yet.

In 1941 the Curtis high school senior of Staten Island was scouted by both the Giants and the Brooklyn Dodgers. He was invited to try out for the *Dodgers Rookies* and made the team. Playing in games around the city including the Parade Grounds, Bobby was highly regarded as a prospect by the Dodgers organization. "The Dodgers had more interest in me than the Giants did," Bobby remembers, so much so that they asked him not to sign with anyone without notifying them , in order to assure they could make a counter offer.

Thomson signed with the Giants without notifying the Dodgers. Why? "I was a Giants fan, that's why," he says. "The money didn't mean anything; it was so little anyway." There is something incongruous about Bobby Thomson being called *A Boy of Brooklyn*. The gentleman from Staten Island, who played for the Dodgers Rookies,and hit the *Shot Heard 'Round the World*, came within a hair's breath of being a Brooklyn

Dodger. What would that have done to history? The mind boggles.

VIII.

The Only Race That Counts

"In baseball the only race that counts is   the race to the bag"
-Ernie Harwell

It has been said that baseball is a reflection of our society at a given time. certainly in this epoch of greed and rampant commercialism, the major league game holds a position in the forefront. In periods of war ballplayers served their country and depleted the ranks on the diamonds; while economic depression brought a time of belt tightening frugality.

Organized baseball stood at the head of the line in segregating the sport as the rest of the country segregated its schools and communities. In the late 1870s and early1880s there were a few black players on professional teams, but it remained for Moses Fleetwood Walker to become the first black player in the Major Leagues, when he played with the Toledo club of the American Association, rival of the National League and recognized as a Major League. Walker was a catcher with Oberlin College and then the University of Michigan before joining Toledo as a professional.

Walker did experience some degree of abuse because of his color, but for the most part seemed to be accepted by the other players and spectators alike. It wasAdrian *Cap* Anson of the Chicago White Stockings who raised objection to Walker's playing in 1883. On this occasion his bluff was called by the Toledo club and Walker was allowed to participate in the game. Anson was the premier baseball man of his day, but just why he was so strongly opposed to black players has never been explained. It remains a mystery to baseball historians.

Moses Fleetwood Walker had the honor of being the first African-American to play in a major league game in Brooklyn. On June 17, 1884, the Toledo club faced Brooklyn at Washington Park. Walker appeared in two games with no reference to the catcher's skin color having been made in the New York papers. By September of 1884 Anson and Albert Spaulding had succeeded in barring black players from the field and the Jim Crow laws effectively commenced in time for the 1885 season. The next time an African-American played in a major league game was on April 15, 1947 when Jackie Robinson appeared for the first time at Ebbets Field wearing the uniform of the Brooklyn Dodgers. Roger Kahn has called this period in the major leagues "a bastion of American apartheid.".(1)

This sixty year delay would not have occurred if John McGraw had his way. The erstwhile *Little Napoleon* , who managed the New York Giants for more than thirty years, had begun his managerial career in 1899 with the old Baltimore Orioles. In 1901, McGraw took his club to Hot Springs,

Arkansas, a popular health resort where people partook of the mineral waters and the hot mineral baths

It was here that he came upon a bellhop working at the Eastland Hotel where McGraw was staying. Charlie Grant was a second baseman that the manager saw working out and immediately recognized as a solid ballplayer. Grant spent his summers playing for the Columbia Giants , a Chicago based team in the professional Negro Leagues. McGraw wanted to sign him believing that the infielder was good enough to play with the Orioles.

In his biography of John McGraw, Charles Alexander notes that having grown up in a small town in a northern state, McGraw had no particular views on race one way or the other and most likely had rarely seen any black persons until his baseball career took him to the south. But McGraw knew his baseball and wanted to win, so he determined to come up with a scheme that he thought would be fool-proof.

He announced the signing of Grant, who was from Cincinnati, as Charlie Tokahoma, a full-blood Cherokee Indian from Lawrence, Kansas. However, his scheme never had a chance. It was Charles Comiskey of the Chicago White Stockings who blew the whistle on Grant. "This Cherokee of McGraw's is really Grant, the crack Negro second baseman, fixed up with war paint and a bunch of feathers," he declared. (2) So it remained for Branch Rickey and Jackie Robinson to break the color barrier in Brooklyn some forty-five years later. Branch Rickey had been contemplating the injustice of the Jim Crow laws in baseball for quite some time, since his days with the St. Louis Browns, but neither the time nor the circumstances were right for any attempt at change, that is, until the mid forties. In his time with the Browns and the Cardinals, the city of St. Louis would not have provided the environment necessary for such a drastic step forward, but in 1942 Rickey landed in Brooklyn.

It seemed that at last the time was ripe. In 1945 the passage of the Ives-Quinn Bill , establishing a New York State Commission Against Discrimination, was supported by NYC Mayor Fiorello La Guardia and his committee appealed to baseball for support. Thus, time and circumstance was on Rickey's side, and place, well, he was in Brooklyn!

It had been said, notably, by Dodger catcher Roy Campanella, that the break-down of the racial barriers in baseball could only have taken place in Brooklyn. Bill Veeck agreed when he said, " If Jackie Robinson was the ideal man to break the color line, Brooklyn was the ideal place." Peter Golenbock in *Bums* notes that immigration had something to do with it. "Brooklyn was different from the rest of the country," he writes. "Everyone came as a minority, and they discovered that when they arrived in Brooklyn, everyone was the same: Everyone was poor. Everyone was struggling. No one felt persecuted, unless he rooted for the Giants or the Yankees instead of the Dodgers." (3) Be that as it may, Brooklyn was tantamount to the ideal for Branch Rickey's *Great Experiment*, and in its people, place and demeanor, ideal for the making of history.

In the post war years the Parade Grounds served as a backdrop for the young players and lessons in racial tolerance. More distinctly, there were no real lessons because none were required. The comradery that existed among ball players at the Park at mid-century was neither contrived nor forced, merely the natural order of things. The proof of it is in the experiences many of the Boys of Brooklyn encountered in areas of the south after leaving Brooklyn and how taken aback they were by them.

It happened to me in 1958 in Orlando, Florida. In a five-and-ten-cent store, I encountered a drinking fountain that was marked "Colored". After taking a drink I noticed the sign and another one over a fountain a few feet away that said, "White". While the impact didn't sink in right away, I told some of the other players when I got back to camp. "Hey," I was told, "this is Central Florida. You're in the deep South." Some of the southern boys I was with explained how life was in their towns. And so I learned something about Selma, Alabama; Turin, Georgia and Winnobow, North Carolina and a social climate that until that time was foreign to me.

Butch Gualberti played in the Florida State League for Orlando at about the same time. He remembers boarding a city bus and stretching out his six foot frame over two seats in the rear of the vehicle. He recalls also the looks from white passengers, looks which were totally alien to him in terms of their meaning. Once again, it took teammates more accustomed to the mores' of white America to point it out to him. He was equally puzzled by the system that allowed the white players to enter diners and restaurants while black teammates ate on the bus.

Butch was a teammate of Clarence "Choo-Choo" Coleman, who had some major league time with the Phillies and the

Mets and who was a native of Orlando. "Choo-Choo" ate on the bus.

Fred Weber was at Cocoa Beach in 1951 and recalls an incident in a store which knocked him for a loop. Buying some assorted sundries like toothpaste and soap he stood in line behind two black ladies. The clerk motioned to him, "come up here boy." Weber pointed out that the ladies were ahead of him. "Listen, boy," the clerk lectured, " you never wait on line behind any niggers." The outcome was that he got into a hassle with the clerk who said, "if you want to get along down here, you better learn how things are done." The assorted sundries wound up on the floor with the admonition, "stick 'em up your ass!"

It is to be understood that these white Brooklyn boys were not crusaders for a cause, nor were they humanitarians particularly. They simply had grown up for the most part accepting people for what they were and were chagrined at attitudes that were so foreign to their way.

Anthony Lembo and Tommy Davis, two of Brooklyn's boys, teamed up at the Dodgers camp in Vero Beach in the spring of 1960. Tommy was an African-American from Bed-Sty and Anthony, a white Italian-American from the Borough Park section. The two ball players were not in uniform when they were accosted by some local rabble in the men's room at Holman Stadium in Vero Beach, Florida. There were white and black rest rooms at the stadium. Both boys were taken completely by surprise, not ever having experienced such bigotry back home in Brooklyn . Davis was upset, then mad.

Later it was Al Campanis who told Tommy, "Don't let it bother you." But it troubled both players.

Lembo was witness to an incident in the Alabama-Florida League when he was with Pensacola. On a trip to Selma, Alabama for a game, the team bus was stopped by the State Police and two black players told to get off the bus. "They're with the team. We're going to Selma." the club protested. "No, they're not, get 'em off the bus." Both players were sent back to Pensacola.

In his autobiography, *Chasing the Dream*, Joe Torre talks about a motel in Bradenton, Florida in the spring of 1961. "And even there they had to feed us in a private room where no one else could see blacks and whites eating together....in Brooklyn there were blacks and whites and there were Jews and Italians -we were aware of our differences - but there was never any segregation."

Incidents like these were troubling to the young players from Brooklyn because they had never experienced anything like it at home. In his book , *Brooklyn's Dodgers, The Bums, The Borough and the Best of Baseball,*" Carl E. Prince, in speaking about the Parade Grounds, comments that , "there was not much race mixing on the Grounds." He is referring to the forties and early fifties when he says, " the Parade Grounds diamonds....seem to have been virtually all white." (4) This statement is misleading. Clarence Irving, an African-American manager offers a contradiction. "When you speak about the Parade Grounds, you are talking about one of the best amateur baseball locations in the city, if not the best at that time. In the 20 years that I was around sandlot baseball I have never seen a manager who would not accept a player on his team because of his race, I have known several occasions when managers would go out of there way to bring a black player to his team."

The Parade Grounds was indeed predominantly white during this era. It was a public park and was situated in a predominantly white neighborhood. However, the inference that it was a segregated playground was erroneous. Another Brooklyn ballfield was Betsey Head Park located in the Brownsville section. This was in a predominantly black neighborhood and the demographics of the park area were correspondently different from those of the Parade Grounds. Norman Root played at Betsey Head in the early fifties with the "5220 Club." He recalls all- black teams like the "Rockaway Giants" and Hispanic clubs like the "Carribeans" in the Betsey Head Park League.

Betsey Head had one field and a huge swimming pool. "If you hit one over the fence, it went into the pool ," Root recalls, "only no one ever hit it over the fence." While the major white players could be found at the Parade Grounds, the same could be said of black players and of Betsey Head. Root remembers no signs of any racial trouble on the field there , in the same way that the Parade Grounds were free of such strife.

Black players like Wally Edge, Willie Randolph and Tommy Davis played a lot of their ball at Betsey Head, as well as the Parade Grounds. There were a number of black players at the Park in mid-century as well as some neighborhood teams ; the Breevoort Senators and the Brooklyn Seals were all- black teams who joined leagues at the Parade Grounds.

In stressing the adage expressed by Campanella, it should be noted that for the most part, none of the Parade Grounds regulars recalls any racial difficulties at the facility. This includes Clarence Irving.

Clarence Irving remains one of the most respected and agile of the baseball minds to have managed ball clubs at the Park. Irving grew up in the Brownsville section, later moving to Bedford- Stuyvesant. He played his baseball with the Brooklyn Black Sox. They played what Clarence calls "country hard ball - you scored 15 runs and you gave up 12." He attended East New York Vocational High School and caught a bad break when he was scheduled to have a trial with the professional Negro League Newark Eagles. Clarence suffered a ruptured appendix and couldn't attend the try-out.

Irving spent the World War II years working as a printer in the Brooklyn Navy Yard and following the war in 1946 he began managing baseball teams. At a local hangout on Ralph Avenue and Decatur Street someone issued a challenge to Irving. In response to complaints the police would come by and break up the stickball games by breaking the bats, Irving balked, "Somebody should do something for these kids," he intoned. "Why don't you?" Someone said.

Taking the kids behind the high school, Irving proceeded to hit some fungoes and teach them the fundamentals. They formed a team they called the Rockets and booked games where they could. After combining with another club, they became the Falcons. Thus began a long and productive career in managing sandlot kids.

With all of the wonderful memories for Clarence Irving, there were some sad moments. One of his players was a first baseman- outfielder named Manford Chandler. Chandler signed with the Dodgers in 1952 and led the league his first year at Shebogan, Wisconsin. Promoted to the Pacific Coast League and triple A ball the next, the young man suffered an illness that ended a promising career. He passed away at age 28.

Another top-notch youngster was Jimmy McGowan , who played with the Pawnee Indians at the Parade Grounds. Having agreed to sign a contract, McGowan was injured severely in a stabbing incident which was never explained. It was thought to be a case of mistaken identity. These two tragedies were never forgotten by a caring and sensitive man whose pride is his "kids".

In 1949 Irving formed a new club. He did it by putting an ad in the *Brooklyn Eagle,* and he got applicants from all over the borough, about 150 all told and he held trials to weed them out. "It was a cross-section of kids from all over the place," Irving recalls. He called the new team The Bisons. "I worked as hard as I could to prepare them for better competition." His Bisons won the Kiwanis League title in 1953, the borough championship in '54, and were State Champs in 1955. They traveled to Abner Doubleday Field in Cooperstown on September 9, 1955, where Irving became the only Black manager at any level to compete at those hallowed grounds, a fact that has made Clarence duly proud. There was no black or white on Irving's teams and they were a further reflection of the atmosphere at the Parade Grounds. Incidentally, Tommy

Davis played in that game and some years later he played at Doubleday Field as a member of the Los Angeles Dodgers, the only time that anyone appeared there both as an amateur and again as a major leaguer.

Clarence speaks of the Jackie Robinson and Brooklyn experience with the same kind of elan as Campanella did. "There is no place in the world like Brooklyn," he says, "Branch Rickey knew what he was doing, both in choosing Robinson and in making his move in the borough of Kings." Clarence Irving recalls getting a job following the war with the father of a buddy, a white man. "Segregation was unusual in Brooklyn," he says of the time. And at the Parade Grounds, which Clarence calls the "most unique place in the world, the Madison Square Garden of sandlot baseball," segregation was virtually non-existent.

"We got along because we respected each other and treated each other fairly. Nobody spoke of Clarence Irving, as Clarence Irving, the colored guy. Nobody said, 'what about that Jewish kid Koufax; or the Italian kid, Torre,'" Irving relates.

Like a select group of that time and place, Irving put his heart and soul into his kids and was rewarded with more than championships. He dedicated himself in any way that suited. Once he managed a young pitcher who seemed to lose his stamina after just four innings or so. Told by the bird dog scout Matty Matheson that the kid was hungry, Clarence said, "Well, it's good that he wants to succeed, but he's gonna have to finish games."

"No," Matty said, "he's hungry, he don't eat breakfast." So he told the pitcher to meet him in the morning before a game and he fed him a big breakfast. The kid went the full seven innings."I told you so," said Matty. Clarence was happy, "but,"he said,"then I had to feed the kid the rest of the year."

His octogenarian mind spins tales of games that took place fifty years ago. He recalls with a chuckle a game in which he had Gallagher, a pitcher who "had the heart of a pawn broker on Monday morning", intentionally walk a slap hitter to load the bases and pitch to a good power hitter. Clarence remembers the sequence of pitches with absolute clarity. "The first pitch was a fast ball down the middle. The hitter couldn't believe it." For pitch number two, "give him some chin music and make him happy." It's now a 1-1 count. The third pitch was low and away and the hitter waved at it for a second strike.

" The next pitch was low and inside", Irving says without taking even a moment to recall. "And then," he says, "the fifth pitch was on the upper part of the plate and on the outside corner, strike three." Managers like Clarence Irving worked long and hard with young players and took an unfathomable pride in their development, not only as ball players , but as men. Perhaps almost as proud as he is of his own son who is a retired Assistant Secretary of Commerce."Those kids were good," he says."Most of them back then were coachable. They were disciplined." Gil Bassetti went as high as triple A ball as a pitcher and then became a major league scout.

Clarence's boys are everywhere. If you tune in to the nightly channel 11 ten o'clock news, you can get your sports from one of them. Sal Marchiano delivers his *Sal's Sports* segment with the gusto and enthusiasm of a kid playing ball at the Park. Probably because he was. Marchiano was a catcher for Clarence Irving's Bisons in the Kawanis League at the Parade Grounds in the mid-fifties. Like most of us he rooted for "our beloved Dodgers". Sal recalls that "Ebbets Field was our shrine, but the Parade Grounds was our Field of Dreams." Although time tends to dim the memory, there are days and scenes that ballplayers never forget.

Marchiano has "vivid memories of sunlit days and games and competitive fun. For instance, " he says, "I hit a bases loaded triple over the left fielder's head. While much of that era has faded from my memory, that moment stands out." Like most of the Boys of Brooklyn, Sal is drawn to those marvelous days of youthful memory. "The Parade Grounds, " he recalls,"like Coney Island, the Brooklyn Paramount and the indoor swimming pool at the Hotel St. George were very much a part of my youth."

Lou Grant lived in Sheepshead Bay and played early kid ball at Marine Park with teams like the Mariners and the Celtics and later in the Police Athletic League. Lou joined Clarence and the Bisons in 1956 and caught and played some second base. But Lou's dreams were artistically motivated; he wanted to create art. He attended High School at Industrial Arts in Manhattan, later renamed The School of Art and Design.

Grant was drafted into the army in 1957 and stationed in Germany and playing every day, Lou played some of the best baseball of his career. A Tank Battalion base field, the same camp where singer Elvis Presley was stationed, Lou recalls that it was "as good as any pro field." Lou completed his education at Cooper-Union college and went into the field working for advertising agencies, ultimately accomplishing his goal of being a free lance artist.

Lou has many memories of the Parade Grounds and youth baseball. He said that Clarence taught them the game, "He was always on your butt." His memory does not include any racial epithets or difficulties, "I had no complaints about race at all," he said. Watching baseball in the professional New York-Penn League today, Grant says that the quality of play is "No better than ours at the Parade Grounds and probably not as good." At seventy-two years old, Lou lives in New Paltz in upstate New York and has art shows of his work in various venues. A good portion of his subject matter is baseball. His art is poignant and engrossing and very, very good. Viewing one of a runner colliding with a catcher at home plate, one has to imagine Lou Grant recreating a memory.

For all of the satisfaction that managers like Clarence Irving realize from the accomplishments of their kids through the years, there is usually one of them that may reach just one iota deeper into the managers heart. For Irving it was Tommy Davis. "A disciplined kid. Could hit blindfolded. In the schoolyard he hit on the roof, all over the place. But," Clarence said, "you had to lean on him. Teaching him cutoffs and all that, he learned very fast. I love Tommy Davis." One of Irving's proudest moments had to be when Tommy Davis got to the Major Leagues and then watching as he put together an eighteen year big league career.

Davis himself remembers softball as being the catalyst for his future baseball days. At age nine playing fast pitch softball with fifteen year olds, made the baseball look easy to hit by comparison when he began playing the hard ball game.

Herman Thomas Davis lived in the Bed-Stuyvesant section of Brooklyn and started out with a local softball team sponsored by a place called "Magic Mart"."We had shirts and it felt Big-Time," he says,"Later I played baseball with Our Lady of Victory before joining Clarence on the Bisons." Tommy was with the championship Bison club of 1955 that traveled to Cooperstown to play at Abner Doubleday Field. It was here for the first time that Davis encountered the kind of bigotry that was alien to the kids in Brooklyn. "Never," Tommy said, "had I ever experienced anything of that kind at the Parade Grounds."

Playing against a team from Watertown, New York they heard racial epithets as well as those directed at the other players; Epstein, a Jew; and Penuzzio, an Italian. Tommy heard the taunts like "Wop" and "Kike" and he was called "Sambo". After the game the Watertown players said that they were just trying to upset them; it didn't work because the Bisons came from behind and won the game, 7-5, but it helped to steel the teen-ager Davis for what was yet to come in organized ball.

Scouted by Al Campanis of the Dodgers, he also got quite a bit of attention from the New York Yankees, so much so that he had a locker at Yankee Stadium and could work out there whenever he wanted to. He anticipated signing with them, but Campanis kept after him. He was expected to sign with the Yanks on a Tuesday but that Sunday a phone call came to the Davis home from none other than Jackie Robinson. Tommy was flabbergasted and completely awed.

Robinson spoke about the advantages of being in the Dodgers organization and even if he had merely read a railroad timetable, it would have done the trick. "It didn't matter what he said," Davis says, "he was Jackie Robinson." Tommy was signed that week right out of high school for a bonus of $4,000 and went to Hornell, N. Y. for his first taste of professional baseball. It was 1956. At Hornell in the PONY League he hit .325 to finish out the season and the next year led the league in hitting at .357 and stolen bases with 68 while at Kokomo. It was at Kokomo, Indiana that Tommy experienced a turning point in his life in the person of manager Pete Reiser.

Reiser was very tough on these kids and apparently managed with the same wild abandonment that he exhibited while playing. Davis recalls how he and two teammates lived at Mama Lutie Brown's Boarding House in Kokomo. "Teapot" Wheeler and Napoleon Savinon were his roommates. Mama Brown had to put a lock on the refrigerator to keep the growing young athletes from dissipating her entire food supply. One night Tommy and Teapot and Napoleon stayed out past curfew. When they returned to their room, Reiser was asleep in Davis' bed. He looked at them, fined each of them $50 and turned over. "Don't wake me up," he ordered. "Where am I going to sleep?" Tommy asked. "I don't care," said the manager, "just don't wake me up." Tom spent an uncomfortable night on the floor. But the impression Reiser made on the young man was deep and binding. "He got me prepared for life," Tommy Davis says now. "He was like a father to me."

In 1958 he again hit over .300, this time at Victoria, Texas in the Texas League. It was here that those lessons in life became more acute. Hardly a day went by when he didn't hear the word "nigger." "It was part of the daily routine," Davis said, "A tough experience." It came from the opposing benches and from the stands. It was a part of the everyday vocabulary there. When Tommy did something good he'd hear, "that's *our* nigger." An old Negro leaguer named Nat Peoples played in the league. When hitting, he had a habit of pulling his rear foot out of the batters box just before the swing.

From the seats behind the dugout came , "Mr. Umpire, can you please keep the nigger's foot in the box?"

At the tail end of the 1958 season Davis was called up to Montreal, the Dodgers AAA affiliate in the International League. Here, like Jackie Robinson, Tommyreceived a wholly different kind of treatment. "It was a good experience especially after being in the south," Davis recalls. "They treated me awfully well."

Davis got to the Los Angeles Dodgers for one at-bat in 1959, and then in 1960 to stay in the big leagues for eighteen years. Incredibly, by 1961, Holman Stadium in Vero Beach, Florida, was still segregated, thirteen years after Jackie Robinson had broken into the majors with Brooklyn. Peter O'Malley was in charge of spring training and Davis and some of the other players brought this inequity to his attention. Black fans were seated down the right field line. Prior to a game Tommy, Willie Davis, John Roseboro and Jim Gilliam went into the stands and very nearly physically removed the people from that section and sat them in seats behind home plate. "No, we can't go there," some of them protested. "Oh, yes, you can," the players told them. One more historic event that went virtually unnoticed. Robinson's crusade was not yet completed.

Davis recalls manager Walter Alston as being a very quiet man, but strong in that silent way. The most hated manager he came across was Eddie Stanky. The players hated him and would enter the clubhouse each day and walk past him without so much as a greeting. Stanky was "a mean dude," Tommy says, " he scared the kids." But, he also says, he was a good manager. "You had to go somewhere on every hit ball. He would ask in the dugout 'Why weren't you backing up third? ' or whatever." Among the best hitters Tom saw there are no surprises; Hank Aaron, Stan Musial. "Willie Mays could do everything, a five-tool guy." Jim Gilliam was the best #2 hitter Davis ever saw. Pitchers are another story. He bows to the legends like Bob Gibson and Juan Marichal, "always tough to hit." But of the "fifty or so guys" who Tommy claims gave him the most trouble, he singles out Joey Jay, Don Cardwell, Bob Purky and Jack Sanford. It was the good sinker ball throwers that gave him fits.

But even for the likes of Tommy Davis there were few slouches at the Parade Grounds. He recalls quality hurlers like Fred Wilpon, Jerry Boxer and Gil Bassetti.

As difficult as the pitching was in the National League, Tommy was good enough to lead the league twice in hitting, having a banner year in 1962 when he led all NL hitters in batting at .346, RBIs with 153, and hits with 230. Normally a line drive hitter he had a career high of 27 home runs that same season. His 153 RBIs remain a Dodger franchise record. After 18 seasons he retired with a lifetime batting average of .294. Tommy authored a book with writer Paul Gutierrez called "Tales from the Dodgers' Dugout" Tommy Davis, one of the Parade Grounds greatest success stories and one of Clarence Irving's brightest lights.

But Tommy was only one of Clarence's *Boys*." They were my sons," he says,"all of them." Judge Alton R. Waldon, once a shortstop, now a retired jurist. Ray Epstein, the third baseman who became a dentist; Dom Anile, currently General Manager of Player Personal for the NFL's Indianapolis Colts; and Lou Grant, an accomplished artist.

Dom Tenerelli was a second baseman on that first Bison's team and stayed through the '55 championship. The son of Italian immigrants, Tenerelli grew up on Buffalo Avenue in the Crown Heights section of Brooklyn. He is a graduate of New York's CCNY and earned a PHD at Stanford. As a Lockheed Martin Fellow, Dom was one of the team who designed the Hubble Space Telescope. They weren't just ball players.

Sebi Pepi lived in Bensonhurst and pitched for New Utrecht High School. His Parade Grounds career mimics that of so many others, beginning in neighborhood ball and progressing to the Unlimited Leagues where he played in that quality competition until he reached age thirty. After that it was softball and ultimately golf, a game Sebi loves and plays as often as he can in Florida retirement.

Pepi was a member of Clarence Irving's 1955 championship Bisons team and the road there was interesting. Sebi started out with the Angels, a team managed by his father. They were a good club and were seldom beaten, until they went up against the Bisons in a championship game. Watching Clarence's team working out Pepi was impressed. He remembers thinking, "No way we're going to beat this club." They didn't, but the following year Sebi's dad was suffering from a cancer that would take his life. One of the last things he did was to make sure his son was set up to play ball the next year. "Who do you want to play for?" he asked the boy. Young Sebi was overwhelmed, considering his father's concerns for him despite his suffering. He told him he'd like to play for the Bisons.

Mr. Pepi called Clarence Irving and left his name with Mrs. Irving. Both Pepi Senior and Irving had been coaches a couple of years before on an all-star team but Clarence did not recall the name. Now Irving owned a small business at the time, a record store, and banks not being cooperative, it became necessary at times to borrow money from other sources; friends, relatives and then some. When Irving asked his wife what the gentleman on the phone wanted, she inquired, "Do you owe anybody any money?"

He knew that he didn't, but a couple of days later at the Park a gentleman approached him. He was dressed in a business suit and Clarence remembers that he was " kind of dark and tough looking." "Mr. Pepi wants to see you in the car." he informed Irving. "What the hell does he want?" Clarence wondered to himself. When he got to the curb, he saw Mr. Pepi, also in a suit and tie sitting in the rear seat. "Come in," he invited, "sit down." He had gotten out of a sick bed, put on a suit and drove to the Park in the interests of his son. The words , "Oh, my God!" popped immediately into the baseball manager's head.

When Mr. Pepi explained his quest, Clarence relaxed, then told him he had indeed had an eye on Sebi and would be glad to take him on his club. Irving knew that Pepi pitched and played first base and the outfield and was a "smart kid."

Sebi played for the Bisons and then for Dave Barrett and the Vikings. He wound up his career with the Open division Senecas.

For Pepi his time with the Bisons was special. Irving had put together a club of ballplayers with no interest in race. Pepi says that in those days at the Parade Grounds there was "never a problem from day one. Not even a passing word. It was baseball only. Color was never an issue. We were brothers," he says in recalling a fondness for his teammates.

The Bisons had a left handed pitcher named Fred Wilpon. Following his graduation from the University of Michigan, Wilpon became a businessman, and ultimately owner of the New York Mets. To his credit, Wilpon never grew too far away from his Brooklyn and Parade Grounds roots. When the Bisons planned a fiftieth reunion to commemorate the '55 championship team, Fred Wilpon insisted upon hosting it. Those Bison boys of Brooklyn were treated to dinner at Wilpon's business address, Shea Stadium in Queens, followed by seats behind the Mets dugout for the evenings' game. Pepi attended as did Tommy Davis. Gil Bassetti who pitched in the Giants organization and then spent 30 plus years as a full time major league scout also showed up. Wally Edge and Dom Tenerelli were there.

Clarence sits smiling in the center of the photograph taken that night surrounded by his boys.

Jim Mosley was an outfielder who played his Unlimited Division ball with Nathan's Famous and with the Eagles in the late fifties and sixties. Jim still lives in the Bedford-Stuy section where he grew up. He began his sandlot days playing for the Bisons and played on Clarence Irving's 1955 championship team. A good defensive outfielder with a fine throwing arm, Jim could also hit and showed some pretty good long ball power.

As an African-American man at the predominately white Parade Grounds, Jim said that he "never had any racial problems throughout my time with the Bisons, the Eagles or Nathan's." There was always mild bantering among teammates that touched on racial and ethnic notes and Mosley recalls jokes of that nature particularly when he was with Nathan's. "There was never anything malicious about it," he declared.

The worst that Jim remembers is overhearing a white teammate use the term "nigger" in a conversation but he let it slide. He didn't think of it as slanderous since "it had always been otherwise pleasant as far as race goes during my time at the Parade Grounds." Jim Mosley, at sixty-eight years old has had a hip replacement, but is thankfully otherwise in good health. He walks with a cane, but says "I feel like I could get out there still. The mind and the heart are willing. I guess I'll have to give it a little more time."

Wally Edge experienced the opposite as the Brooklyn boys going south. He came from a segregated environment in Heflin,

Alabama where he was born in 1936, and lived until he was in the eighth grade. His first team was the usual neighborhood group, called the "Greenhat." He moved to Brooklyn's Bed-Sty section and at thirteen joined Clarence Irving's Bisons, and was a member of the 1955 championship aggregation. Wally was the captain of the team while playing center field. He attended Boys High and was a part of the '54 team that was the runner-up to city champs, Clinton High.

Edge was scouted and in all likelihood could have signed a pro contract had he chosen to do so. But for Wally the path led in a different direction. His mom wanted him to be a teacher and didn't want him to sign a contract and he acquiesced to her wishes. He graduated from Brooklyn College and taught math in the NYC system, eventually becoming an elementary and a junior high school principal. In later years his mom said, "Wally being a principal was a bonus for me. I only wanted him to be a teacher." He concluded his teaching career as the Bronx Deputy Superintendent of Schools.

His Parade Grounds baseball career however, continued to have highlights even after he outgrew the Bisons. He played with teams like the Senecas, the Cardinals and the Eagles, in the Parade Grounds League, the Queens Alliance and the Twi-light League.

Wally was in the time and the place when the integration of organized baseball began to proliferate. He played at both the Park and at Betsey Head. The Parade Grounds was predominately white during the fifties, actually Italian dominated, but African-Americans who played there like

John Rucker, Manford Chandler, Rueben Alexis, Tommy Davis and Sonny Williams all played in the pros.

After making the transition from segregated southern teams to Brooklyn where he was the only African-American on the Brooklyn college team, and then one of a few on the sandlots, Wally doesn't recall there ever being a racial issue. "There were none in my time," he says. As a member of the Senecas, Edge traveled with the team to tournaments in other states, some in the south. "I was simply part of the team,"he says, " we transcended racial stuff. I was cushioned by my teammates, absorbed into it and never faced any problems, even in the south."

He considers himself very fortunate to have played for Clarence Irving, "one of the great baseball minds, he broke new ground." Sports has opened up so many avenues of understanding for Wally and so many other sandlot kids at the Parade Grounds. The experience was a character builder for those boys and anything that Wally Edge gained by those he came in contact with, he gave to them as much or more. "I'm glad to have been a part of Brooklyn baseball," he says now, echoing the deep sense of fulfilment that is shared by everyone whose spiked shoes touched the dusty ground on Coney Island Avenue.

The inability to make any discriminatory racial distinctions for most of us playing at the Park may best be expressed by one who spent many years there. Richie "Rebo"Lupardo, he of the legendary walk-off grand slam, remembers his years with both white and black teammates with no adverse incidents whatsoever. "I played with Sonny Williams, Jim Mosley,

Reuben Alexis," he said, "and for fourteen years in the same outfield with Wally Edge, that, having been among my fondest memories."

Incidentally, Lupardo's only son, Taylor Robinson Lupardo, is named for Jackie Robinson. "The only hero I ever had," Lupardo says. "Brooklyn was indeed a special place and our fields, sacred places."

IX.

Warts And All

"If you're not having fun in baseball, you miss the point of everything."
-Chris Chambliss

Human beings are flawed. This is the proof that baseball was never invented, but created, created by a God with a wry sense of humor. Yes, you can hit a home run today, but tomorrow you will strike out three times. That diving stop was a thing of beauty; but how come you let that easy ground ball go through your legs? Ironically, it is the flaws in men, the lack of perfection that makes baseball so perfect a game. Don Larsen can dispute this and point to his own moment of perfection. True, but once in over 100 plus world series; once in over 600 games makes it a rare occurrence at the very least. It is no wonder that a few years ago when Larsen was asked if he ever got tired of speaking about his accomplishment, his surprised and purely honest answer was ,"No, why should I?"

The God of human frailty tossed a bone to the Brooklyn Dodgers' Cookie Lavagetto in game four of the 1947 World Series. With two out in the last of the ninth inning and Yankees' pitcher Bill Bevens trying to protect both a game and a no-hitter, Lavagetto delivered a pinch-hit double that kayoed both for Bevens and the Yanks. The next day with the game once more on the line, and Lavagetto again pinch-hitting, the mighty *Cookie* struck out. Giggles from heaven. And so it goes. A batter who is successful need only achieve that level of success a mere 30% of the time. The most prolific home run hitter of all time was George Herman *Babe* Ruth, and he averaged only one every 11.7 times at bat. The highest winning percentage among hall of fame pitchers is Whitey Fords' .690; most in fact are under .600; a success rate of between 50% and 60%.

Is it any wonder that baseball has grown up as everyman's game, that we see the flaws in even the greatest of players. It seems that baseball may have been created for the purpose of reminding men of their shortcomings. I have seen the best at the sandlot level come up short and yet go on to stellar achievement; and I have also seen pros humbled in the same venue.

On a Saturday afternoon ,typically on Diamond #1, we were playing a game against the Cadets. Joe Torre was at the plate with the bases loaded and two out and a count of 3-1. Our pitcher was John Lepik, the same Johnny Lepik with whom I went on the Cyclone at Coney Island. He wore the same reddish crew-cut and had the same smiling disposition, but he had grown to about 6' 2" and weighed about 190. John would soon join the Parthenon of Parade Grounds ballplayers who played in the pros, spending two seasons in the low minors.

At that moment he was a prospect, a strong hard throwing left-handed prospect. I was playing shortstop. Tiani called for a fastball and I wondered if that was the best pitch to give Torre. Lepik delivered and Joe swung and missed, - strike two. Vinnie called a fast ball again. This time I was sure I closed my eyes and may have missed strike three completely.

As it happens, that night I was at a gathering with Cookie Lorenzo and as always, Cookie and I talked baseball. I told him about the game. I didn't question Torre's ability, wondering only whether good pitching could stop him or perhaps slow down his progress. Lorenzo was, as always, very high on Joe and told me in no uncertain terms that he was going all the way.

In his first year of pro ball, Joe Torre hit .343 at Eau Claire, Wisconsin. He came to the majors with the Milwaukee Braves in 1960. He spent eighteen seasons as a big-league ballplayer and hit .297. He won the National League batting title in 1971 while with the St. Louis Cardinals, hitting .363. He hit 252 home runs in his career. He hit safely over 2300 times. Once he was struck out by Johnny Lepik with the bases loaded at the Parade Grounds. It could have happened to any one of us and it did many times. Everyman's game!

Jerry Casale came home to Brooklyn after his major league stint, which included a 13-8 season with the Red Sox. He called Weber and asked if he could throw a game for the Eagles. His arm bothered him a bit but he wanted to pitch.

He stood on a Parade Grounds mound facing the Pollio Cubs, not particularly potent at that time. He gave up four runs in the first inning. When two got on in the second he called Weber out to the mound. "Fred, get me out of here," he told him. Fred turned to the bench and clutched his right elbow to indicate an injury. Baseball! Everyman's game.

I was having a terrific year, but my flaws were conspicuously evident. I didn't have much of a throwing arm. I switched to second base for that reason. But I was playing a lot of short. One of my meager assets was a pretty good pair of hands. I reasoned that I was better off getting rid of the ball as quickly as possible, rather than straightening up and throwing overhand with nothing on the throw. It worked fairly well. Weber said that I was the first shortstop he'd ever seen who threw the ball with that sidearm motion. It helped me at second base also on plays to my right.

However, on a cutoff I could not make a strong throw to third or home from the cutoff position on the outfield grass. We solved that one by having Castaldo, the shortstop, go out for the relay on balls hit to the right center gap.

My arm could create some levity. Once, I somehow wound up playing in left field. This was a couple of years later when we were the Cardinals. Wally Edge, was out in center fielder that day. I camped under a routine fly ball with a man on third. The shortstop, Floyd Joiner, was yelling "Home! All the way!" I wound up and threw a three or four hopper to the plate. I looked over my shoulder and saw Wally down on his knees laughing. I had to go over and help him to his feet.

Over the years I had difficulty with pop flies, not often, but it came in cycles, sort of like a batting slump. And I had one about mid-season. I would lose the ball or run out from under it. To compensate I would catch pop-ups with a basket catch, not quite Willie Mays style. A fly ball to the outfield has a different trajectory, but in the style of Giants' infielder Bill Rigney, whom I had seen do it and so I adopted the method. It gave me more confidence to engulf the ball this way.

Flaws are not the same as errors. Everybody makes errors, the better the player, the fewer errors he makes. Fortunately, I didn't make too many, aside from the pop-ups. When I did, it was usually because I hadn't gotten low enough on a ground ball, or got down to the ground and miscalculated, and came up too soon- not an excuse, but the infields were shrewn with pebbles and holes. The problem in the outfield was to avoid stepping into a hole while running after a ball.

We had an outfielder named Willie Giovanelli, a very big guy, tall, wide and heavy. One day he and Chick were chasing a ball hit between them. As Willie crossed in front of Chick, he stumbled and hit the ground. Unable to stop and not wanting to collide with the fallen behemoth , Chick leaped over his teammate and continued after the ball.

When he came into the bench, everyone was laughing. Chick explained, "When Ifelt the ground shake, I knew he went down, so I timed my jump. " Then he said, "It was like jumping over a fallen water buffalo." The *Telegram* reported thatMonday that "Willie Govenerella knocked in eight runs with a triple, double, and two singles as the Seafarers Virginians out slugged Gragnanos 19-9." It was a good thing that Chick was able to clear his hurdle.

There was one error that I made that really stands out because it is an insight into the disposition Bobby Stone . He was pitching and getting hit pretty hard. The knuckler was high, not fluttering very much, and the hitters were leaning into his pitches. However, the outfielders, particularly Chick and my old friend Eddie Conti , who had joined us after coming home from college, were hauling in long drives all over the outfield. On one ball Eddie went to the four foot fence in center and leaned over and took away a home run.

The upshot is that in the fifth inning, Bobby held a three to one lead. Freddie kept at me to tell Bob to get the ball down. So with the bases loaded and only one out, I went in to the mound. "Bob," I said."Get it down, willya. We'll get a ground ball and get two and get the hell outta here." He looked at me with that expression he always had that seemed as though he was about to break into laughter. "Ok," he said obediently.

Sure enough, on a pitch below the belt, a sure double play grounder came my way, and sure enough, it went through my legs. Tied the score. I felt terrible, but figured I had to say something. I went in to the mound, tail between my legs. Before I could say a word, Stone said to me," Maybe I should go back to throwing it high. At least those guys out there were catching them." And then he broke into laughter. Not a guy easily rattled.

In the Sunday league we were keeping pace with Sacred Heart and St. Bernadette We took turns having the lead. A

Jimmy Murphy column had Bobby Stone turning in a four-hitter with the aid of Tommy Castaldo, who doubled, tripled and singled in four runs. We were one game behind St. Bernadette, with Sacred Heart now one behind us.

In the same item, Joe Torre out pitched Joe Silomate as the Cadets nosed out Our Lady of Peace, 3-2 to remain undefeated in the senior division. Joe fanned thirteen.   We played in a Saturday league that had no age requirements. As a result, senior teams like the Cadets were among our opponents. It was in this competition that I came up against the younger players who would go to the pros. The Cadets had Joe Torre, Matty Galente, and Rico Petrocelli.

Nathans Famous had a team in that league. This was the Coney Island Nathans of hot dog fame. I think the only guy on that club who had not played any pro ball up to that time was a first baseman named Joe Pepitone. He could hit the heck out of the ball and hit it very hard. He is a left hander, so at second base I played him in the hole and very deep, usually a few steps back on the outfield grass. He hit the ball so hard that I threw him out from there more than a few times. These were tough clubs, the reason that baseball at the Parade Grounds was so lofty.

I was building myself a little scrapbook and I did enjoy seeing my name in print, I think because it always meant something positive. I think my favorite clip was the one in the *World Telegram* that said, "Frank Chiarello led the attack with three for four, two doubles and a home run, to drive in six runs. Andy Mele also collected three hits in three times at bat." It linked me with Chick, one of the best hitters I ever saw at that level. Another club in the league was the Senecas. They were managed by Harry Trimmer and Ken Avalon. Sebi Pepi pitched and played first base and Wally Edge and Richie Lupardo played in the outfield. We all loved to play the game . This is obvious when you see fellows in their twenties and thirties playing four or five games a week and not getting paid. After working all week we couldn't wait to get to the Park. If it rained we were crushed, but there was something worse than being rained out, and that was to be *muddied* out.

It meant that even though it was a beautiful day the night rain had made the field unplayable. There was a solution, however. Weber would go across Coney Island avenue to the ESSO station and buy a can of gasoline. Then he would spread it over the muddy area and light a match to it. The flames would burn for a couple of minutes and when they died the ground would be dry. What an innovative idea! On a particularly wet day, Fred figured that he needed more than a can of gasoline, so he took a couple of us with him and brought back six or seven gallons. Dutifully, we covered the whole infield with the highly flammable liquid. Weber ceremoniously dropped a lighted match and the whole thing went up like a Redwood Forest.

The flames leaped to about twenty feet while the air was black with billowing smoke, and we all scattered. A lady at her window on Caton Avenue called the fire department and they responded with screaming sirens to quell the blaze. The up side of the whole experience was that they didn't arrest Weber. We were already calculating how much we'd have to chip in to make his bail.

The umpiring at the Park wasn't bad although there were always times when certain umps would walk on the field and you'd look at each other , roll your eyes towards heaven and say, "Oh, jeez!" I especially respected Pete Larkin and Steve Albanese Tommy Corrodo Pete Bellone., and Pitsie D'Angelo.

At times the word would go around the Park that someone was about to sign a contract. I happened to be there when we heard that Joe Torre would sign with the Braves "this week". I was on my way to one of the open diamonds to play a game, walking along the cinder path between diamond #1 and 13. Joe was coming toward me dressed in white shorts and tee shirt and jogging. He was sweating profusely and as he approached me he slowed to a walk. We exchanged some words for a few seconds or so and both went on our way.

I remember being very impressed with this young man that day. He was a top prospect; his brother was playing in the major leagues; scouts had their eyes on him for a while and now he was about to sign a contract to play professional baseball himself. You could say that "he had it made". Torre was kind of a chubby kid and here he was trying to sweat off a few pounds to be in the best shape possible to start his pro career. It told me something about attitude and dedication and kept me in a rooting mode for this young man.

To be honest, I rooted for everybody who signed out of the Parade Grounds. Of all the pros I associated with I never had a bad word for any of them. No one shunned me on or off the field. No one came in spikes high or pulled anything low. We could follow them through the *Sporting News*, baseballs "Bible", the publication from St. Louis that carried the averages of players throughout the minor league system. We could assess their progress on a week-to-week basis.

I had a similar experience when Joe Pepitone signed his first contract. The word came down and one evening that week Chick Chiarello and I came out of the clubhouse on our way to one of the fields. The blaring of a car horn stopped us short and we watched a brand new black Ford Thunderbird turn into the driveway and rev up to the front of the clubhouse. It was Pepi. He must have had the car on order as we heard that he got about twenty grand to sign. He was pumped up and we congratulated him. His career didn't go the way it should have gone. He was a loose cannon even at Manual Training High School.

Pepitone came to the majors in 1962 and spent eight years with the Yankees before being traded to Houston and then the Cubs and Atlanta. In twelve seasons he hit more than twenty home runs five times, hitting a personal high of thirty-one in 1966. He drove in one hundred runs in '64. A great natural talent, Pepitone was a smooth and elegant fielding first baseman as well. He is also credited with being the first major leaguer to use a hair dryer in the locker room.

He has been described as fun-loving and carefree, which is all well and good , but not, it seems , at the expense of a career. He hit two home runs in one inning on May 23,1962 against Kansas City and a sixth game grand slam in the 1964 World Series against the St. Louis Cardinals. In the eighties he was arrested on gun and drug charges. The picture I have of Pepitone is that of a hard hit ball slammed my way and the infield dust kicking up into a cloud where the missile struck.

I remember a manager named Dave Barrett, whose club was the Vikings and I recall a kid who played for him. In the big leagues, he had the nickname "The Bull",but at the Parade Grounds, Al Ferrara was called *KiKi.* Young Kiki was a pianist. At age twelve he gave a performance at Carnegie Hall in New York City. We talked about it at the Park , "no kiddin', Carnegie Hall? Wow!" After he got to the major leagues it was written about, but in 1971 Al explained, "All that stuff that has been written about me being an accomplished pianist has been overplayed. When I played at Carnegie Hall, it was during a recital....but I have not played since I was sixteen." (1)

At 6'1" and 200 pounds, a teammate once said that Al looked more like a piano mover than a piano player. Al signed with the Los Angeles Dodgers and made his way all the way to the top.

Ferrara put in eight seasons in the major leagues and compiled some interesting career highlights. On May 15, 1965, Cubs pitcher Dick Ellsworth threw a one-hitter at the Dodgers, but the hit was a three-run home run by "The Bull". Following a trade to the Reds in 1971 for a player named Angel Bravo, Ferrara had a tough season, hitting only .182 for Cincinnati. He quipped, "What did you expect to get for Angel Bravo, Willie Mays?"

The 1958 Open Division All-Star game was another major thrill for me. It was the selection process that made it so uniquely special. The managers picked the players with one reservation: they could not vote for anyone from their own team. That meant that your opponents made the choices, the ultimate complement. Fred was to be the field chieftain of the National Division. Our club had Carl Hottinger pitching along with Billy Litras of Sacred Heart and Joe DiGeralomo from St. Bernadette and Vinnie Tiani as one of the "lads to handle their offerings."

In the infield we had Vinnie Marino at first and Castaldo at short beside me. In the outfield both Chick Chiarello and Putsie DeBernardo were selected. The *Telegram* had me down as hitting .400, the second highest batting average on the whole squad behind Moe Palazzo's .510.

Teddy Trance, a fine ballplayer was the other second baseman and Frank Yurman was at third, rounding out the Sacred Heart triumphant infield. Yurman and Palazzo had both played in the pros, Moe the next year and Frank having already had his shot with the Cleveland Indians.

We were to go against the American Division that had the Sabres and the Brooklyn Eagles. They would be managed by Mike Rubino of the Sabres. We would be going up against Moose Morrissey and Sonny Williams of a club called the *Seals*. Little Peter Rabbit was the shortstop. They had a pitcher named Walter Kolowanski, a very hard throwing right hander against whom I would hit my one and only career home run later in the season.

Walter had a tremendous arm and also played in the outfield. It is unfair to denigrate him by talking about my home run, but it was the only one that I have to talk about.

It happened on Diamond Five. There were two runners on and I caught a fast ball out over the plate. I hit it pretty hard, but not far and it went into the right center field gap. I circled the bases before the relay throw came in and crossed the plate standing up.

Chick, who, had he done the banquet circuit in the off season would have made a living telling stories about my hitting. He loved to make fun of my lack of power, to josh about my bloop hits and seeing eye squeakers through the infield. As I came back to the bench, he keeled over in a mock faint. Taini threw his hands up in frontof his face as though I might use my newly discovered power on him.

I didn't have to lie about the blow in future years. If anybody doubted it, I could pull out the clip from the next days' *Telegram.* " Carl Hottinger spun a five hitter and turned back nine on strikes....Andy Mele led the attack with a home run and two singles that sent four home."

I learned a lesson in this All-Star game from pitcher Tom Morrissey. The Moose had walked me. I liked to run and Freddie often gave me the steal. Iwas pretty quick; I'd run 220s and 440s at Erasmus Hall high school. As a result, I determined how big a lead I could safely take and get back if the pitcher threw to first. For me it was three strides. Habitually I began to step off three strides towards second as soon as I hit the bag.

Morrissey had noted this in the past, so when I hit the bag and took one stride, then two, he threw over. I just did get back and altered my method in the future. They played with their heads as well as their limbs at The Park. Most knew "how to play the game." Fundamentals and basics were the way of things back then and one reason why someone like me with limited talent could usually hold his own.

There were valuable lessons to be absorbed, and I was benefitting from them ever since Al Fortunato had made us recite the infield fly rule. We won the All-Star game as a headline stated. "Nationals Win PG All-Star Title 7th Time." We won it 11-4 and the hitting stars listed were our Virginians, Vinnie Marino and Frank Chiarello, along with Moe Palazzo and Frank Yurman of Sacred Heart. No surprises there. Billy Litras, who followed Irving Friedman to the mound got credit for the victory.

Each Monday the local newspaper, the *Brooklyn Eagle* would report the previous days game highlights. Early in 1955 the *Eagle* went out of business and the loca lsports were picked up by the *New York World Telegram and Sun*. On a given day one could read the names of several players who either went on to the pros or had returned home. In one column I noted the names of six such players: "Jerry Boxer spun a four-hitter and retired nine on strikes." "Matty Galente chased across three runs with two safeties." Moe Palazzo and Frankie Yurman were the hitting stars for Sacred Heart as was Frank Chiarello for the Virginians. "Joe DiGeralomo lost a heartbreaker to the Virginians" on this Sunday.

On another day there were four *different* names highlighted; those of Angelo(Putsie) DeBarnardo, Reuben Alexis, Ron Salomine and Vinnie Tiani. There were six minor league classifications ranging from D to AAA, and more than 50 leagues, but only sixteen teams and approximately 400 major league jobs. It wasn't easy to get there and the low minors were especially tough, with long overnight bus rides and minimal pay. But the Parade Grounds remained one of the most prolific producers of professional baseball talent in the nation.

The decade had lost a man who is undoubtably the greatest athlete America has ever produced. Jim Thorpe passed away in March, 1953. In '55 the Brooklyn Dodgers won the World Series by defeating the Yankees in seven games. On the afternoon and evening of October 4, Brooklyn was assuredly the place to be. On July 1, 1958 Alaska was admitted into the Union as the 49th state. In March 1959 Hawaii became number 50. In November of 1953 Welsh poet Dylan Thomas died. It was from a Thomas poem that Roger Kahn extracted the phrase *Boys of Summer,* which he used to immortalize the Brooklyn Dodgers of the fifties, and, for that matter, all of the summer game participants.

Ernest Hemingway received a Pulitzer prize for his novel *The Old Man and the Sea.* In it the fisherman Santiago lauds the *Great DiMaggio* - baseball in literature. In the mid-fifties, a full length fur coat at Gimbals sold for $239. Drive-In movies were *Passion Pits* to the teens and the Russians sent a dog into space, while America's space program had yet to "get off the ground."

The boroughs of Staten Island and Brooklyn were linked incontrovertibly when the Verrazano-Narrows Bridge opened in 1966. Tens of thousands of Brooklynites relocated, including a great many of the borough's ballplayers. Most of them took to playing softball and touch football on the Island

and were soon assimilated into the Richmond County sports scene. But lesser noted was that the tie-in between the two boroughs through baseball had a history that was decades old by the time the Verrazano was opened for business.

Staten Island has a long and eminently successful baseball history of its own. Island natives who went to the major leagues are familiar names to the local fans. Hank Majeski, Bobby Thomson, George Bamberger, and Terry Crowley are just a few. But what may be less known is that the borough link existed in reverse, and it did so through baseball, with the Parade Grounds playing a part. Thomson and Crowley both played there. Larry Bearnarth was a native Islander who played at the Park on his way to the majors.

Jack Tracy, a member of the Staten Island Sports Hall of Fame, played high school ball at Curtis in the New Brighton section and with a sandlot team called the "Violets" in the American Legion. An outstanding infielder, Tracy and his high school mates got to play in Brooklyn, including the Parade Grounds. "We played a lot of play-off games at the Parade Grounds in those days," he recalled. And "those days" meant traveling by ferry boat. In addition to the "Dodger Rookies" and the "Yankee Rookies", there was a team of all-stars put together by the newspaper, *The Journal American*. The JA All-Stars toured the city often playing in Ebbets Field and certainly, the Parade Grounds. Jack played for the JA team and also for the Yankee Rookies under the tutelage of scout Arthur Dede and bird dog Jim *Mac* McElroy. That was in 1960.

Tracy attended Seton Hall University in New Jersey and in 1964 signed a contract with the New York Mets. As a college ballplayer, he set a Seton Hall record for errorless chances by a second baseman. Assigned to the low minors at Auburn his first year, Jack did well and was elevated to AAA Jacksonville soon after. Though spending several seasons in the organization and going to spring training with the big club in 1966 and again in '69, Tracy never got to play in the majors.

With a touch of humility, Jack speaks of the players around him as being so much better. He roomed with Bud Harrelson and Tom Seaver and played with the likes of Don Baylor and Bobby Grich. In retrospect, Tracy thinks he may have been moved up too quickly. "Maybe it would have been better for me," he said, "if I had been brought along gradually." Nevertheless, he is grateful for the career he did have. "It was a very enjoyable experience", he says in the throes of fond memories.

A sore spot for the young second baseman came in 1967 at Jacksonville. Hitting at a .350 clip, he was benched when the big club sent Sandy Alomar down to AAA. Jack confronted manager Bill Virdon who told him, "I get orders too." That was the way of the minor league experience in those days. The memories linger. "I played behind Tom Seaver, Jerry Koosman and Nolan Ryan," he remembers. Jack became friends with another Park alumni Ted Schrieber and also with catcher Choo-ChooColeman.

"Chooch never got excited," Tracy recalls, "he was a regular Yogi Berra ." Jack has a favorite story he regales us with about Choo-Choo. Tracy, Schreiber and Coleman were teammates with Buffalo, the Mets AAA affiliate in the International League, when Teddy was traded to Baltimore, during a series with Rochester. Schreiber simply switched clubhouses and the next day played against his old friends.

According to Tracy, Coleman was trying to steal second and Schreiber went over to cover the bag. He held up his bare hand at the approaching runner, "stand up, Chooch," he said, " no throw." Choo-Choo obediently refrained from sliding and Ted tagged him out. Both benches were in an uproar as Choo-Choo was chewed out by manager Kirby Farrell.

Jack came back to serve as a physical education teacher at Tottenville High School near his Staten Island home. Like so many others, Jack Tracy is not obsessed with what might have been, but revels in the experiences he did have. Terry Crowley was another Staten Islander who played at Brooklyn's *Field of Dreams*. Larry Anderson has a clear memory of a game on Diamond # 13 when he played center field and Jack Tracy was at shortstop for a sandlot team called the Staten Island Chiefs.

In an Alliance championship game that day, a fifteen-year-old Terry Crowley hit two home runs out of the enclosed diamond. Crowley also played at the Park with Nathan's and went on to a fifteen year major league career with the Baltimore Orioles. He turned to coaching and carved out a new life as a big league hitting coach. Employed at Baltimore, Crowley once said with humility, "Even the Robinsons' come to me," referring of course, to Frank and Brooks.

A superb writer of sports on Staten Island is Jay Price of the Staten Island Advance. Jay is another ballplayer who grew up on the other side of the Narrows. Somehow these young Staten Islanders managed to get to Brooklyn to play ball, usually in tournaments or championship games. Jay never did quite make it to the Parade Grounds, but he did get to Bay Ridge. His Tompkinsville Blue Devils won the P.A.L. juniors city championship and what a ferry ride home those boys must have had.

Larry Anderson is the Chairman of the Staten Island Sports Hall-Of-Fame. As a student at Curtis high school, he and Tracy and Frank Fernandez, another future major leaguer were with the team that lost the City Championship to Bryant high school 3-0. Anderson played football also and was a member of the *Journal-American* All-Stars in 1960. They faced the *USA* All-Stars at Yankee Stadium where Nathan's Howie Kitt struck out seven of the nine hitters he faced in his allowed three innings.

The *USA* battery was Mike Marshall and Bill Freehan, two more major leaguers to be. In this game the *JA* team took lead into the ninth when a three-run home run by *USA* Joel Taggard won the game 6-5. Anderson, a good athlete himself had the opportunity to play alongside some of the best of the locals during his time. Larry played in the last official game at Ebbets Field, the home of the Brooklyn Dodgers, in 1959, preceding the razing of the fabled old ballpark in February 1960.

Incredibly, in the fifties, there was still debate raging in some quarters about whether or not a curve ball actually curves. In "scientific" tests conducted in 1941, it was established in a report in *Life* magazine that the results "failed to show the existence of a curve....the possibility that this....is after all only an optical illusion." Obviously, the tests were conducted by people who never played the game, and baseball people scoffed at the notion.

Since the conundrum was not solved to everyone's satisfaction, *Life* had another go at it in 1953. They were getting close. This time the conclusion was, "Yes, a curve ball does curve, but in a gentle arc. No, a curve ball does not break!" Stillnot satisfying everybody, the scientific community tried again; in '59. And this time they got it right. A baseball does indeed curve and break, "as much as 17 ½ inches between the mound and the plate. "

I learned my aerodynamics at the Parade Grounds facing pitchers like Butch Gualberti and Tony Balsamo. And I did it without having a Doctorate degree. How about that!

X.

Good Enough To Dream

"He could reach for a star or two, see what you have seen; because his heart was full of hope, and he was good enough to dream"
- unknown

There was a time when all of us could dream. There was no college or high school drafts, or qualifying lists or designations. There was only the game you played. When you played it there may be scouts or bird dogs to watch you. At the Parade Grounds in the years that I played there scouts were bountiful. It was before *Moneyball* and baseball executives who were not baseball oriented. And, thankfully there were no radar guns. Pitchers were evaluated by how well they pitched, not solely by how hard they threw. The radar gun misses a lot. It tells you speed but not movement. Big leaguers can hit fast balls, it's location, control and movement that make the difference. And perhaps the greatest blessing of all. No Pitch-Counts!

At the Park in those years the Dodgers had Art Dede and Steve Lembo. Matty was bird dogging for the Giants. Joe LaBate was with the Phillies. Botts Nicolaof the Boston Red Sox signed Ted Schreiber and Rico Petrocelli out of the Park. He also has signings of Carl Yaztremski and Chuck Schilling to his credit. I once shook hands with former N.Y. Giant shortstop Buddy Kerr scouting for his old team. His hands were so huge the fingers nearly reached my elbow.

You played your game and they were watching and if you did well you could imagine someone coming over to you with a pen and a contract. So we all could dream. But some could dream more than others because their talents brought their dreams closer to reality. Some of them came just so close.

Arthur *Archie* Schwartz grew up in the Crown Heights section of Brooklyn, on Sullivan Place, a fungo distance from Ebbets Field. He played for Erasmus Hall high school and the Daytons in the late forties. The 1949 Daytons were Kiwanis League champs and went all the way to the last round of the city championships before losing to a team called the Millmachs for the title. They were managed by another Erasmus alumni, a catcher named Lennie Morris.

Archie was a skinny 145 pound outfielder who could run and as he says, "my greatest asset was a cannon for an arm." Schwartz thinks that he may hold the record for the greatest number of releases from professional teams. His buddy, Al Fortunato had an invite to a N. Y. Giants tryout camp in Florida and coaxed Archie to go along. "What have you got to lose?" So Archie went.Upon arriving he was told that no one gets in without an invitation, something neither he nor

Fortunato had realized. While trying to con the Giants into letting him stay, former Giant pitching great and head of the scouting system, Carl Hubbell unexpectedly came on the scene. Overhearing Schwartz's plea, he said,"find him a bed." Archie wound up signing his first contract and was assigned to Oshkosh, Wisconsin, a class D affiliate. Over the next five years he was released by the Giants and signed by the Browns, released by the Browns and signed by the Braves, released by the Braves and signed by the Yankees.

It was in the Yankees organization that Schwartz had his best year. At Bristol, Virginia in the Appalachian League on opening day he pinch-hit in the eighth inning and hit a home run. The next day in the starting lineup he hit another home run. Archie was not a long ball hitter, he wound up with five on the year, but those home runs got him into the regular lineup , and he hit .301. He is proudest of the fact that he struck out only 27 times, lowest in the league. This was 1954.

After the Yankees released him , he was picked up by Kansas City. Archie calls himself *The Kosher Busher*, but says that he has no regrets. There were memorable moments doing something he loved to do. At Wellsville in the PONY league, he once chased down a long fly in right center field and made a running catch. The next day the newspaper called it an "impossible catch". He played in a game against the Kansas City Royals while with Norfolk and got two hits off of big-leaguer Alex Kellner. The year was 1955 and Kellner was 11-8 that season.

Schwartz recalls being on the same field with the likes of Vic Power, Gus Zernial, Andre Rodgers and Leon Wagner;

Tony Kubek and Bobby Richardson. And playing in towns like Grand Forks, North Dakota; Jenkins, Kentucky; Homer, New York, a town Schwartz says incredulously, is a *suburb* of Cortland; and particularly Graceville, Florida. A town on the Florida-Alabama border in the class D Florida State League. For it was at Graceville where Archie Schwartz picked up his most indelible memory. Anyone who has ever pulled on a pair ofspikes has stories to tell and Archie's is a doozy.

Playing every night in the excessive heat was tough enough, but in the daytime it would be unbearable. After a particularly tough loss, manager *Onion* Davis did the unthinkable - he called an afternoon workout. Player protests went for naught but Schwartz figured he had to make a point. "What the heck," he says now, "I'd been around awhile by then so why not have some fun."

He waited until everyone was on the field and Davis was throwing batting practice. He hid behind a fence until the right moment and then he strode up to home plate ready to take his cuts. He carried his favorite bat over his shoulder, his cap was on his head, a pair of white sanitary stockings up to his knees and a pair of spikes on his feet. And that was it, the rest of him was "balls-ass naked".

Onion Davis said nothing. He wound up and threw and with the first pitch hit Archie in the butt. The next one was behind him about waist high. "You know where he was aiming," says Schwartz. He wound up getting his five swings and then strolled away from the batter's box content in the knowledge that he had made history.

On a sunny morning in mid March, with the temperature at 51 degrees, I met Jim Fanizzi at the Bagel Baestro on Victory Boulevard in Staten Island. It was across the street from "Going Places Travel", the company Fanizzi had started and was still associated with, though his son Peter now runs the day-to-day operation.

Fanizzi was born in 1935 in the Flatbush section of Brooklyn on Rutland Road. As happens with people at this age, the question of health often begins a conversation. Jim had recently had a knee replacement and spoke about the importance of diet in health. "When we were kids," he remembered , "we ate good because we ate cheap. Escarole cost about 40 pounds for a dollar. Now," he says , *Shca-dole*," as the Italians say it, "has become a delicacy in restaurants. "

But health problems have not deterred Fanizzi as he was preparing to join an over 70 hockey league. Hockey was one of Jim's passions growing up in Brooklyn. He played roller hockey; hockey on roller skates; at 53 street and Ft. Hamilton Parkway and at Farragett Park with a team called the "Hawks".

His memory begins to go back-back-back like he did when retreating for a flyball during his days as a center fielder. He recalls going to the Parade Grounds in those very early years. "Parents didn't drive you," he says. "you got there on your own. You walked or rode your bike." Those years of kid ball, Jim spent with the "Bonnies". In 1955, Fanizzi took a train ride to Winter Haven, Florida to attend a camp run by the Chicago White Sox. He showed well and was tended a contract by scout Zack Taylor. Taylor, at the time 58 years old, was himself a sixteen year major league veteran, who had some good years in Brooklyn, hitting .310 in 1925.

The contract they offered Fanizzi called for a $1,000 bonus, a fair offer for the time. However, the bonus was for $500 down and as far as the other $500 went, "We'll see how you do." Jim was sent to Madisonville, Kentucky in the Class D KITTY League. In mid-season player-manager Bill Close was leading the league in hitting when Jim passed him by climbing to an average of .418 in the process.

It seemed to him to be a good time to bring up the remaining bonus money. Close said, "I don't know." Then reluctantly, "I suppose we'll have to give it to you." And just in time, the league folded a few weeks later and Fanizzi was assigned to Superior, Wisconsin in the Class C Northern League. Then came one of those breaks that all minor leaguers dread; a career threatening injury. In those days, Fanizzi says, "If you got hurt you fixed it yourself or it didn't get fixed."

In 1957 Fanizzi and a buddy from Brooklyn, Dom Tursellino were prepared to head south for spring training when they missed their train. The next one was leaving early the following morning, so they slept the night in the railroad station. Jim awoke to a sore and aching throwing arm that plagued him throughout the spring. So much so, that his performance suffered and he was released by Chicago.Not willing to give it up yet, he "hooked up with one of those baseball bums" who travel from camp to camp looking to sign on with somebody.

They traveled to Lake Charles, Louisiana and Jim signed on with an Indepen-dent club in the Evangeline League. He played two more seasons and then determined that it was time to plan a life away from the game. He married in September of 1957. It was at this point that Fanizzi returned to the Parade Grounds and played with the Sabres into the early sixties. A rotator cuff injury from a fall on the ice while playing hockey at age sixty has slowed him down a bit.

Old ball players remember games and specific at-bats but time does dim the memory and those fellows who played in the pros have that many more games and teams and cities to recall. Nonetheless, the mind seems to restore some special events. For Jim, a day on Diamond # One stands out. His Sabres defeated the Virginians 3-2 with Fanizzi driving in a couple of runs with a double and a single. The mind recalls such days , or maybe it is the heart that remembers. Jimmy never doubted that he could sign a pro contract, never doubted hisability, and in his early seventies, he is tossing a baseball and getting back on the ice once again, content in the knowledge that he gave it his best and there is nothing more that you can give.

Standing at home plate at the Polo Grounds and wearing the home uniform of the New York Mets with the number 43 on the back of his jersey, Ted Schreiber had to feel pride. Pride in accomplishment, Pride in achievement, and pride in the knowledge that a long and arduous journey had come to a successful and fruitful conclusion. Ted Schreiber had made the big leagues.

Ted had to be thinking back to his days growing up in the Marine Park section of Brooklyn and playing baseball at the sandlot fields of Marine park and then at the historic site of the Parade Grounds at Prospect Park. Ted was one of many who signed professional contracts after playing in Brooklyn during the forties and fifties, but one of the few to complete the trek and hurdle all obstacles inherent in the journey, and make it all the way to the crest of the mountain.

Theodore Henry Schreiber attended James Madison high school while playing for a sandlot team called the "Avons". Ted was a good ballplayer and a definite prospect. While a student at St. John's University, he also excelled at basketball. While playing the infield at the Parade Grounds for the Flatbush Pontiacs, Teddy received an offer from scout Botts Nikola of the Boston Red Sox to play pro ball.

Before signing he was approached with an offer by the St. Louis Cardinals. At the time Ted was playing in a college league in South Dakota where he was hitting a lofty .393. Having given his word to Nikola, Ted signed with the Red Sox and accepted a bonus of $50,000.

The player signing a professional contract is usually a stand-out at the level of competition he is at, but once in a pro league he is thrust in with athletes who are as good or better and sometimes the player is in for a rude awakening. Schreiber, however, had no reservations about his ability and tackled his first assignment at Allentown, Pennsylvania in the class AA Eastern League with relish. Then came the adversity every player dreads. In an early season slide Schreiber broke his wrist. He came back with a vengeance, getting five hits in his first five times at bat, including two home runs, one of them, a tenth-inning game winner. But it was a false omen. His wrist was weak and prevented him from swinging properly and his first pro year turned out to be a disaster. The next year Ted was sent to Danville, Illinois; Class D, the bottom of the professional ladder. Arriving just prior to a game, the manager welcomed him. "I'm glad you're here," he told Ted, "you're playing tonight." Then he scanned the clubhouse and pointed to one player. "You. You're released. Give this guy your uniform." Years later Schreiber was still incredulous at the memory. "He looked for a guy my size to release," he said, "even made him give me his sanitary stockings."

Schreiber did well over the next two seasons and made it to Seattle, the Red Sox AAA affiliate, the top of the minor league heap, a mere stride away from the major leagues. But that small step is, in fact a *giant leap* and more setbacks awaited. At Seattle, a conflict developed between the young ballplayer and his manager, Johnny Pesky, an occupational hazard in any field.

Schreiber now had a wife and two small children. His wife had driven from New York to Seattle with the children only to find that Ted had been hit by a pitch, suffered another broken wrist, and had been reassigned to Johnstown, Pennsylvania. In a professional baseball family, this may be considered "par for the course", so it was back in the car and another cross country trek to Johnstown.

Ted's first visit to a big league clubhouse finally came in Boston where he reported for a spring workout. He entered the locker room; empty, except for one player. Jim Piersall looked at the rookie. No hello, or good luck, only, "get every dollar you can out of them, kid!" Welcome to the big time!

Back in Seattle, Schreiber made the All-Star team but his ongoing feud with Pesky hadn't abated and Ted was placed in the minor league draft at the end of the season. Selected by the New York Mets as their number one pick, Ted was the choice of general manager George Weiss and scouting supervisor Johnny Murphy. He had gotten the thumbs down, however, from manager Casey Stengel, who had his eye on pitcher Allan Worthington. The front office won and Ted was a Met. Not being on Casey's favorites list, Schreiber didn't get much of a chance in New York.

He figured the writing was on the wall, when on the last day of the season, in the last inning with most of the players already left for an early start home, Casey scanned the bench for a replacement player. Finally, with some reluctance in his voice, he told Ted to go in the game. "I was the only guy left on the bench," Ted says, "and it was still a tough decision for him." Schreiber reported to Buffalo the next year and was traded to Baltimore and decided to call it quits.

But one year in the majors is more than most players ever accomplish. Ted opted to go home to continue his education and to commence the life after baseball that came sooner than he had hoped. He carries the dubious distinction of being the last major league out at the old Polo Grounds when he lined into a double play. On April 24, 1958, Ted Schreiber hit the next-to-last home run ever hit at Ebbets Field before it was demolished. It was a two-run game winner into the left field seats enabling St. John's University to defeat Manhattan College by a score of 2-1.

As a standout basketball star at Madison high school and St. Johns University, Ted calls to mind the feeling he experienced coming out on the court at the start of a championship game, knowing full well what he was capable of accomplishing. "Baseball is different," he said, "it's a tough game. You get a good hop and you're good, a bad hop and you're a bum. A good pitch and you're the hero."

While there is always the lingering sense of the "what ifs" and the "if onlys" ,Ted Schreiber is content in the knowledge that he was good enough to go the route. It doesn't happen often.

Between Sunday doubleheaders at the Parade Grounds, where he pitched and played first base and the outfield, Ed Jordan made a number of trips to another type of athletic domicile. Places with names like *The Eastern Parkway Arena* and *St. Nicholas Arena* and *Madison Square Garden.* As *Irish* Eddie Jordan, who by 1959 was still an undefeated welterweight, Jordan was just as much at home in the boxing ring as he was on the diamond.

On March 6, 1959, Eddie Jordan climbed through the ropes at Madison Square Garden in New York City for a ten round main event against Stefan Redl. Jordan wore a purple robe with gold trim and was flanked by his manager, Rickey Fasano and two corner men. Even today the memory of that night is still fresh for the Brooklyn native born, as Eddie says, into a fighting family. Two of his three brothers were boxers,

Billy fought while in the Marine Corps and Joe had several pro fights. It was Joe who took Eddie into the gym for the first time and began to teach the teen the rudiments of the fight game.   As an amateur, Jordan won 18 fights against two defeats and made it to the semi-final round of the Golden Gloves Tournament. A fine athlete , Eddie played for Sacred Heart-St. Stephens in the Open Division of the Parade Grounds League. He turned pro boxer in 1954 when he out pointed Lou Fusco at the Eastern Parkway Arena. After just two bouts, Jordan was inducted into the Army and put his budding career on hold until his discharge in 1956. Going into the fight with Redl, Eddie had won 16, had not lost, and had fought twice to draws. A natural lefty, he was converted for the ring.

Gene Ward in the *New York Daily News* described the fight as the "bull vs the matador", Jordan being the more stylish boxer. Redl carried the fight through the first five rounds opening up a cut under Jordan's left eye. Eddie began the second half of the fight by using his powerful left hook and stabbing jab to gain an ultimate draw.

In 1960 when Eddie and I were teammates, he decided it was time to see if he could stay in with a contender. He went to New Orleans to face Ralph Dupas, the *Baby Bull*, and ranked as the divisions number four contender by Ring Magazine .Dupas already had 101 fights on the way to a career total of 135 and would, in 1963, win the World Junior Middleweight title. Jordan stayed the course, but lost a ten round decision. He knocked out Ronnie Cohen at St. Nicholas Arena in New York, and in turn was KO'd by another ranked contender, Jose Stable, at the Garden.

Following that fight in March of 1961, "Irish" Eddie Jordan decided to hang up his gloves. His 29 pro fights broke down as 20 wins, 5 losses, 4 draws. A classy boxer and a scrapper, Jordan is proud of his forays in the square arena and the friendships and memories that were generated as result. He continued his Parade Grounds baseball career into the sixties. Each summer Eddie travels to Canastota, New York to visit the Boxing Hall of Fame. On one such trek, he met, strictly by chance, his nemesis from all those years ago, Stefan Redl. They embraced like long lost brothers, joined in the memory of a battle fought in a time and a place that no longer exists.

Two warriors worn by time remembering when each of them was "good enough to dream."

In the Red Hook section, on the edge of Cobblehill at Woodhull and Columbia streets, a career began for Gasper "Butch" Gualberti. Mike Rubino managed a group of neighborhood kids who called themselves the Sabres. They started out as all the young ballplayers did through the mid-century years. They played their baseball on rock filled lots, there were such vacant lots, all over the city of New York. For the Red Hook kids it was the "Rock Fields".

For Butch and his buddies; his brother Joey, Tommy *Moose* Morrissey, Vinnie Bonacure, Sal Brocco and Peter *Rabbit* Vacari it was only the beginning of years together. Years of playing ball and the after years, of reunions and Florida trips, and gathering at an old hangout, Nick's sandwich shop, still run by the Delfonte family, now into the third generation. Of laughing and sharing and remembering.

They took their club into the Parade Grounds and went through the Senior and Open competition as teammates and friends. At Alexander Hamilton high school, Butch and Peter Rabbit were teammates on the city championship team of 1956. But for Butch Gualberti the road turned soon after and very nearly culminated in a dream come true.

Playing in a Parade Grounds game on Diamond # 1 , his Sabres went up against one of the Park's Classics, Nathan's Famous. The wooden bleachers were full and the crowd overflowed behind the outfield fences. The scouts were there in abundance because of an exceptional prospect playing first base for Nathan's. The youngster's name was Joe Pepitone and Joe looked to be able to do it all. He was as smooth as a cat's coat around the bag and could hit; oh, how he could hit.

But when Gualberti toed the rubber that day, he wasn't cognizant of the fact that those scouts were very much aware of the 6' 2" right hander with the blazing fast ball. He struck out Pepitone twice, although he did hit a long foul, "about 500 feet," Gualberti remembers with a laugh. A scout for the Philadelphia Phillies came to the Gualberti house and proceeded to have a few drinks. The more he drank, he higher his offer went. By the time it reached $30,000, the scout had to be helped into a taxi and sent home.

Butch's mom worried about the business her son might be getting into. "What's wrong with that man?" she asked. The next day the scout didn't recall making any offer at all, let alone $30,000. So Gualberti accepted an invitation for a personnel try out at Ebbets Field with the Dodgers. Told to bring his own catcher, he brought along his brother Joe. Butch believes he was one of the very last to throw off the Ebbets Field mound before the demolition. But throw he did. In the empty ball park, his fast balls exploded into Joe's mitt. "What a beautiful sound," Butch says now.

The outcome was that Dodger scout Steve Lembo inked Gualberti for $2,000. Therewere several offers after that , six or seven as Gualberti remembers, some over twenty thousand dollars. However, it was no longer a concern and the young blazer looked ahead. His first year was spent in Class D Orlando in the Florida State League. Among his teammates was a future Mets catcher Choo-Choo Coleman and another Parade Grounds alumni, Al *Kiki* Ferrara. He and Ferrara once overslept while with Orlando and missed the team bus. Somehow the dilemma was conveyed to the state police and they hustled the two players into a squad car and caught up with the bus.

Gualberti hung around for a time with minor league legend Steve Dalkowsky. It had been said by some, like Hall of Fame manager Earl Weaver, that Dalkowsky threw harder than any pitcher who ever lived. Even Ted Williams called him the "fastest ever, I never want to face him again." Some said his fast ball reached 110 miles per hour. But he was extremely wild. In 1960 in the California League he struck out 262 batters in 172 innings, and walked 262.

It was in Kingsport when a pitch from Steve tore off part of a hitter's ear. Many believed that his fear of killing someone contributed to his wildness. But to Gualberti he was "a nice guy and fun to be with."

By his third year as a professional, Gualberti reached the roster of the Spokane club, the Dodgers AAA affiliate, and the highest level of minor league ball before the big top. He had already traversed such minor league towns as Great Falls, Montana, Green Bay, Wisconsin and Macon, Georgia.

At Vero Beach, Florida that spring, the consensus of opinion among Dodgers coaching and scouting personnel was that Gualberti was the hardest thrower in camp. In those pre " radar gun" days, it was decided that he was clocking 100 miles per hour with his fast ball. Speed, however, is not the determining factor in evaluating the fast ball. It is the movement that is the key. The ball thrown by a right hander should move up and in to a right handed batter.

Robert K. Adair, in his scientific treatise , "*The Physics of Baseball*", explains that a baseball thrown overhand and with a backspin can *hop* up to four or five inches. The problem for the hitter, however, is in the realization that "*half of the hop deviation occurs in the last 15 feet of the flight.*" Imagine a 90-mile-an-hour fast bal lcoming at you at shoulder height and you must initiate your swing when the ball is about halfway to the plate when the deviation is about one inch. You begin to stride and swing and when the ball is virtually upon you , it jumps , apparently quite suddenly , another three inches. (1) Of course, a good hitter will stay in there and even hit the ball safely with some degree of regularity. A good hitter like Tommy Davis. Davis, also from the Parade Grounds, faced Butch Gualberti in an inter-squad game at Vero Beach. Butch's jumping fast ball hit the peak of Davis' cap *spinning it around*. The Dodgers players started howling, "get him out of there!" Butch loved to hit and was good at it. "I never hit less than .300 in any league," he said proudly. One newspaper called him "the pitcher who wants to be a hitter."

It was in this spring that Dodgers manager Walt Alston offered some welcome advice. "Take care of yourself, " he told the young fireballer, " looks like next year you'll get your shot."

The pain in his shoulder began at Macon that season. Unable to quell it, by seasons end it had grown to "unbearable" proportions. Doctors were at a loss to treat sports injuries in those days and all that they could offer was "exploratory surgery." The arm never quite came around. The Dodgers offered the good hitting pitcher a chance to play first base. But, as Butch relates, the club had, "Gil Hodges at first and a good prospect in Tim Harkness behind him." Seeing no other alternative, Gualberti went home.

The depression he felt passed in time as he played some more ball at the Parade Grounds and over the years has stayed close with his friends from the Sabres. Often baseball ties are not easily forgotten. Some forty years later the group took a Florida trip to view some spring training games. At the camp of the Atlanta Braves, Gualberti confronted Braves pitching coach, Leo Mezzone, and asked him to mention to Bobby Cox that he was there to see him.

The manager of the Braves stepped out of the dugout, took one look at his old roommate, 60 pounds heavier. "That can't be you!" Cox exclaimed. The two then embraced, the forty years that separated them gone quicker than one of Butch's old fast balls and the old memories as fresh as today.

Jim Ursillo was another fireball throwing pitcher, this one a lefthander, who simply blew away the hitters. He started out as a first baseman from 84 Street and 14 Avenue in Bensonhurst where he played his kid ball for St. Bernadette. He captained the New Utrecht high school team where he played for three years and joined the Ty Cobbs while a senior in high school. The Ty Cobbs played in the Parade Grounds League and also in the twi-light Industrial league where Jim got to face Unlimited level competition. It was during those teen years that Jim became a pitcher.

Sonny Giordano was a neighbor and friend and a good ballplayer who played some pro ball in the Braves organization and was also a fixture at the Park where we'd played together on the Virginians. Giordano knew how hard Ursillo could throw and thought he might have a better chance as a pitcher. "You're too skinny for a first baseman," hetold him, "they look for power at first base." Jim started pitching at the Park and had a try out with Jimmy McElroy's Cadets, but didn't make it. McElroy said he was too wild. Later that season when Ursillo shut out the powerful Cadets, McElroy admitted to Jim that he should have taken him on the club, "that was the biggest mistake I ever made," he bemoaned.

Ursillo continued to improve. In a twi-light league game ,pitching for the Ty Cobbs against the Bonnies, Jim threw nine innings of no-hit ball. The left hander was attracting attention and was soon the recipient of a contract offer from scout Bubba Genard of the New York Mets. The year was 1964 and Jim began to rub elbows with some future greats. Playing rookie league ball he was teammates with a flamethrower named Ryan. Nolan Ryan was a kid from Refugio, Texas. At Marion, Virginia, he once lost a 1-0 game after striking out ten. Depressed and dejected, the kid wanted to go home. Ursillo saw him packing a bag."Where you going?"

"Home," Nolan said, "I can't win here."

Ursillo said, "before you leave, let's go to a hospital."

"A hospital?"

"Yeah," Jim said, "I want to get a doctor to switch our arms. Then you can go home and I'll be a superstar. They don't care if you win here. You're throwing 105and striking out 12 guys a game. That's what they care about." To satisfy any curiosity, note that Nolan Ryan decided to stay around just to see how things would turn out.

Ursillo went to Cocoa Beach and Auburn in the N.Y.-Penn League. It was in spring training in 1964 that Ed Kranspool said, "Hey, aren't you the great Jim Ursillo?" "Why do you say that?" Jim asked. "Well," he was told, "your name has been floated around the organization for the last six months. " Throwing at 101 with an 89 mph curve ball, Jim began to think that it really could happen. It turned out that the Met brass was thinking the same way; Ryan as right handed starter, Jerry Kooseman, lefty starter; Tug McGraw , short relief and Jim Ursillo and his almighty speed as a lefthanded long reliever.

At Auburn , pitching coach Cot Deal, a major league veteran pitcher, taught Jim a more effective curve ball and how to set up the hitters with his speed and breaking pitch. That season Ursillo was sent to Jacksonville, AAA, and anticipated to be one year away from the bigs. But at Jacksonville in 1965 something in his arm snapped.

How? "Who knows," Jim says now. "Maybe walking home from New Utrecht high school on winter evenings", where they let the pro work out. "The sweat and the cold, maybe it did something, I don't know." Jim wouldn't quit yet, he gave it all he could. The next spring he was traded to Cleveland where he roomed with a young Lou Pinella, before going home for good. "There was no point anymore," he said."The arm was totally blown out."

Regrets? "Only that I was so close. If I tried and couldn't cut it, okay, but to end with an injury, it was tough too take." So many fond memories, though. A minor league Rod Carew, on his way to the Hall-Of-Fame, after being struck out by Ursillo, told Jim, "if I had to face you all the time, I'd never make it."

Jim misses the "great comradery we had in the minors. Who knew what was in store?" He is inclined to prefer the game before pitch counts and six inning *quality starts*. "It's a different game today. Pitchers don't protect the inside of the plate." He remembers knocking down hitters after a home run. "These guys today are leaning in and nobody loosens them up," Ursillo said.

At age 47 Jim went to a Mets fantasy camp and got out on the mound once again. Former major league player and coach and native of Brooklyn Joe Pignatano was there as an instructor. Watching Ursillo throw, he said, "Hey, where you from, Lefty?" "Brooklyn!" came the reply.

"No kiddin'" Pignatano said. "You look like Koufax out there."

And a thought went through the mind of Jim Ursillo, "I almost was....almost."

Ed Mathieson of Dahill Road

Al Fortunato at Erasmus Hall HS - 1949

Frankie "Bo" Taylor at Ebbets Field 1942 sand lot All-Star game

74 police pct softball team circa 1940s - Paul Mele (back row-r)

Welterweight boxer "Irish" Eddie Jordan

Arthur "Archie" Schwartz - the "Kosher Busher"

Parade Grounds League Director "Cookie" Lorenzo, Joe Torre,
And Dodgers scout Steve Lembo (l-r)

Cadets' Jim McElroy (l), PGLs Arthur Bellone and
Frank Torre *

Chuck Connors during recitation of "Casey at the Bat"
Courtesy Barney Stein Photo Collection LLC Photo

Ted Schreiber with the New York Mets – 1963

Frank "Chick" Chiarello gets congrats from teammate Barry
Frazita after grand slam home run on Diamond # 1

Richie "Rebo" Lupardo - "The Legend"

Gaspar "Butch" Gualberti (l), Macon Dodgers with manager   Ray Perry ®)

Sal Marchiano of Channel 11 News Courtesy CW 11 (WPIX 11)

Gov. Mario Cuomo as a Pittsburgh pirates farmhand -
1952 Courtesy Mario Cuomo

Parade Grounds umpires Tom Corrodo (I) and Steve Albanese *)

Gabe "Red" Verde - manager Brooklyn Royals

Cadets manager Jim McElroy (l) and former Cadet Joe Torre (r)

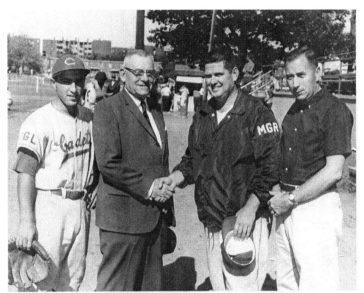

Asst GM Houston Astros Matt Galante (l) Jim McElroy
(Second from right) with two regional directors AAABA

The Aspromonte brothers, Ken (l) with the Chicago Cubs,
And Bob ®) Houston Colt 45s - 1963

The "Old Boys of Summer" Bill Langsdorf - 2006 Photo

Parade Grounds ribbon-cutting Grand Re-Opening June 26, 2004

Sandy Koufax, one of 2 Hall-Of-Fame players from the
Parade Grounds, after signing Dodgers contract 12/22/54
courtesy Brooklyn Public Library Collection

Clarence Irving (l) Bisons manager with former Bison Tommy Davis *))

The Dodgers at Vero Beach, Fla. 1951 includes 3 Boys of Brooklyn: Jim Romano (lower middle with pipe) Tommy Brown (Fr middle with pipe) and Steve Lembo (standing middle)   Courtesy Barney Stein Photo Collection LLC

Yankee Rookies - scout Art Dede (back row -I);
Jack Tracy (second from r) ; Sal Campisi (front row I)

The Bisons 50th reunion 2005 (front row second from L)
Tommy Davis, Fred Wilpon, Clarence Irving (photo size   App 3.5x5)

The Parade Grounds... The Future

XI.

Did Anybody Here Play In Brooklyn?

"Whenever anybody asks me where I'm from, I never say New York , I always say Brooklyn." -Fred Wilpon

All roads are supposed to lead to Rome, but any that don't, apparently lead to Brooklyn. It is said that five or six of every ten Americans have some roots in the City of Churches. The Lone Ranger's faithful Indian companion,Tonto, lived in Brooklyn. Actor Jay Silverheels married a girl from Brooklyn and lived there for a time.

Vitagraph Studios set up shop in the Midwood section and made silent films in the early days of the twentieth century. Cecil B.DeMille and Rudolph Valentino called the borough home for a period of time. Comedian Henny Youngman used to step out of his bedroom window on the second floor of his families' apartment on at 51 street, onto the roof of the tailor shop below and practice his violin. The *King of the One-Liners* proclaimed himself the first "Fiddler on the Roof."

Vincent Gardinia lived at 77 street and 17th Avenue even years after he was a noted actor preferring Brooklyn to California. Although apparently not a ballplayer, Gardinia did a superb job as manager Dutch Schnell in the film *Bang The Drum Slowly.*

Carmine Orrico came from 50 street and eleventh avenue and played his early baseball as a catcher with the Ty Cobbs at the Parade Grounds long before embarking on a Hollywood acting career as John Saxon. He went on to appear in several dozen films and TV dramas, including a starring role in the cult classic, *Nightmare on Elm Street* in 1984.

If you should happen to stop for gas in Staten Island at Walter's Sunoco station at the corner of Arthur Kill Road and Arden Avenue, you may run into Tony Russo. Tony is retired from the NYC Sanitation Department and spends a few hours a week pumping gas at Walter's. Tony is still a fan of the New York Yankees and loves to talk baseball. No wonder, he started out at 82 street between 14 and 15 avenues in Bensonhurst, Brooklyn, in the Catholic parish of St. Bernadette.

Born in 1951, Russo did get to go to Ebbets Field once with his Dodger fan father, also a ballplayer from South Brooklyn, before they departed the borough.It seemed all the kids of that era grew up playing baseball. For Tony, it was first with the Pee Wee League Allied Sanitation team at Dyker Park on 86 street.

A product of New Utrecht High School, Russo joined the ranks of Parade Grounders in the early sixties when he played shortstop for one of those legendary Park teams, the Ty Cobbs. Tony continued his baseball career until he entered the military in 1969 and did a tour in Vietnam with the U.S. Navy. After his discharge he went the route of so many sandlot ballplayers and into softball where he played fast pitch and windmill into his forties.

Author Bernard Malamud spent early years in and around Prospect Park and the Parade Grounds. His 1952 novel, *The Natural*, is a bittersweet tribute to the game from one of America's foremost writers. Mr. Malamud had been the recipient of the *National Book Award* and a Pulitzer Prize. Although popularized in the film which starred Robert Redford, it fell short of capturing the passion and mysticism of the novel. Harry Sylvester in the *New York Times* called it "a brilliant and unusual book."

Certainly one of the most illustrious of the Park's alumni ultimately spent twelve years in the Governor's Mansion in Albany, New York. Mario Cuomo grew up in Queens and like the rest of his generation began playing baseball on a vacant lot near his home. He did get to play at the Parade Grounds while a student at St. John's Prep in the Bedford-Stuyvesant section of Brooklyn and recalls playing on Brooklyn's principal *Field of Dreams*, Diamond # One. Cuomo also played there with a sandlot team called the "Austin Celtics."

But the young man's political quests were not the first step on his life's agenda. Before that came Mario Cuomo, prospect! A student at St. John's University, Cuomo was signed for a bonus of $ 2,000 by the Pittsburgh Pirates. He first had to convince his father, Andrea Cuomo, who thought playing games was for the kids. Mario was keeping company with Matilda Raffa who was less than enthusiastic about a life with a ballplayer. "When I said I'd never marry a baseball player, he looked at me with this funny look, as if I'd slapped him." (1)

Somehow his persistence reached them both and Mario got his shot. The contract was signed at Cuomo's grocery store in 1951. Robert S. McElvaine describes the signing scene in his biography of Cuomo. "At a little table with provolones and salamis hanging from the ceiling above , Mario Cuomo signed to play for the Pirates." He went to Brunswick, Georgia in the class D Georgia-Florida League for the 1952 season. (2) A Pirates scouting report read that he was "a below average hitter with plus power. He uppercuts and needs instruction.... potentially the best prospect on the club and in my opinion could go all the way....he is aggressive and plays hard. He is intelligent." Cuomo lived up to his hot-headed reputation in a game at Tifton. While at bat, the catcher made an ethnic slur and Mario turned and punched the opposing catcher, who was still wearing his mask. "That's not hot tempered," the governor said years later, "that's stupid." (3)

He crashed into an outfield fence and was hit in the head with a pitched ball. This was before players wore batting helmets and fortunately, the resulting blood clot ultimately dissolved. He wound up playing 81 games and hitting .244, though an excellent fielder and base runner.

The following season he decided not to return to baseball because he says, " I didn't think I was good enough. And we learn from the rest of our lives , you can't make it anywhere unless you go all out and that's part of baseball too. You've got to give it everything." The Pirate organization wanted him to change his mind and did not give him his release until 1965, by then a thirty-three year old successful attorney.

He and Matilda were married in 1960 and he turned to politics, ultimately serving three terms as Democratic Governor of New York State. Highly respected , Harvard's Kennedy School named him "the nation's most gifted philosopher-politician." The New York Times regarded his tenure as Governor, "one of the lengthiest and most celebrated Governorships in recent history." (4)

Never far from his baseball roots, Governor Cuomo enjoys repeating a comment made by Yankee great Mickey Mantle. "The two dumbest scouts in America signed me and Cuomo. They signed me for only $1,100 and I went to the Hall of Fame. They signed him for $2,000 and he still couldn't hit a barn door with a paddle."

On the flip side Brooklyn sandlot baseball missed out on a supreme major league ball player. The Washington Senator's excellent third baseman, Ed Yost was born in Brooklyn, but his family moved to Queens when he was four years old. Ed played in the CYO and Queens Alliance Leagues and attended and played ball at NYU. Yost also played some semi-pro ball in the New York area before signing with the Senators. His major league career spanned 18 years. As baseball's premier lead off man; he was known as *The Walking Man*; Yost led the American League in On-Base-Percentage twice, in 1959 and 1960 while with Detroit. His batting average those two seasons was .278 and .260 while his OBP was a whopping .435 and .414.

Brooklyn Dodgers outfielder Gene Hermanski and New York Yankees' pitching ace, Whitey Ford both found those Brooklyn roads. Ford pitched in a game at the Parade Grounds for the Ft. Monmouth Army team . The future Hall-Of-Fame Yankee threw three innings on Diamond #1 against the Nathans team and struck out eight of the nine men he faced. Considered something of a "junk" pitcher in the majors, on-lookers that day had a different memory. Fred Weber said, "don't you believe that junk stuff, he could really bring it."

Hermanski was stationed at Floyd Bennett Field with the Navy when he appeared for the service team at the Park in 1943. He also played with the semi-pro Bushwicks at this time as pros often did under assumed names. Gene played under the name "George Walsh." I had been told that he had hit a home run out of Diamond One . "I don't remember that," He said, "but I'll tell you what I do remember." Hermanski, now in his mid-eighties is extremely lucid in speech and memory. " I was stealing home and the son-of-a-gun swung the bat. He almost killed me. That I remember, " he said. "He almost killed me." That same year , having applied forflight school, Gene was given a two months hiatus in which time he played 18games for the Dodgers and hit .300 in 60 at-bats.

Always popular with the Flatbush Faithful, after the war Hermanski played in Brooklyn from 1946 until he was traded to the Cubs in 1951 in the deal that brought Andy Pafko to the Dodgers.

Like Waite Hoyt, Tommy Holmes completed the circle from the Brooklyn streets and the Parade Grounds to his final major league season in Brooklyn in 1952. Holmes lived on 57 street off Ft. Hamilton Parkway and played with a neighborhood club called the Overtons. There were fields all over Brooklyn and many local teams had fields that they called home. The Overtons used Overton Field in Bay Ridge as well as the Parade Grounds. Tommy's eleven big league seasons wound up in a .302 lifetime batting average. Holmes had a brilliant year in 1945 with the Boston Braves. He led the National League in hits with 224, 47 doubles and 28 home runs. He was second in RBIs with 117 and his .352 batting average was second in the league to Phil Cavaretta of the Chicago Cubs.

But that year Tommy also set the baseball world on end when he hit safely in 37 consecutive games to break Rogers Hornsby's modern National League record of 33.Willie Keeler had hit safely in 44 consecutive games in 1894 and Pete Rose broke Holmes' record in 1978.

Although a Brooklynite and a favorite son, when push came to shove, the Dodgers fans reacted in support of their beloved *"Bums."*   While managing the Braves in 1951, his club swept a doubleheader from the Dodgers on September 25, reducing the Dodgers' seemingly insurmountable lead to one game over the New York Giants in their staggering come-from-behind pennant victory that year. Holmes reported receiving threatening calls and letters from the fans of Flatbush. He was shocked. "But I'm from Brooklyn!" he declared.

In truth, Tommy remained an honest- to- God Brooklynite . When they began the heart rendering destruction of Ebbets Field in 1960, Holmes was there. When the first blow crushed the dugout roof, both Holmes and Carl Erskine turned away. "As soon as that wrecking ball came down," Tommy said, "I said to myself 'Let me get the hell out of here. No one wants to see this.' And I left." (5)

Jimmy Ring was born in Brooklyn in 1895 and pitched in the National League for twelve years. He was a part of an incident which preceded the infamous *Black Sox* scandal of throwing the World Series in 1919. Ring was a rookie pitcher with the Cincinnati Reds in 1917. The first baseman was Hal Chase. Gambling and selling out ball games was rampant in the early days of the twentieth century and Chase was flagrantly notorious at the practice. In many cases he was known to have cut out the gambler completely , placed his own money on a game, and tossed it out by himself.

On this day, young Ring came in from the bullpen with the score tied and two runners on base. Eliot Asinof relates the incident in his definitive study of the 1919 Black Sox, "Eight Men Out". "Chase walked over from first base and with incredible gall told him (Ring), 'I've got some money bet on this game, kid. There's something in it for you if you lose.'"

Although Ring ignored him, he wound up losing the game anyway. The next   day Chase slipped him $50. Ring reported it to his manager, Christy Mathewson, who reported the incident to National League President John Heydler. The hearing that followed acquitted Chase for lack of evidence. Such was the temper of the times. (6) Ring, however, did ultimately contribute to the suspension of Chase from the major Leagues. The next year, 1918, Chase's transgressions were becoming all too blatant. After kicking away a ground ball in particularly disgraceful fashion in a game that Ring was pitching, the big pitcher exploded in the clubhouse. "I swear I'll never pitch another game for Cincinnati as long as Chase is on this club." The episode was followed with Chase's suspension. (7)

The writer Donald Honig was a great admirer of Ring and was told these stories by Jimmy in one of the sessions they had near their homes in Queens when Ring was long retired and Honig an inquisitive teen.

In 1919 Ring pitched game four of the World Series for the Cincinnati Reds against the Chicago White Sox. He pitched a complete game 3-hit shutout. It was soon revealed that the White Sox were the *Black Sox* and had thrown the World Series.

Writer Don Honig was a ballplayer also, growing up in Maspeth, Queens. He played in the Queens-Nassau League and recalls fondly how "we shoveled off the snow on the empty lots in order to play." He was with a club called the St. Mary's Browns and played Saturdays, Sundays, and evenings in a twilight league. Born in 1931, as a youngster he was a bat boy for the famous Brooklyn Bushwicks, who played most of their baseball at Dexter park. Don was thrilled by Bushwick stars Sam Mele, Phil Rizzuto, Sid Gordon, and Gene Hermanski. Many were already in the pros and played under assumed names to pick up a few dollars. Honig says Rizzuto used his own name, "he couldn't hide, everybody knew who he was."

Honig was signed by the Red Sox when he was only sixteen years of age and assigned to Milford, Delaware in the Eastern Shore League. A pitcher, he failed to make it out of the Boston spring training camp in Melbourne, Florida. He tried again later with Cincinnati and Washington, and played semi-pro ball in the New York area and this brought Honig into Brooklyn and the Parade Grounds.

Just about anybody who played ball played at the Park in the days through the1950s. It was the largest facility around and offered some of the very best competition. Don wasn't broken up about not playing in the pros however, "my heart wasn't in it," he said, "I wanted to write." And write he did. Honig began writing novels and short stories for *Alfred Hitchcock* Mystery Magazine, some of which made it to the TV show, *Alfred Hitchcock Presents.*

Donald Honig didn't write his first baseball book until he was forty years old, and that one is a classic. It's called *Baseball When the Grass Was Real.* "It was a great experience," he said. " I traveled around the country meeting baseball stars and talking about the game. What could be better?" In a forward to the book,Lawrence Ritter writes, "The best thing about baseball today is its yesterdays."

Honig echoes that thought with the more than 70 books he has written about the greatest teams and the greatest players in the game's history. He speaks of sitting and listening to the players talk about their careers as though he was still a wide-eyed teen as he listened to veteran Jimmy Ring regaling him with *war* stories of the diamond. Indeed, Honig has become as much apart of baseball history as his subjects.

Like so many of us who reach back 50 years or more, Honig bemoans the state of baseball today, but he also sees the positive. "I never saw such outstanding defensive play," the writer said. "The leaping, and diving; the players today are naturally better than ever." But the pitch counts and the lefty-righty switches bother him. In Donald's time hitters didn't know that they could not hit a lefty or a righty,"we thought we were supposed to hit everyone." Honig echoes the thoughts of so many of the greats that he interviewed over the years. "The ball still has to come over the plate," he says.

A. J. Buddy Fortunato is the owner and publisher of a weekly newspaper , *The Italian-Tribune* of Montclair, New Jersey. The paper is circulated in the state of New Jersey and in New York City. Mr. Fortunato is an old ballplayer who grew up in Montclair and made the New Jersey All-State baseball team three years as a student at Montclair High School, the only player in the history of New Jersey to hold that distinction.

A center fielder in those years, Buddy injured his throwing arm in a football mishap, and, rather than succumb to it and forcibly give up baseball, a game he loved to play, the determined young man taught himself to throw with his left hand. Throwing well enough to still play in the outfield, he did alternate at first base when playing ball at Ryder College.

Playing for a ball club in Clifton, NJ in 1967, Buddy and his team traveled to Brooklyn's Parade Grounds to play a game against one of the borough's top clubs, the Brooklyn Cadets, managed by Jim McElroy. Though much of those days have drifted from memory, Fortunato recalls quite clearly, a drive he hit that cleared the right field fence for a home run on Diamond # 13.

Recently several newspapers picked up an item about a softball league on Long Island that featured a couple of octogenarian pitchers. Paul Rotter is 86 years old and continues to pitch in the league. A graduate of Lincoln high school and a resident of Bensonhurst while growing up in Brooklyn, Paul played most of his baseball on the Bay Parkway diamonds, but remembers how three neighborhood ballplayers would drive him to the Parade Grounds so the teen-ager could throw batting practice to the wanna-bees. One of them, Hack Willis got to play third base for Buffalo in the AAA International League.

Another youngster whose dreams of baseball glory were nurtured on the Parade Grounds was Fred Wilpon. Fred loved the game and like so many others, wanted to be a ballplayer. Not achieving that ultimate dream, he decided to own a whole major league ball club instead. On January 24, 1980, it was announced that Nelson Doubleday and Fred Wilpon headed a group of investors who purchased the New York Mets for a reported $21.1 million, at that time, the highest price paid for a major league franchise.

Fred grew up in the Bensonhurst section of Brooklyn and attended Lafayette high school along with his friend Sandy Koufax. A left handed pitcher, Wilpon played ball in the Coney Island League with a team called the Blue Jays, and then with Clarence Irving's Bisons. Wilpon remembers the Parade Grounds as a "very special place. One that allowed us to play and develop in an organized way."

Wilpon himself was a pretty good pitcher, Tommy Davis called him one of the "best left handers at the Parade

Grounds." Not a particularly hard thrower, Fred's forte' was in the breaking stuff and he may have had a chance to sign but his direction was to complete his college education.

It is particularly interesting to note that a man as successful as Wilpon is would give such credit to experiences and people from those early years as being so significant to his ultimate success. He is not being trite when he says that sportsmanship and integrity were woven into his Parade Grounds development and they are valuable lessons to cling to in whatever field these young men venture into in their adult lives.

He is ample in his praise and regard for two men in particular that the young Wilpon encountered in his early baseball experience. Ted Meyerstein founded the Brooklyn Kiwanis League and was instrumental in Fred receiving a scholarship to the University of Michigan. Meyerstein was "a wonderful man" and Wilpon says that he will always "honor his memory."

Another gentleman from his sandlot past who looms so largely in Wilpon's life and career was his Bison's manager Clarence Irving. Fred refers to him as "a lifelong friend and a remarkable man." His regard for both of these legendary Parade Grounds notables is shared by anyone who knew them; and this includes most who played in and around Park Circle during the mid-century years.

Mr. Wilpon's business was real estate and his success placed him in a position to become a purchaser of the Mets when the opportunity presented itself. In 1986 theDoubleday Publishing Company sold their 80 % interest in the club to Fred

Wilpon and Nelson Doubleday. It was an uneasy partnership that was finally terminated in2002 when a deal was completed to transfer full ownership to Wilpon.

Wilpon's business success has not taken him far from the friendships he cultivated in Brooklyn and by his own reckoning have held him in good stead through the years. He remains in close touch with individuals and organizations in his native borough. The affiliation of the New York Mets with a short season team in the class A New York-Penn League, the Brooklyn Cyclones, has further served to keep Fred Wilpon's ties to Brooklyn as strong as when he toed the rubber on the Parade Grounds diamonds fifty years ago.

Although baseball was the dominant sport played at the Parade Grounds from early in the century, by the late thirties football was a mainstay at the Park. The grassy area in the center of the tract with thirteen diamonds around the perimeter was marked out for the growing sport. A number of high schools played games there and sandlot teams were in abundance in mid-century.

I played a season as an end, both offensively and defensively during my junior year at Erasmus Hall. There were a lot of high school players that participated and the club I played for was made up of players from the Erasmus and the Midwood high teams. One of the schools that played a share of its games at the Parade Grounds was Lafayette high school and one of Lafayette's stars in the early fortieswas Arthur Pinto. Pinto came from Avenue P and East second street and gained a following for his prowess on the gridiron. His wife recalled how in later years Arthur was still recognized and approached by people he didn't know, just to say that they remembered him on the football field.

John Dockery was a student at Brooklyn Prep High school and played baseball and football at Park Circle. Dockery was a prospect in both sports having signed with the Boston Red Sox after attending high school. Dockery went to Harvard on an academic scholarship and then captained the football squad. He then spent several seasons in the pros, appearing in fourteen games with the 1969 New York Jets; Joe Namaths' Super Bowl winners. Dockery played six years in professional football before going on to a long and successful career as a broadcaster.

Sam *Sonny* Rutigliano was born in Brooklyn on July 3 1933. Before playing football at Tennessee and Tulsa, he played at the Parade Grounds. Sam went on to a coaching career, first as an assistant at Denver in 1967. Over the next eleven years he was with the New England Patriots, the New York Jets and the New Orleans Saints before taking over as head coach for the Cleveland Browns in 1978. Rutigliano led the 1980 Browns to the AFL Central Division Championship with an 11-5 record. After being fired by the Browns in the 1984 season, Sam did some broadcasting and coached at Liberty University in Lynchburg, Virginia. He is currently working for NFL Europe.

Basketball was not one of the sports played at the Parade Grounds, but a number of the Grounds athletes excelled at the hoop game. Sandy Koufax at the University of Cincinnati and Ted Schreiber at St. John's University were standout basketball stars. Carl Braun was born in Brooklyn on September 25,

1927 and played baseball at the Parade Grounds for one of the venerable Park organizations, the Bonnie Cubs. Braun spent 13 seasons in the NBA, the first twelve of them with the New York Knicks. He was a player-coach for the Knicks as well in 1961 and '62.

The Parade Grounds League's Cookie Lorenzo remembers facing pitcher Marius Russo. The left hander was a first baseman in high school and for three years at Long Island University before taking the pitchers mound. Russo said, "what a lucky break it was for me the day I gave up trying to play first base and decided to try my hand at pitching." The great Yankee catcher Bill Dickey after handling Russo's serves when he came to the big leagues in 1939 had this to say , "He is a control pitcher, knows how to pace himself, and has a good change of pace delivery....he's a great prospect." (8)

Marius was a member of a great team at Newark in 1937. Called by many the greatest minor league club ever, the 23-year-old was used sparingly that year, but went on to have a 17-8 season in 1938 also for Newark. Before being called up to New York in '39, Russo was only 5-4 but with a sparkling 1.97 Earned Run Average,the result of being on the short end of 1-0 score on three occasions.

Russo came to the Yankees where he spent six seasons before being drafted into the army in 1944. He won 14 games each in 1940 and 1941. In a memorable World Series moment Russo faced the Brooklyn Dodgers and was opposed by pitcher Fred Fitzsimmons in game three of the '41 series. With a scoreless tie and two out in the seventh inning at Ebbets Field, Russo hit a line drive off of Fitzsimmons' left leg. The ball was hit so hard that it popped high into the air and Dodgers shortstop Pee Wee Reese was able to catch it for the third out.

But the Dodgers pitcher had to be removed from the game. Reliever Hugh Casey was rushed into action and gave up two Yankee runs in the top of the eighth inning. Brooklyn scored one in the bottom half of the inning and Russo came out on top by a 2-1 score. Although jubilant in victory, Russo expressed regret over the opposing pitcher's injury. " It's too bad Fitz was hurt," he said. "He pitched a great game and I'm sorry he had to come out that way." (9)

The next day was the famous third strike to Tommy Henrich and catcher Mickey Owen's passed ball which led to another Yankee victory. Brooklyn fans to this day bemoan both games for the tough breaks that may have cost their Dodgers a World Series victory. Russo spent two years in the military and completed his major league career with a record of 45 wins and 34 loses.

Players who had major league careers proliferated at the Park over the years. Tommy Brown will forever be in Brooklyn baseball lore because he played with the Brooklyn Dodgers when only sixteen years of age. "A Brooklyn boy who had been discovered at the Parade Grounds along Prospect Park; Brown was called up to play the infield in July '44 at the age of 16 years, 7 months." (10)

On August 20,1945, Tommy hit a homer at age 17, making him the youngest major leaguer ever to hit a home run. He hit it against the Pirates and off of a future teammate,

Preacher Roe. Tom came from the Bay Ridge area and played his kid ball with the Ty-Cobbs. Brown had a tremendous arm, but was saddled with the sobriquet, *Buckshot* because of the erratic nature of his throws. Brown played nine years in the majors, seven in his native Brooklyn, always as a versatile utility player.

He was so young when he broke in that manager Leo Durocher took a carton of cigarettes from him. The Dodgers had a sponsor, Old Gold cigarettes, and every time that a Dodger player hit a home run, someone would roll a carton of Old Golds' down the screen behind home plate to be given to the player. Once when Tommy hit a homer, Durocher grabbed the cigarettes, "Give me the cigarettes, he's too young to smoke," he explained.

The Dodgers reactivated retired and popular star Babe Herman in 1945. At one point , Herman pinch-hit for Brown. Tommy, in awe of the old star asked him when he first started playing for Brooklyn. "1926," the Babe told him. "Wow," Tommy said, "that's two years before I was born."

Herman looked at the youngster, "well, then," he decided then and there, "I think I'd better quit." (11)

Mike Chiappetta grew up in the Midwood section and went to church at the parish of St. Rose of Lima. He remembers how Sam Ainbinder put together a youthful club in the neighborhood and called them the "Dwarfs." Later Mike played for the Bonnies and then the Parkville Boys Club. He recalls the Parkville lineup had Erasmus Hall high school basketball star Billy Cunningham as the number four hitter.

Cunningham was from the same Midwood neighborhood as Chiappetta and is remembered as a good baseball player, although the 6'7" high school standout was seen as all "skin and bones" when he got to Chapel Hill to attend the University of North Carolina, by Dean Smith, the Tar Heels basketball coach.

Of course Cunningham's career has become legendary. An All-American and All Atlantic Coast Conference selection three times while at North Carolina, Billy was drafted by the Philadelphia 76ers in the first round of the 1965 NBA Draft. Teaming up with Wilt Chamberlain, he helped the Sixers to the Eastern Division title in his first year. In the 1966-67 season the 76ers rang up a record of 68-13 and went on to capture the NBA finals.

An injury ended Cunningham's brilliant career in the early stages of the 1975-76season. He turned to coaching and in eight years with the 76ers, never finished lower than in second place. Cunningham went on to become a top analyst for CBS broadcasts of NBA games.

Billy Cunningham, basketball star and Parade Grounds baseball player was elected to the Basketball Hall of Fame in 1986.

Anthony Ferrante was nicknamed *Egghead* by his buddies, because of his knowledge of baseball. Anytime there was a tough question, someone would say, "Ask Egghead." Anthony is from Park Slope, Union Street at 4 and 5 Avenues. He was a catcher for the 78 precinct in the PAL. They called their club , the "Happy Rabbits". Ferrante attended Manual Training high school and played at the Parade Grounds from age 11 until he graduated from high school. "The place was always packed," is how he remembers the Park. "Those were sunny days, it never rained in those days," he says now. "We were also fanatical Brooklyn Dodger fans," Anthony recalls with relish.

Richie Wunderler caught for the Vagabonds and grew up at MacCarron Park in Williamsburg. "My friend Bobby Williams would wake me up at six in the morning so we could go out to get a field to play on. Born in 1948 Richie was in time for the Little League generation. At 12 years old , an all-star team of Little Leaguers was formed and they played Babe Ruth League ball and got Wunderler to the Parade Grounds. His twin brother Tom also pitched for the Vagabonds. Richie remembers Park Circle as a "bunch of dirt fields with dust flying all over."

The Williamsburg group hung out at Stevey Jack's Pool Room and reveled in the Brooklyn Dodgers. Richie says that "Bobby would kill if anyone said anything bad about Sandy Koufax." They were at Ebbets Field when Gil Hodges hit his fourteenth grand slam home run. "....and Bobby slipped and fell down a flight of stone steps."

The twins were drafted in 1967 and Richie was sent off to Viet Nam, where he served at Da Nang and Mai Lai at a helicopter base landing zone. When he came home in '70, Wunderler's baseball was done, but not his love for the game nor his contributions to the flack at Stevey Jack's.

Major League careers were so often begun at The Parade Grounds that a complete picture is difficult to achieve.

Saul Rogovin signed with the Detroit Tigers as a third baseman in 1941, he played his Parade Grounds baseball through the thirties. Saul hit .297 in 95 games at Beaver Falls in the Pennsylvania State League. It wasn't until 1944 that he appeared on the pitchers' mound and threw two innings in his debut giving up no runs, one hit, and striking out one. He shuffled between Detroit and Buffalo from 1949 until 1951when he stuck in the majors. Rogovin won 12 and then 14 games his first two years, and was traded to the White Sox in 1951. He spent eight years in the big time where he had a five hundred record , 48 wins and 48 loses.

Harold Seymour was a teacher , author and highly respected baseball historian. He is most known for his groundbreaking three Volume, " History of Baseball."The first volume, *Baseball: The Early Years,* was an outcrop of his PhD dissertation at Cornell University. In 1956 he became Vice President and Director of the State University of New York at Buffalo's Office of Information Services. The Society of American Baseball Research awards the *Seymour Medal* each year to the best book of baseball history or biography.

Even more important, Cy Seymour came from Brooklyn. He began making his mark as a player and coach at Drew University which he attended before Cornell. He was the star first baseman with a four year average of .425. Along the way Cy an boys' teams at the Parade Grounds, among them, the Falcons and the Crestons. These teams played in the late twenties and thirties and players still remember Seymour.

Francis "Skipper" Raguson of the 1929 Falcons said, "I will never forget Cy Seymour. I admired what he did for the youth of his day....he was a great role model for youngsters."

Cy scouted players around the Parade Grounds and asked them to join his teams. He did some bird dogging for the Boston Red Sox and recommended pitcher Bill Lohrman and Harry Eisenstat, both of whom went on to have major league careers. George "Bucky" Schneidmuller was one of Cy's boys who played in the pros.

Another of his kids was Joe Trimble who became a well-known writer for the *New York Daily News*. Jess Furlan, a catcher at Erasmus Hall high school, also played with the Falcons. "Harold taught us a lot of baseball - and respect for one another," Jess said.

Harold Seymour, as scholar, teacher, historian may well be secondary to Cy Seymour, bat-boy for the Brooklyn Dodgers, player , coach and respected mentor to hundreds of boys.

New York City police detective Robert Leuci wrote an account of his twenty years on the street from 1961-1981 in a book called "All the Centurions". His life inspired a motion picture, *Prince of the City* which told his story as a real life cop. But Leuci made a stellar contribution to the sandlot baseball history of Brooklyn as well. In the book "Reaching for the Stars", Leuci authored a chapter called "Hooks". The reference was to his father , James *Hooks* Leuci, who would head off to Prospect Park and the Parade Grounds. "It was on those great old Brooklyn fields that he discovered baseball."

He earned his nickname because "he was the only kid on the block that could throw a curve, hence 'HOOKS.'" Hooks grew up playing stickball on Hull Street and Hopkinson Avenue in East New York, a block from Brownsville. He'd say that kids learned hand and eye coordination at the game. When he got old enough to play baseball, he said "that ball looked as big as a basketball and no matter who was throwing it , it would never break as much as a spaldeen, never."

Hooks played semi-pro ball at places like Dexter Park in Queens and Dyckman Oval in the Bronx. But young Robert was pretty good himself. He pitched in the Queens-Nassau League and the American legion. (12)

Larry Napp had a distinguished twenty-three year career as an American League umpire. On a number of occasions Napp was in the right place at the right time. He was umpiring at third base when Don Larsen pitched a perfect game in the 1956 World Series. He was behind home plate as Nolan Ryan broke off a curve for a called third strike at the first World Series game ever played at Shea Stadium. "Napp drove a clenched fist toward the sky" and officially declared the Mets a winner .

All told, Larry worked in four World Series and four All-Star games. During a military hitch, Napp was stationed on Staten Island at the Navy's Frontier Base, Pier 6 in Tompkinsville. After the war he and his wife Phyllis decided to purchase a house and make Staten Island their home. Between 1942 while in the service and 1961 when he retired to Florida, Napp was a Staten Islander. In 2004, he was honored with induction into the Staten Island Sports Hall-Of-Fame.

But Larry was, after all, from Brooklyn. Born and raised in Sheepshead Bay. He attended Abraham Lincoln high school where he was a star at baseball, football, and swimming. He undoubtedly played at the Parade Grounds as a sandlotter and later as a semi-pro. His son, Larry Jr., however , was unable to confirm this."I only know he lived on Avenue U," he said. "I grew up on Staten island and that's all I can remember." Napp was born in 1919 and there are so few left of Larry's time. Larry Yaffa, 90 years old in 2006, recalls Napp, but cannot specify if he played at the Park, although, as Yaffa says, "everybody played at the Parade Grounds back then."

Napp was also an amateur boxer and was the Kings County AAU Champion in the light-weight division as he compiled a record of 38-2. Later on, while playing baseball professionally and working as an umpire, he was licensed as a boxing referee and despite being available for only five months of the year, was still considered a top-rated referee and assigned featured bouts in Madison Square Garden.

Larry signed with the New York Giants out of Lincoln high school as a catcher/outfielder in 1938 and spent time in the Giants' organization at Pocomoke City, at Olean in the PONY League and at Batavia before joining the Navy during World War II. He coached two Golden Gloves championship teams and was the player/manager of the baseball team, in addition to serving as chief physical training instructor for self-defense (judo and boxing) while stationed at the Frontier Base on Staten Island. After his discharge he was put on the 1946 Giants' roster, but never appeared in a major league game.

Realizing that his age was now against him, Larry enrolled in Bill McGowan's School for Umpires. He graduated in 1948. Napp was moved along quickly, serving only in the Middle Atlantic League and the International League before the American League took an option on his services in 1951.

And the list goes on. Ballplayers and writers and businessmen from Brooklyn, playing baseball on the fields at Coney Island Avenue.

If the numbers are correct and forty percent or so of Americans have some hold on Brooklyn as a home, odds are a fair amount of ballplayers had a domicile at Prospect Park's Parade Grounds, a real-life Field of Dreams.

XII.

The Dream

"I was just supposing. That's all dreams are anyway-Supposing"
                                                      -Paul Gallico

In Brooklyn in the fifties, there was Coney Island and fireworks every Tuesday evening that exploded above the beach. There was a bicycle path along Ocean Parkway on one side of the street and a bridle path for horseback riding on the other. A pound of ground beef cost 33 cents and one pound of coffee 73 cents. We went to the movies to see the *Duke-* John Wayne, and Bogart and Cagney, and new sensations James Dean and Marilyn Monroe.

The season progressed following the All-Star game and we continued to jockey for position with St. Bernadette and Sacred Heart. For some reason I became more friendly with the players from the Sacred Heart team and played with them for one season in 1960. In a 1958 article it said, "Eddie Jordan, undefeated welterweight boxing contender, pitched

Sacred Heart-St. Stephen's to a 9-6, nine-inning nod over the Lancers."

Eddie was indeed an undefeated welterweight boxer during these years. When I played with Sacred Heart we had a ritual that I tried to be a part of each week. There was an idea that a professional prizefighter could be charged as a felon if he used his fists, his "lethal weapons", on another person. With this in mind, we wanted to protect Eddie from any such problems. Every game two teammates were assigned to the boxer. In the event that a fight broke out on the field, it was their job to prevent Eddie from getting involved.

I volunteered for this job every week. It was a legitimate way to keep myself as well as Jordan out of harm's way. We would pull Eddie as far away from the action as possible, ourselves as well. "Stay over here, Ed. You'll be OK." Eddie would protest, "I'm not gonna fight. Don't worry about me." He was no dope. But it kept me out of a few rhubarbs.

There were rivalries that seemed to develop naturally like the ongoing one with the Sabres. Another was with Sacred Heart-St. Stephen. There was never any animosity between these clubs, only on the field rivalry. Sacred Heart had a good bunch of boys from the Red Hook section where they played as a neighborhood team for their parish. Al Marchese was there from the onset, coming from Strong Place and DeGraw Street. Following the familiar pattern they organized their first local team which they called the Clippers.

They played in the Police Athletic League (PAL) and according to AL, early every Saturday morning the boys would stop by the 81 precinct house, wake up the officer and pick up one baseball for the days' game. From there it was to the Red Hook "Rock Fields" to play. There were obstacles, not the least of which were the conditions indicated by the name of the playing field. The adjacent lumber yard was guarded by a couple of mean "junk-yard" dogs and if the ball was hit there it meant some innovative and courageous actions were needed to retrieve the only ball they owned. Someone had to distract the dogs while another of the players retrieved the ball. Marchese believes the boys learned the meaning of team work there in Red Hook.

Al attended high school at the New York School of printing in Manhattan and played third base for the school team. Marchese played every inning of every game for three years. The Printers were one of those industrial units that fielded teams in the Parade Grounds week-night Industrial League. This was not a fly-by-night operation. In 1898 the ball club traveled by stagecoach to Pittsburgh, Pennsylvania for a three game set against the local Printers nine.

While employed as a printer, Marchese played twi-light ball with his printing buddies; Tommy Siracusa of our Virginians, Pee Wee Parascondola and Joe Geraffo. He remembers how "Cheezy", who was a catcher with Nathans Famous, also pitched in the week nights and once threw shutouts against the Printers on Tuesday and again on Thursday. "We didn't get a run off of him in a whole week!" Al recalled.

It was in the Sunday Parade Grounds League that the Red Hook Sacred Hearts team fielded Eddie Jordan , Teddy Trance , Billy Gates, pitchers Billy Litras and Joe Clark, as well as Al Marchese. They boasted two pros in Emilio Palazzo and Frankie Yurman. Yurman had signed with Cleveland as a pitcher, but a sore arm brought him back to the Park where he played centerfield. A good all-around ballplayer, Frank got a short-lived shot as an outfielder in Batavia, New York.

In the next few years Marchese played with Gravesend, where he encountered Ron Salamini who signed with the Yankees, one more pro off of the legendary sandlot. Apparently you can go home again as Marchese wound up back in Red Hook with a club called "Malabee", a trucking firm who sponsored the team. Al played baseball until he was 36 years old before turning to softball.

As with all of us, once the conversation starts, a floodgate of reminiscences is unleashed, and not just about baseball. Al remembered how we got our hair cut by barbers instead of beauticians. He recalled with a laugh how "Nick" would be cutting his hair when the vegetable man with his horse and wagon would come by. The barber would step outside and trim the horses eye lashes and come back inside the shop and finish cutting the boy's hair, all with the same scissors.

Even after so many years Marchese recalls pitchers Joe DiGeralomo of St. Bernadette and Carl Hottinger of our club as being particularly tough. Hottinger was "very smart and had good control", he says "he came a little bit from the side and that made it tough on right handed hitters." But like me , Al found the Moose, Tommy Morrissey to be particularly intimidating.

Marchese played third base with Sacred Heart and also did some pitching. According to a May 11, 1959 report in the *Telegram*, "....Al "Pee Wee" Marchese tossed a four- hitter in Sacred Heart's triumph."

Al Marchese and I reconnected in 1984 when we put together a softball team and won several titles in the ten years we were together.

Mr. Staub was always with me. He never missed a game and most of the time his son Allen was there also. Allen was a college student, not very athletic, but a brilliant kid. He loved baseball as his father did and he would keep the scorecard while sitting on our bench or in the seats behind when we were on Diamond One. Chick loved to test him. He 'd come back to the bench after an at-bat and say, "Hey, Al , I'm now 26 for 71; what am I hitting?" With no more than a few seconds to ponder, Allen would say definitively, ".366." Chick just shook his headd laughed. We all marveled at Allen's mental acumen.

I was amazed that I kept hitting and coupled with the fact that we kept winning, was having a glorious season. I had pretty much gotten the knack of slapping at the ball and didn't mind it at all that I almost never hit to the left side. It meant that I would have to swing that split second sooner and lose the precious extra time to see and make contact with the ball. There was plenty of room on the right side of the field. It is extremely difficult to defend against a hitter like I was, as Al Marchese knew.

Al was playing second base for Sacred Heart. With all that room from the first base line to the second base bag to cover, it was a tough spot to defend. On one afternoon, I bounced one over the bag at second, then hit a two hopper in the same place. On the third at bat, I hit a soft liner that bounced just beyond the bag. With each time up, Al moved a bit closer to the middle of the diamond. Finally on my fourth time up, he went over and planted himself with both feet firmly on the bag.

"Come on, you Punch n' Judy, hit it here now!" I slapped one through the right side and we both got a laugh. Later in the locker room, Chick was talking about my "power". "If you put all four hits back to back," he was saying, "they didn't go 120 feet on the fly!"

I was gaining a reputation for popping base hits into right field and bouncing ground balls through the right side. My teammates had fun at my expense. One day the "old pros", Chick Chiarello and Putsie DeBarnardo watched as I hit one up the middle. Still looking straight ahead, Putsie said flatly, " he really got around on that one, didn't he." Chick grunted in agreement.

I was content, however, to be getting my hits, without being concerned about how far they were going or how hard they were hit as long as they were dropping in. It wasn't until many years later that I realized why I wasn't hitting the ball more sharply. I had quit softball after the 1994 season and with a few friends began tossing a baseball around one morning every week. We called our group the *Old Boys Of Summer* and we grew to having eight or ten of us. With plenty of time and opportunity I was able to concentrate on the mechanics of hitting as I had never really been able to before.

I came to realize that I had never put the weight on my rear foot, but always hit evenly balanced on both feet or even leaning forward a bit. This prevented me from getting any power behind my swing. Although I would never hit for any distance, in my late sixties, I was hitting the ball harder than I had in my twenties. There is nothing like twelve years of batting practice to improve your swing!

Eddie McDonough started the season for the Virginians and then moved over to third to make room for me. Everybody called him Eddie Mack. He was the same age as the others, but I always thought of him as older. Not because he looked it or acted it, but because he seemed to me to be the "old pro" type. He always knew what he was doing and if he said something you tended to listen.

Mack was from South Brooklyn; tenth street between third and fourth avenues; and was born in 1932. He began his baseball with St. Thomas Aquinas, where he went to elementary school. That was in the CYO League , one of the many leagues conducting organized ball around Brooklyn. One of Eddie's teammates was Jerry Casale, a neighbor hood friend who would go on to the major leagues.

Sportswriter Tom Knight, known as "Brooklyn's Baseball Historian" was from the same neighborhood parish. Tom was active in the church and in planning activities for the youth of the area. He organized softball games, which Mack says "kept us out of trouble" and away from the youth gangs of the time. Eddie was an infielder from the start, short, second , or third base and says that the Parade Grounds "was our home for years. We spent our life there."

McDonough recalls how he played Saturday mornings at the Park with an American Legion team; afternoons with a team that competed in the Kiwanis League and week nights in the Twi-light League. By the time he was in Alexander Hamilton high school, he had joined the Virginians in the Parade Grounds League.

This was in the late forties and the PGL was "tops - like the major leagues, "Mack remembers, "there were so many people came out to see our games, and scouts all over the place."

Like the rest of us , Eddie followed the pattern of selling chances to raise money for uniforms and league fees and equipment. Then up the age ladder; fortunately for us there was no Little League, so we gravitated from the local lots to kid ball, beginning at ten or twelve years old. At the senior level, sixteen to eighteen years old , things began to get serious and in Open ball there were the returning minor leaguers and some of the best prospects around.

Mack remembers how we always started in February , often when remnants of the winter snows were still in evidence. "We couldn't hit," he said, "our hands were so cold. Only Chick and Putsie hit the ball. How did they do it? " he wondered still. Another Park legend ran the Virginians, Pete Cavallo. Petey and some of the other boys joined the Marine reserves at the armory on second avenue because they could play softball in the building all winter. Mack didn't join because he was playing basketball at St. Thomas and didn't have the time for the Marines softball.

In 1950 the Korean war broke out and Cavallo and the others were activated. This broke up the Virginians for the duration so Eddie joined a club called the Senacas. He played shortstop alongside of another of those "unforgettable characters " that baseball produces, John Chino, at second base. By 1952 Mack was drafted also and when he came home the Virginians were up and running again. Eddie swears that the best hitter at that level was Putsie DeBenardo, and as for pitching, he believes that Carl Hottinger was second to none. He had that "good fastball" and playing behind him you never worried. "Even if he was behind the hitter 3 and 0 he could come back ." His recollections generated thoughts of Larry DiPippo who played for Manual Training HS and bounced home runs off the refreshment stand roof from Diamond One more than once. DiPippo was another alumni who spent time in the minor leagues. There was a pitcher named Kelsey Moffett who "struck me out three times throwing that junk."

The memories flow like fine wine once the corks are popped. Name a player and here is a memory and a story. Eddie Jordan. "Oh, yeah, the fighter," Eddie recalls. "Good fighter. We went up to the Garden and saw him fight. Left handed hitter. Used to slap the ball to left." Eddie stops to ponder. "Spiked me once, the son-of-a-gun."

A young prospect had just signed with the St. Louis Cardinals out of one of the Catholic High Schools. He was a very hard throwing right handed pitcher named Paul Speckenbach. According to the word around the Park, his bonus was considerable. The financial details were not made public in those days and even the published major league salaries were estimated. We were to face Speckenbach in his final game before being assigned by his club. It was a Saturday afternoon on Diamond Thirteen.

I was the lead off hitter in the top of the first inning and on a fastball out over the plate, I lined a single to right field. The young hurler got the next 21 batters without giving up so much as a hit or a walk. The papers said that my hit had "spoiled the gem." I saved the clipping so that I could one day prove to my grandchildren that I had gotten the hit off of a big league star.

But it was not to be. As often happened in the days before such things as "Tommy John " surgery , the young phenom went down with a sore arm in his second season of pro ball and sadly ended his career. One of the positive things about today's game is the ability and knowledge to surgically repair this kind of affliction to a pitcher's arm. Often the shoulder or the elbow resulted in a finished career. It claimed a great many victims over those years, and Paul Speckenbach was just one of them.

Another dream that wound up an apparition belonged to Butch Strange. Butch played a few games with us at the end of the season after he decided to pack in his pro career. He was a powerful looking guy who played third base and had a tremendous throwing arm. In the infield workout he burned my hand with his tosses. In the game that first time he hit a home run and two doubles and every one hit like a rocket. I was amazed that he was giving up and I asked him why. He told me that he was 28 years old, and after two years in triple A ball in the Yankees chain, and watching infielders like Tony Kubek and Bobby Richardson going to the big club, that it just wasn't in the cards for him. This was another dream-breaker. Not injury or getting on with life or self-destruction. There was simply no room at the top. Not enough major league jobs.

Aside from my teammates there were former and future pro ballplayers on the field virtually every game we played. For the most part the competition was very tough. Highly touted prospects were noted because they were being talked about. You'd be in a game and there would be scouts there and you knew it was because of Joe Torre or Matt Galante or Tony Balsamo. One name that was familiar was Chuck Shilling.

Schilling was not from Brooklyn, he lived on Long Island. He attended St. Mary's high school in Manhasset and played for the New Hyde Hawks in the Queens Alliance League. Chuck got his degree in engineering from Manhattan College and during this time was scouted by Botts Nikola of the Boston Red Sox. It was Nikola who suggested to Schilling that he play some of his baseball at the Parade Grounds. The scout valued the quality of play there and thought that it would be of benefit to the young infielder.

So Schilling, with Nikola's help, hooked up with Mike Auletta and Nathan's Famous. This was in 1958 and it was at this time that I played against him. I always took particular note of infielders, being one myself, and Schilling was an excellent glove man playing second base. With the additional service at the Park under his belt, Nikola signed him in the fall of 1958 to a Red Sox contract.

His first pro season in 1959, Schilling traversed the typical minor league trail hitting three cities that year alone; Raleigh in the Carolina League, Alpine and ending up the season at Minneapolis, Boston's AAA affiliate; hitting a collective .330 for the year. Chuck spent the next season at Minneapolis, hit .314 and made the move to the big club in 1961. That year, playing in 158 major league contests, Schilling tied a record for the fewest errors by a second baseman, committing only eight. He spent five seasons with Boston before being traded to the Minnesota Twins in the spring of 1966.

The end of the story was written with a swift hand. The Twins had a full roster and assigned Schilling to Denver in the AAA Pacific Coast League. "It was a difficult decision," Chuck said, " but you have to think of your family." A husband and a father by now, Schilling decided to pack it in and start to make use of his education. He worked as an engineer for seven years and made another decision. He went back to school nights and got a certificate to teach and spent the next 24years as a Junior high school math teacher in Suffolk County.

Living in Long Island now, Chuck plays ball in a Senior Softball League near his home. "It always feels good to swing the bat," he says. Like so many others, Chuck has memories to last a lifetime. His best friend on the Red Sox was his roomie, a highly regarded young outfielder who broke in the same year as Chuck did, Carl Yastremski. He recalls teammates like pitcher Bill Monbouquette and outfielder Jackie Jensen. Schilling came to bat over 1900 times in the big leagues, and has experiences that are never far from one's thoughts no matter where life takes him.

Our top pitchers were Carl Hottinger and Mike Tagliafaro and they pitched most of the major games especially in the Sunday Parade Grounds league. However, we carried a full staff that included Bobby Stone, Joe Galetta, Jimmy Volkland and Georgie Hahn. Hahn was from South Brooklyn, the same as Eddie Mack. Georgie was an enigma shrouded in a mystery. He always carried a wad of bills rolled up so that they filled his hand when he took them out. He worked in construction, and was never chintzy with his money.

We later played on the Pollio Cubs in time to win the division title in 1963. Bob Stone and I went into the Caton Inn a couple of times after games and George never let us pay a dime. He was just as generous with the others. We would at times play games where we'd bet some money; for the players it usually was two or three dollars a man. Georgie loved to pitch these games and he's put up $25 or $50 and then would be a nervous wreck throughout the games. "We gotta win," he'd tell us, "there's money riding on this game." He'd light a cigarette between innings and pace the bench puffing away.

We got a laugh out of his attitude because he always seemed to have a chunk of money so the bet didn't seem to mean that much. One day with the Pollio Cubs, our catcher Richie Broker asked Georgie why he was so worked up over the bet.

"It's the challenge," he said, "we gotta win because it's a bet. I don't want to lose. You understand." Richie just laughed and said no he didn't understand. But that was Georgie and we always tried as hard as we could in those games, " so Georgie won't go jump off a bridge," Broker said.

Our Sunday games in the Parade Grounds League as well as the Kawanis and other leagues were written about in Monday's newspaper. The *Brooklyn Eagle* gave our games coverage from scores to highlights to the current standings. When the *Eagle* folded for good early in 1955, the *World Telegram and Sun* picked it up.

In rereading clips from the fifties and early sixties there are an abundance of names of fellows who played some professional baseball. In one such article alone pitchers Jerry Boxer and Joe DiGirolamo are highlighted along with the games' hitting stars Moe Palazzo and Frank Yurman, Frank Chiarello and Matty Galante. In another report "Reuben Alexis wielded the big stick....",while Ron Salomini blasted "two home runs, one with the bases loaded," and "Angelo DeBernardo tripled and doubled to "spark the Virginians' winning attack." Although there was a repetition of names because of the quality of their abilities, nonetheless, these articles consistently showed off the preponderance of talent that permeated the Parade Grounds over the years , particularly during mid-century.

Playing in the Saturday league I came across a slew of great young ballplayers. Teams like the Senecas and Nathans' Famous played in other leagues like the Kiwanis, the Shore Parkway or the Coney Island Leagues, so on Saturdays we got the chance to see them all. Also, since there was no age breakdown, senior teams could also compete on Saturdays. One of the finest organizations was the Cadets, the senior club managed by Jim McElroy. In these years he had great prospects like Joe Torre, Matty Galante and a young man I was exceedingly impressed with named Rico Petrocelli. Rico was a shortstop who signed with the Boston Red Sox in 1961 and went on to a successful major league career.

You might say that the impression he made on me one Saturday afternoon at James Madison High School field was a particularly lasting one. I played third base in the doubleheader and Petrocelli was zinging line drives around me all afternoon. He hit two over the left field fence into Avenue P and slammed a couple of liners past my ear. I think the only time we got him out was on a ground ball to me. It was a one bouncer that shot out of the ground like a missile and whacked me in the chest.

I picked it up and threw him out, but later Chick said he could read the "A.G. Spaulding" label tattooed between my ribs. It hurt. In his book about the 1967 Red Sox, Petrocelli spoke about hitting. He explained that in the minors he had hit a lot to the opposite field, which surprises me because of the way he used to sting the ball to left in the Park, using those great wrists. When he came up, they wanted him to take advantage of the *Green Monster* by pulling everything and hitting home runs. He did hit the long ball, but he feels that his average suffered for it. He hit .251 in his thirteen seasons in the majors, but also hit 210 home runs and drove in 773 runs. He had a fine career and I was happy for his success. (1)

There is something perpetual in all of these young ballplayers. Be it a dream, a wish or just a fervent hope with little touch to reality. I probably came in the dream class. There was nothing in my earlier years to perpetuate that dream, savea love for the game and for my idols, the Brooklyn Dodgers. There was something also about a game at the Park which at times took you out of the realm of an amateur and created the illusion that it might be something more.

At one point on the Virginians we had a bat boy. A kid about twelve years old who loved hanging around so Fred gave him the job. One of those illusions for me came while kneeling in the on-deck circle on Diamond #1 leaning on a bat with the kid kneeling beside me as he often liked to do. I would glance over my shoulder at the overflow crowd in the bleachers, and people standing between them, and marvel at whatever it was that put me in this position. A dream, a wish, call it what you will, I only know it was special, the place, the event, the time, and I was there not just to savor it, but to be a part of it.

Growing up on the streets we always played some version of baseball. There was punch ball, stoop ball or slap ball, and ,of course, stickball; a staple on the streets of Brooklyn. When I wasn't playing ball, I was reading about it, in the *Sporting News*, *Sport* magazine or the novels of John R. Tunis. Consequently, I was always trying to learn and to improve myself. Which is the reason that I was so willing a pupil for Al Fortunato and later Mr. Staub, as well as for anyone willing to impart a word or two of baseball wisdom.

This energy and desire coupled with the instructive efforts of Mr. Staub put me in a position in 1958 that I never could have anticipated. I couldn't throw andI hit bloopers and bouncing balls , but I was having one hell of a season . Not surprisingly, I nurtured the dream during the excitement and success of that season. This brought me to one game late in the year. The culmination of the work, the dream and the desire. A concurrence of all the phenomenon in one place at one time. An alignment of the planets; an age of aquarius, so to speak.

We were out on Diamond #5 and a good crowd had gathered. Some fans followed specific clubs and the Virginians had a following. Others just expected to see a good ball game. Still others would stroll from diamond to diamond, stopping if the game was in a particularly exciting moment. When they came by Diamond #5 that Sunday afternoon and heard that Carl Hottinger was in the fifth inning of a no-hit game, they stayed to watch.

The games were seven innings so Carl was in the final stage of his gem. In addition to the usual fan, we also attracted scouts. Always on the lookout for potential signings, sometimes they simply enjoyed the ball game. At the Parade Grounds you couldn't go from the clubhouse steps to Diamond # 1 without tripping over one or two of them. Fellows like Joe LaBate of the Phillies, Herb Stein of the Twins and Honey Russell of the Braves were always around.

A bird dog scout named Jim McElroy spent a good deal of time at the Park. This is not the Jim McElroy who is manager and director of the Cadets. This McElroy came from the East Flatbush section and lived at Church and Utica Avenues. He pitched and caught with a neighborhood team. Jim entered the military in 1944 and after being discharged went to Colby Academy under the GI bill where he pitched for the school team. From there he began umpiring at the Parade Grounds until he joined the New York Yankees as a bird dog scout in '58 and stayed until 1971.

It was here that his observations and experiences with the players were so acute. He recalls a "pudgy Joe Torre hitting one over the clubhouse." He also ran across a pitcher from the Park named Howie Kitt. Howie pitched for Nathan's and signed with the Yankees. McElroy tells about the day while pitching a game in the minors, Kitt went to the dugout water cooler to get a drink. "There was an electric wire going from the outlet to the cooler and was laying across the floor of the dugout." It seems that Kitt stepped on the wire and his spikes cut through the insulation. "There was a spark, and his foot was burned and because it was his front foot it interfered with his delivery." In trying to adjust he had to change his delivery and apparently the pitcher never regained his old form. As Mac says, " true story, you can't make up stuff like this."

McElroy was one of many to recognize early the talent of Rico Petrocelli. He watched a bunch of kids tossing a ball around and noted one who stood out. It turns out that the kids were going to be the baseball team at the new Sheepshead Bay HS and the kid of course was Rico. The Yankees watched him for four years, through high school and then with the Cadets. Jim says the Yanks wanted to sign him, but Botts Nikola slipped past everyone and got the Petrocelli name on a contract.

And then there was Joe Pepitone. Pepi had suffered a gunshot wound in an accident while in high school. McElroy saw his first game after he got out of the hospital between Nathan's and Gravesend and Joe hit one into Gravesend Bay.

But there were only two clubs still interested, "us and the Dodgers and you know the rest."

The Yankees had a similar program to the "Brooklyn Against the World" one of the Dodgers'. They called it the Yankee Rookies. Jim McElroy spent a few seasons on this project along with scout Arthur Dede. Among the kids who got through the try-outs at Yankee Stadium was Sal Messina whom the Yankees signed and an old teammate of mine named Jordan Gatti. After choosing the final 15 for the squad, a 26 game schedule was initiated and games were played throughout New York, New Jersey and New England.

In West Haven, Connecticut they needed to replace an injured outfielder and found a local kid who was pretty good named Butch Cretara. In the game that night "The guy pitching against us was throwing blue darts, and none of our guys could touch him," remembers McElroy. But Butch kept fouling him off. "Dede was coaching at 3rd and I was at 1st. Dede yells over to me, 'if he fouls him again, I'm gonna sign him.' As it was Butch fouled him and Dede signed him at the end of the tour. True, you can't make this stuff up!"

On this day on Diamond 5 there were three scouts standing behind our bench on the first base side. Matty Mathieson, bird dogging for the San Francisco Giants was there along with Steve Lembo of the Dodgers and with Steve was Al Campanis. Campanis was at that time the Dodgers' farm director. Fellows at his level would be called in to give an opinion about a player a scout had recommended and there must have been someone at the Park that day that the Dodgers had their eyes on.

My day was going well. I had two hits in my first two at-bats and was gliding over my position at second base gobbling up everything I could reach. With two men out, Hottinger threw a fast ball that was hit on the ground to my left. I took off after it but it was a bit beyond my reach. I timed my dive perfectly and hit the ground just as the ball hit my glove.

I rolled over to my left and threw from the ground and we just did get the runner at first. I jogged off the field to a thunderous ovation and was feeling pretty good at that moment. Then above the din I heard a voice that I was sure belonged to Lou Shalaba. It said loud enough for everyone to hear, *"When the hell is somebody gonna sign this kid?"*

I looked up and saw the scouts, all three smiling broadly and applauding, but I couldn't help but notice that not one of them held a pen in his hand. My dream ended in a euphoric blaze of glory. I secretly thanked Lou for his comments, knowing that I would never in future years have to say to myself, *"What if ?"* To add insult to injury, Carl lost his no-hitter the next inning.

XIII.

Legends In Their Spare Time

"....many legends, and many different interpretations of the legends exist. The truth cannot be known for certain, and perhaps the best course is to accept the version one likes best, and leave it at that." -Walter Umminger "Supermen, Heroes, and Gods"

There is a propensity to use the terms "legends" and "legendary" liberally throughout this narrative. It is, according to Mr. Webster, "a story usually concerned with a real person, place or event believed to have some basis in fact." If there was an encyclopedia of Parade Grounds baseball listing the greatest games ever played there, everyone who ever frequented the Park would have an opinion. Some, undoubtably, would recall a game played sometime in the year 1949 or 1950 between the Flatbush Robins and a club called Grazianos. The latter was a team sponsored by Irving Cohen, at the time the manager of boxing champion Rocky Graziano.

The minor league season ended earlier than the majors and players would often return in September to play a few late season games with the local clubs. On this day Diamond # 1 was unavailable and so the contest was placed on Diamond # 3, where two pro pitchers squared off. Hymie Cohen took the mound for Grazianos, a hard throwing right hander with a fast curve that broke from head to toe. The Robins had Don McMahon, later to go on to an 18-year big league career. According to a bird dog scout in attendance, McMahon had a fast ball that was a *blur*.

Diamond 3 was an open field and the crowd that gathered had to roped off to prevent them from coming onto the field of play. Money bets went through the crowd as quickly as "mega millions" hopefuls dispense with it today. It was a low hitting game in which Cohen struck out 16 and McMahon 15, Don winning it 1-0.

There were legendary teams as well, one of them being *Nathan's Famous*, named for the world renowned Coney Island hot dog emporium. In its glory years the team was managed by Mike Auletta and was, for the most part, a lineup of veterans of the pro ranks.

The second baseman was Stanley Rosensweig, at short was Benny Galante, the brother of Matt Galante, and the third baseman, Jack Elias, had played AAA ball. They had pitchers named Stabitz, Bassetti and Howie Kitt. We also faced Larry DaVita in a Nathan's uniform. A catcher whom we knew as *Cheezy*, had also been in the pros.

Gil Bassetti forged a remarkable career in baseball going back to his youth in the Gravesend section of Brooklyn. His early baseball was at the Parade Grounds with Clarence Irving's Bisons and the Towanda Indians. At Lincoln high school Gil was teammates with a shortstop named Phil Caruso who would one day head the Patrolman's Benevolent Association (PBA) of the New York City Police Department.

At 15 Bassetti was already establishing a reputation. Pitching for the Indians in a game in the Open Division, Gil struck out 19 of the 21 batters he faced. The New York Giants signed him out of high school in 1952 and Bassetti, a right handed pitcher embarked on a seven year minor league odyssey. At Sandersville in the Georgia State League, he was teammates with another Giant hopeful, WillieMcCovey, and it was here that Gil witnessed the future hall-of-famer hit his first professional home run.

That season Bassetti won 21 games and four more in the play-offs; three as a starter and one in relief. A remarkable achievement, at one point in the season he made eight consecutive mound appearances. His Parade Grounds friend, southpaw Larry DaVita also signed with the Giants and the two pals found themselves team-mates one season at Danville. It was here that they shared an experience that Gil does not let his friend forget, even to this day.

The club's center fielder Manny Mota was unable to play one day, and as Larry explains, "they only carried sixteen or seventeen players on the roster," so DaVita found himself out in center field in a game that Bassetti was pitching. In an early inning, Larry misplayed a routine fly ball and it dropped untouched. "I put the glove up," DaVita explained, "and the ball dropped twenty feet away." In the dugout Larry apologized to his buddy explaining that the ball had "hit a wire upthere."

The next day while shagging flies in the outfield, Bassetti couldn't resist taunting his friend. "Hey, Larry," he called, "there are no wires up there." DaVita scanned the clear skies and reasoned, "it must have hit a bird." Now, some fifty years later, Larry says in mock hurt, "if the situation was reversed, I would have taken his word and not checked for wires." Incidentally, the reason Gil keeps ragging his pal is that the dropped fly was the only hit Bassetti gave up that day, going the complete nine innings.

Caught up in a not-yet-completely-desegregated baseball of the fifties, in spite of it being several years since Jackie Robinson had broken baseball's color barrier, Gil had an experience he would not soon forget. It was at Winston-Salem in the class B Carolina League on a club managed by Dave Garcia. Heckled one day by a fan using ethnic slurs, Garcia pointed at the leather lunged fan and said, "Don't you leave until after the game. I want to see you." Bassetti had pitched the first game of a doubleheader and was instructed by his manager to go sit in the stands and "make sure that guy don't leave." Gil did as he was told and when the fan pulled out a knife, Bassetti went at him. Fortunately his old pal Larry DaVita was again on the same club and he went into the seats and held Gil back. The fan left the park but was picked up by the local police.

After getting to the pinnacle by playing AAA ball, plus winter ball in Nicaragua, it seemed that Gil was on the verge of getting *the* break that they all wait for. Leo Durocher, Giant manager sent word to his front office that he was in need of a right handed starting pitcher. The decision rested with Carl Hubbell, the Giants' farm director. He narrowed the choice to Gil Bassetti and Stu Miller. It happened that Miller had already spent some major league time and Hubbell's decision was motivated by that bit of big time experience and he opted for Miller.

And so, once more, a single choice not of his own making made the difference in one man's life and career. Bassetti went home to Brooklyn and the Parade Grounds and hooked up with the Nathan's team. He got a job in the Post office and did some work with some kid teams. It was here that the ex-pro began to take special notice of young ballplayers. He remembers being very impressed with a high school junior named Rico Petrocelli, who later was signed by Botts Nikola and the Boston Red Sox.

But all of the experience for Bassetti paid off. He was soon offered a scouting job by an old friend, Benny Bonghnan, with the St. Louis Cardinals. When Bonghnan moved over to the Minnesota Twins, Bassetti followed him. He spent a year in the Pittsburgh organization where he recommended a hard throwing 16-year-old kid at the Parade Grounds named John Candelaria. The Pirate organization wrote him off saying he was too young to consider. Candelaria ultimately did sign with the Pirates, but by that time Gil had gone to the Los Angeles Dodgers.

It was here that Gil's new career flourished. He spent the next twenty-five years scouting the northeast for LA. Gil owns two munificent World Series rings; from the 1981 and

'88 seasons. Among others, Bassetti signed Eric Young from New Brunswick, New Jersey. Young put together a thirteen year major league career and hit .285.

Gil also was involved along with Steve Lembo in the signing of John Franco. Franco would achieve fame as a closer for the New York Mets, ultimately recording 424 saves, in the top five on the all-time list. Bassetti called Matt Galante a heads-up ball player and recalls how Fred Haney had his eye on Joe Pepitone when Hamey was with the Phils, but waited until he joined the Yankees to recommend signing the young first baseman.

Bassetti is "old school" in that he sees today's pitchers as unable to pace themselves. "They go all out for five innings and have nothing left." He says that pitch counts do not allow for arm development. One reason pitching is so different today, according to Gil, is the reliance on the radar gun to record speed. "That's all it measures , is speed, and that's not enough."

Bassetti has a hatful of baseball memories, like scout meetings with Dodgers' chief scout, former pitcher Ben Wade and remembers Clyde Sukeforth supplying those meetings with lobsters sent from his native state of Maine. He recalls a game at the Parade Grounds when Nathan's faced a US Army team from Ft. Monmouth, New Jersey that had a pitcher named Whitey Ford.

On June 23, 2005 at the Richmond County Ballpark at St. George in Staten Island, the Staten island Yankees placed four plaques on the grandstand wall behind first base, dedicated to four area scouts. One of them is Gil Bassetti. His plaque reads in part, "Gil Bassetti has worked in baseball for over 44 years, first as a player, then as a scout....and has had seven players reach the big leagues during his career."

Still active, Bassetti covers the local area for the Baltimore Orioles. One of the most heartening results of Parade Grounds baseball has been the lasting relationships that have developed. One example is the friendship between Gil Bassetti and Larry DaVita more than fifty years after their youthful sandlot days.

Larry was born in Brooklyn but moved to Floral Park and attended high school on Long Island. He played basketball at Scwanhaka high before returning to Bensonhurst at 292 Bay 19th Street.

At the Parade Grounds Larry began showing the stuff that would net him a pro contract. He remembers with mixed emotions a game he lost on Diamond # 13. He pitched a gem against future major leaguer Gerry Casale. Casale, a good hitter even in the majors, hit a home run that beat DaVita 1-0. In another 1-0 play-off victory in which he was the winning pitcher, Larry remembers with amusement how the opposing manager tried in vain to protest the game with the claim that the pitcher's mound was less than 60 feet from home plate.

"Where did your pitcher pitch from?" Larry asked, "second base?"

DaVita signed with the Giants in 1951 and went to North Carolina and later posted a 14-2 record at Danville. Muskokee, Oklahoma was the next stop, then came an army hitch and Larry played his baseball for Ft. Casson in Colorado. He picked up his career following his discharge in 1953. At St. Cloud, DaVita faced a young shortstop named Henry Aaron who played for Eau Claire, Wisconsin that season. "Don't ask me how I did against him," Larry said, "I can't remember." Then by way of explanation for his memory failure, "How did I know he would turn out to be Hank Aaron."

DaVita was assigned to Yucatan, Mexico for the '56 season, but he refused to report. "No dice," he said and took off the whole year. He came back to the Parade Grounds and pitched for Nathan's, among others, and was surprised when the Giants wanted him back the following year. He played in Dallas and Springfield and then in spring training of 1958 came up with a sore arm.

For all intents this ended DaVita's pro career, although Cleveland made an offer the next season, but Larry was still the property of the Giants organization and they refused to release him, though they wouldn't use him because they had knowledge of his arm trouble. And so it goes around and around with the player in the swirling eddy.

Both Larry and Bassetti agree that ball clubs baby pitcher's arms today. They recall pitching every fourth day with a regular schedule of work. Day two after a start they'd throw batting practice, day three would be for running and day four, you were back on the mound; expected to, and intending to throw nine innings.

Larry loved working with kids and was coach at Brooklyn's Poly Prep for ten years. He pitched batting practice to both the

Mets and the Yankees for five seasons. The game is so different today, Larry muses. It was much tougher then. He laughs at the memory of Roy Campanella dropping dirt into Willie Mays' shoe when the outfielder was in the batter's box because it frustrated him and might help to break his concentration.

DaVita says that it was Warren Spahn, the winningest lefty in baseball history who told him that Little League baseball would kill the sport. "Too much pressure, too little good coaching. Kids come off the field crying," Spahn told him. "That's not good."

Larry currently works for the Brooklyn Cyclones at Keyspan Park in Coney Island. One day Parade Grounds alumni and Mets owner Fred Wilpon entered the locker room and caught a glimpse of DaVita. "Larry," he exclaimed. "What are you doing here?"

"I'm your clubhouse man!" Larry told the old Brooklyn boy proudly. Two more Boys of Brooklyn still in baseball and loving it.

Joe Pepitone came from Park Slope, a tough neighborhood at the time and even tougher, according to Joe, was his father. William Pepitone, known as Willie Pep, after the former featherweight champion of the world, had been a Golden Gloves fighter and not adverse to using his skills outside of the ring. Joe says in his auto-biography, *"Joe, You Coulda made Us Proud"*, that his dad was "the toughest guy in the neighborhood. I saw him fight , in the street, at least fifty times. He never lost. *Never.*"

Joe was a street kid, in addition to hanging around with the Washington Avenue Boys gang, he played a lot of Brooklyn's number one street game, stickball! It wasn't until he was 14 that Pepitone began playing baseball; mostly pick-up games at the Parade Grounds. "Gee, I loved it," he said. By the time he was starring at Manual Training high school, he had a steady following of 13 big league scouts. It was that season, 1957, that he tried out for, and made, the Nathan's team.

Being among the first of lots of things, Pepi was possibly the first player to have a steady agent. Around this time, John King, a Yankee bird-dog scout became close to the 15-year-old. Helping him with advice on how to improve, King also got close to Joe's parents, and had all three of them sign a contract for King to act as Joe's agent. He would receive "something like fifteen per cent of everything I earned until I was about forty-four years old." (1)

It happened in 1958 in a high school hallway. One boy had a gun, a .38, and it went off, seriously wounding Joe Pepitone. It took nine hours of surgery and six days before he was off the critical list, but he pulled through. In the aftermath, he lost ten of those scouts that had been watching him. Only the Phillies, the Dodgers, and the Yankees retained an interest. Joe had grown up a Yankee fan, so he took their $25,000 bonus.

Pepitone had been described at the Park as being a "wild" sort of guy and so it was natural that he would team up with similar types in the pros. His first roommate was Phil Linz, whom Joe described as "one of the flakiest, wildest people I ever met, my kind of guy." (2) Pepitone broke in with Auburn, a class D Yankee affiliate and by spring training of 1961 was sitting next to manager Casey Stengel in the Yankees dugout. "Watch Skowron at first, Pepperone," the *the ole professor* would say, utilizing his famous *Stengelese* dialect.

Joe Pepitone spent 12 seasons in the majors, yet never achieved what he seemed capable of accomplishing. He was the victim of his own excesses and despite clubbing 31 home runs in 1966 and 27 in '69, he fell far short of what his potential predicted. In a 1971 column, Chicago sportswriter Jerome Holtzman wrote a story that was vintage Pepitone.

When Pepi joined the Cubs in July 1970, he immediately began pestering manager Leo Durocher to let him steal. "I'm fast," he would say, "let me steal." This continued for a couple of months. Finally in a game in late September first basecoach Joey Amalfitano gave Pepi the steal sign, which was a wink. Pepitone just looked at him. He had forgotten the sign. Amalfitano winked again, then again. According to Holtzman, "Pepitone then did what comes naturally. He blew Amalfitano a kiss." (3)

At shortstop for Nathan's was Benny Galante. Both of the Galante brothers, Ben and Matty ultimately played professional baseball. Benny was the older by several years. The boys grew up in the Sheepshead Bay section and both attended James Madison high school. The elder Galante spent his early teen years playing for the Cadets under Dan Hill and Jim McElroy, until he signed with the Milwaukee Braves. Ben played a couple of seasons in the low minors and then came home to Brooklyn and the Parade Grounds. An excellent shortstop, Ben hooked up with the Nathan's team , part of the legend that fielded a club with six or seven pros in the lineup each game.

Until the post World War II years semi-professional baseball proliferated through-out the country and was the epitome of quality baseball outside of the major leagues, often exhibiting equal status with levels of class A or better. Paying to play at that level declined into the early fifties with the spread of televised coverage of major league ball into areas that did not previously have such access. Though in some cases, as with Nathan's, a stipend was paid out for special player services. Larry DaVita recalls getting $25 a game to pitch for them. Winning was important at the Parade Grounds and at times there were wagering dollars at stake.

Rising costs also contributed to the demise of the semi-pros and although fans still came out in solid numbers to watch baseball at local diamonds, they would no longer pay for the privilege. Yet a game at the Parade Grounds at mid-century say, between Nathan's and the Eagles, might reveal 10 - 15 former pro ballplayers on the field at the same time. Astounding baseball for the sandlot level of play , thus rivaling the quality of former semi-pro teams like "The House of David" or The "Bushwicks" of old. Ballparks like Dexter Park and New Farmers Oval were gone by the early sixties, relegated to local baseball folklore, but the Parade Grounds still offered games that sustained the quality seen at those historic venues.

On any given Saturday or Sunday, in addition to the teams mentioned above, fans could come out and see Jimmy McElroy's Cadets, or our own Virginians battle it out on Diamond #1. The wooden bleachers would be packed with several hundred onlookers with standees three deep beyond the stands along the foul lines. In center field, the early arrivals would get a front row spot leaning on the four foot cyclone fencing for a panoramic view of the Elysian plain.

Incredibly, the Brooklyn Eagles under manager Joe Schwartz fielded virtually an entire team of former professional players in the mid-sixties, and they extended to a variety of organizations. Paul Gargone, a catcher, had been in the farm system of the Minnesota Twins; Danny D'Oca with the Pittsburgh Pirates, and Sonny Pace had signed with Cleveland. Jerry Rosenthal received a hefty signing bonus from the Boston Red Sox, while Tony Tjera went with the Giants. Tjera was a top defensive second baseman who could handle the bat; going to the opposite field with a good deal of precision. In the ensuing years, Tony played in the highly regarded Puerto Rican League.

Even more amazing were the pitchers who stood on the Parade Grounds mounds in the gray flannels of the Eagles. Sal Apria, Larry DaVita, and Chuck Feinstein all pitched professionally. Apria was a Journal-American All-Star winning the Lou Gehrig Award as the year's outstanding player. Feinstein, a side-arming right hander who possessed a sharp breaking curve ball, played in the Cleveland Indians organization before returning to the Park and the Eagles.

Jerry Boxer was one of the highest rated pitchers in the long Parade Grounds history. When players are asked who were the toughest pitchers they faced at Park Circle, Boxer's name is invariably among those mentioned. Jerry was a very hard thrower who broke off a wicked curve ball. At one point he was called the most promising pitching prospect in the entire system of the Kansas City A's.

There was, however, one overriding cloud on the horizon for this gifted pitcher. Jerry Boxer marched to his own drummer; a bit of a "flake" in baseball parlance. He seemed to be always mired in pursuits other than baseball which often took his mind, not too mention his physical presence away from the game. As an example, Jerry loved to paint and tended to put valuable baseball time into this favored activity.

Fred Weber, coaching with the Eagles during the sixties, once was sent to Boxer's house to retrieve the errant pitcher on a day that he should have been taking the mound. Trying in vain to convince the pitcher turned artist to come out to the game, he finally in exasperation said, "Jerry, you have great talent for baseball, but your painting stinks. Why don't you concentrate on baseball?" The pitcher just shrugged. "I love to paint," he explained simply. Some of his old teammates have heard that Boxer is currently somewhere in East Asia in the company of a guru, presumably one who prefers oil paints to rosin bags.

Lou Gatti was half of another brother act playing at the Parade Grounds. Lou was a first baseman from Bay Ridge who started out with the Sheridan Boys Club before moving on to the Brooklyn Royals under manager Joe Tomiselli. This was in 1957. Lou attended high school at Brooklyn Tech, following his older brother Jordan, whom he later joined on the Open Division Eagles. Lou was a graduate of City College and in 1966 he accepted a position with the Atlas Chemical Company in Wilmington, Delaware. "People thought I was falling off the end of the Earth,"Gatti said. "They would tell me, 'I went to Delaware, but it was closed.'"

Lou left baseball behind in Brooklyn, but in Wilmington turned to slo-pitch softball where he played competitively until he was 48 years old. "And," he said, "Somehow I'm still in Delaware after almost 40 years."

Pete Scarpati played with Spokane in the Pacific Coast League, a AAA Dodgers affiliate. Scarpati was a good pitcher with only moderate speed, but an outstanding assortment of breaking stuff and excellent control. "Definitely a major league prospect," said Jim McElroy, his coach at St. Francis College and also Pete's manager with the Park team, the Cadets. Pete Scarpati was elected to the St. Francis College Hall-Of-Fame and signed to a Dodgers' contract by scout Steve Lembo.

At Spokane in 1970, Scarpati played with a number of Dodgers prospects who ultimately played in the big leagues. First baseman Steve Garvey hit .319 that yearat Spokane, and Bill Buckner .335. Bobby Valentine was the PCL batting champ at .340. Along with Scarpati on the pitching staff was Charlie Hough who won 12 games and Jerry Stephenson who led the league with a record of 18-5.

But for Pete, a decision had to be made. He was married and his wife was expecting their first child. Facing a common crossroad for young minor league players, the traveling, and the uncertain future motivated Scarpati to give up the game.

A number of the Parade Grounds organizations followed similar paths by establishing several teams beginning at the "Grasshopper" level of 10 years ,allowing them to keep boys in their organization through senior and even Open Divisions.

Teams like the Bonnies, Ty-Cobbs, and the Cardinals, in addition to some fine ball players , developed as well, some outstanding young men.

Probably the most "legendary" of the sandlot baseball clubs is the Cadets and their "legendary" manager and executive director, Jim McElroy. The Cadets have been in existence for more than sixty years and have won at least one championship in one division at some level in *each and every one* of those years. An incredible achievement that is an irrevocable, undeniable, almost unbelievable truth. Although perhaps not so unbelievable when the quality of the organization and the man behind it is considered.

Jim McElroy was born in 1930 in the Marine Park section . In those early days, Jim and his friends played on the lots that would become the Marine Park sandlot baseball diamonds, built as a WPA project. Jim's teams were the Shamrocks and then the Good Shepherd Cadets which he joined when he was 14 years old. This was in 1944 the first official season for the Cadets Baseball Club. McElroy began his unbroken string of sixty plus years associated with the organization. In 1949 they went to the semi-final round in the American Amateur Baseball tournament played each year in Johnstown, Pennsylvania. Frank Torre was the first of the Cadets to reach the major leagues and he won the tournament batting title that year. His brother Joe won it in 1958, the only brothers to have accomplished that feat. Jim was a player and coach to manager Dan Hill. The '50 and '51 teams won the New York City Federation championships, with the '51 club also winning the Journal-American tournament. There was definitely a dynasty in the making.

In the mid-fifties, Hill retired to Florida and McElroy took over the running of the entire organization. At that time there were two junior and two senior teams playing at the diamonds on Shore Road at 96th street. Jim remembers taking two buses and two trains to get there. By 1954 the Cadets had joined the Parade Grounds League under Cookie Lorenzo and played their senior team at the Park.

The PGL was in the throes of expansion and additional fields were needed. The solution was to establish a spin-off league at Marine Park which McElroy was instrumental in helping to get started. Over the years the Cadets put out so many winners , obviously because of the incredible array of talent that the organization was able to put on the field. Players like Sal Campesi, Frank Tepedino, Jack McCabe and Jack Dalton all played ball professionally.

My own experience knowing the Cadets was limited to the years I played with the Virginians, but it was worth remembering. Facing the Cadets in the late fifties was to play against a remarkable group on the threshold of achievement. Joe Torre Matty Galante and Rico Petrocelli were on the field at the same time. There was Hank Pascone who signed with the Red Sox, later to spend his career years as a police detective on Long Island. Jimmy MacDonald was one of McElroy's top pitchers and George Kalafatis ultimately became an attorney and a baseball and soccer agent. Torre pitched and played first and third base before going behind the plate. A chubby kid, Jim watched his great throwing arm in action and his development as a hitter from the time he was fourteen years old. When Joe came to the majors with the Milwaukee Braves in 1960, McElroy spent a week in that city to see Joe and wish him well.

McElroy says that Rico Petrocelli was "the most powerful for his size that I ever saw." It seems that no one who saw him play at the Park had the slightest doubt about his ability. Matt Galante was a little guy with a thick pair of thighs, giving him the power behind his swing. A good hitter and a top notch second baseman.

Like all of the Boys of Brooklyn, Matt started out with a neighborhood team, the Bay Cubs when he was thirteen. After one season, he went over to the Cadets and stayed with them until he signed with the Yankees in 1966. Playing with the senior Cadets, Matt got to play against Open Division teams in the Twi-Light Industrial League and in Saturday travel leagues. McElroy considered it an invaluable asset to have his teenagers compete against the older and more experienced players, especially with so many ex-pros in the ranks.

Galante felt it essential to his development. "We did it to learn," he said, "it was a great experience." Being a part of McElroy's organization was for Galante a chance to be educated in the game. "I learned how to play baseball with the Cadets. It was my upbringing." Sandlot ball in those days was all about learning, which to some extent, may account for Galante's later success as a coach and a manger.

As a senior at St. John's University, Matt hit .402 and helped his club reach the College World Series in Omaha, Nebraska. Galante was signed to a Yankee contract by scout Arthur Dede and embarked on a minor league career that traversed a path similar to so many of the other boys after leaving the Parade Grounds.

After playing AAA ball, he hit .340 in spring training in a Yankees uniform before being traded to the Milwaukee Brewers in 1972. In spite of his minor league success as a player, it seems that playing in the majors was just not in the offing for Matt, yet he built a long and successful career in baseball. He is currently special assistant to Houston Astros general manager, Prior to his services as a coach for the New York Mets from 2002-'04, Galante had spent 21 years with the Houston organization from 1980-2001, before returning in 2004.

Matt began a minor league managerial career with class A Newark in the New York-Penn League with the Milwaukee Brewers organization. His team won the class A Midwest league title for Danville in 1974 and he stayed with Milwaukee through 1977. Galante managed thirteen years in the minors and followed that with sixteen seasons as a coach at the Major League level. In 1997 he went back to the minors to manage and led the Houston Astros AAA affiliate in New Orleans to a second place finish and a play-off berth in the Pacific Coast League.

Galante has seen a "sea change" in baseball and notes that "players today don't have the fun we had. It's all business now." He considers how much the game has changed, citing pitching as an example. "It used to be that you picked out your five best starters for the rotation and everybody else went to the bullpen.," he said. "Now, the game is all bullpen. And you have to adapt to the changes." The bunt has become a little used strategy, though in play-offs with top pitching, clubs have often reverted to playing for one run, Galante recalls the period from 1997-1999 when Houston made the play-offs each year. "We didn't bunt or steal all year,and so we played it the same way." The Astros were defeated in the first round each time.

As an Astros coach, he was assigned to teach Craig Biggio, a catcher turned infielder, how to play second base. He worked also with Jeff Bagwell at first base, and Ken Caminiti at third. He had under his wing as well, Julio Lugo, a shortstop who played at Matty's old haunt, the Parade Grounds.

In 1999 when manager Larry Dierker suffered a stroke and was hospitalized for a month, Galante took over as interim field boss. He never got another chance to manage in the majors, though in retrospect , Matt said he would have liked the opportunity. Galante managed the Italian team in the first World Baseball Classic in March, 2006 and was honored in '02 with a "Matt Galante Day" in the city of Houston. As Jim McElroy said of Galante."A great kid. The nicest guy. He never forgot where he came from." And the Boys of Brooklyn never forgot Matt Galante.

Frank and Joe Torre lived on Avenue T , just one block from Marine Park in East Flatbush. Frank was signed by the Braves' Honey Russell in 1950 as a pitcher/first baseman while playing with the Cadets, receiving a bonus of $6,000.Frank hit home runs in games four and five of the 1957 World Series as the Braves defeated the Yankees in seven games. He and teammate Don McMahon, another Parade Grounds alumni teamed up to help Milwaukee to another pennant in '58.

As younger brother Joe is quick to point out, Frank had an enormous influence on the young man's development. Having a brother in the big leagues exposed the teen-ager to major league players, their lives and attitude, allowing Joe the opportunity to move into that world far more easily and effectively than would have otherwise been possible.

Frank was a stickler for passing on his knowledge and experience to his kid brother. As a pitcher, first or third baseman, scouts were not particularly impressed with Joe. But once he went behind the plate, they viewed him with renewed vigor. Honey Russell wrote him off as a "fat kid with no speed to play first base or third base." After graduating from St. Francis Prep in downtown Brooklyn, having hit .500, the scouts remained cool to Joe. (4)

We had all seen the same chubby, slow kid, but how he could hit. The switch to catching made all the difference to the scouts. Frank and Joe discussed the idea with Cadets manager Jim McElroy. Frank saw it as the best opportunity for his brother and Jim made the change. Although, as McElroy points out , he never doubted that Joe's bat could carry him all the way even as a first or third baseman.

One of the young Torre's first games as a catcher was against the Senecas, McElroy approached Ken Avalon of the opposing team. "Who's your fastest man?" he asked him. "Earl McAllister," was the reply. "Do me a favor," Jim said. "If you get the chance, make him run. I want to give Joe a shot behind there."

The chance came and the Senecas sent McAllister on a steal attempt. "The ball hit the dirt in front of Torre," Avalon recalls. "It bounced up and hit him on the chest protector. Joe picked it up and fired to second. Poor Earl didn't have a chance." And so Joe Torre was a catcher.

In August of 1959, Honey Russell gave Joe a contract with a bonus of $22,500 and Joe was a Milwaukee Brave. He hit .344 at Eau Claire, Wisconsin , in class C ball the next year. His major league debut came that same season when on September 25, Torre pinch-hit against the Pirates Harvey Haddix and drilled a single up the middle.

In '61 Torre caught the 300th victory of the great southpaw Warren Spahn, and in 1971 won the National League batting title and Most Valuable Player Award. But there would be even more memories to dwell upon when Joe came home to New York in 1996 as manager of the New York Yankees. Having had little success managing the Mets, Braves and the Cardinals, Joe won four World Championships in his first five years at the helm of the Yankees.

But Joe has done more than merely pass through the Yankee scene. Larry Brooks of the *New York Post* wrote of Torre in August of 2006, "it's difficult to believe that any manager has ever come to represent the Yankees as much as Joe Torre." Joe Torre, whose trek from streetball on East 34th Street in Brooklyn to World Series champion included a stopover at the Parade Grounds, Brooklyn's *Field of Dreams*.

Aside from the quality of his ball clubs and disregarding the players that Jim McElroy sent into professional ball, his would still be an incredible story. In the thirties and forties and until 1953 when Dr. Jonas Salk announced his discovery of a vaccine to combat it, Infantile Paralysis; polio; was a dread disease that struck fear into the hearts of families. It could be fatal or crippling and it thought to be contagious. Young Jim McElroy contracted polio as a three-year old child.

His leg was put into a cast for the purpose of halting the spread of the disease, but it retarded the development of the leg area instead. Yet growing up Jim played baseball and coached it. He coached the St. Francis College nine for seventeen years and managed the Printers Union ball club in the Twi-light Industrial League while employed in that trade. Over the years the disease was responsible for an increasingly noticeable limp and he has not been seen without an ever present cane for some years. One of his supports is a Louisville Slugger bat made into a cane. When he leans on it, baseball cap pulled down over his forehead, sturdy jaw jutting forward, he resembles an on-deck hitter anxiously awaiting his cuts.

Baseball has formulated a part in all aspects of McElroy's life. When the 1963 Cadets traveled to Johnstown, Pennsylvania for the national tournament, Jim stayed at home. His wife was expecting a child and went to the hospital on the very night of the championship game. While awaiting the birth of his son and the outcome of the game at the same time, Jim got the press box at Johnstown to arrange a hook up with his home telephone.

He listened to the entire play-by-play, a game won by his team, 6-5 despite a home run by opposition player Ron Swaboda. Jim got a new son and a $185 telephone bill to help remember the evening. "Thankfully," Jim said, "mother and son were doing fine, at least before hearing about the bill." Jim speaks of the days past with great fondness and entertaining memories. "The umpiring was basically good," he said. "Pitsie was the last ump to throw me out of a game," indicating that it had happened more than once. He recalls also how race was never a factor at the Park. "Never," he states emphatically, "we just played baseball."

Among his collection of autographed baseballs, he has one signed by Babe Ruth. It was in 1938 and Ruth was a Dodgers' coach. "It was my first game ," Jim recalls. " I just reached out and asked him to sign it, and he did." McElroy is duly proud of all of his teams and their achievements, but there is a "soft spot for that1951 team, " who won seven consecutive games on the way to the All-American Baseball Championship. McElroy carries the title of "Chairman" of the Cadets Baseball Club; he is a member of the board of the NYC Baseball Federation; and Executive Director of the Brooklyn Catholic High School Athletic League.

There are now fourteen Cadets teams competing in the NYC metropolitan area including at the Parade Grounds. Jim McElroy was the recipient of the 1979Parade Grounds League Hall-Of-Fame Award. In looking back over the years and the teams and the players and the games, he says now, "They were good times. Everybody should be as lucky as we were!"

XIV.

Wings Of The "Eagle

"*Baseball, because of its continuity over the space of America and the time of America, is a place where memory gathers.*"
-*Donald Hall*

The borough of Brooklyn had its own daily newspaper since 1841 and the tabloid reported the news and the events on a day to day basis to the inhabitants so every Brooklynite was able to keep well informed about daily life in his neighborhood and those of his friends and family.

The first issue was published October 26, 1841. It began as a morning paper called *Brooklyn Eagle and Kings County Democrat* and never missed a single edition for the next 114 years. Among other items in that first issue was one that informed readers that the trustees of Erasmus Hall in Flatbush, four and a half miles from New York" are happy to announce to the public that they have engaged James Furgusce as Principal of their Academy." (1)

Founded by Isaac Van Anden and Henry Cruse Murphy, the paper was first conceived as a political forum for the 1842 elections, the *Eagle* at one point actually became the nation's most widely read afternoon paper. It played a role in helping Brooklyn to identify itself as an independent entity separate from Manhattan, which it remained until incorporated into New York City in 1898. The paper coined a ubiquitous phrase when it called Brooklyn "the borough of homes and churches." Named editor in 1846, Walt Whitman lasted but two years before being fired and it was his successor, Samuel G. Arnold, who reduced the name of the paper to *The Brooklyn Daily Eagle*.

Over the years the *Eagle* reported events that often were significant beyond the borough's borders. When Civil War broke out in 1861, the *Eagle* and several other newspapers were charged with being guilty of disloyalty, and encouraging the enemy in urging that the North give in to the demands of the South. The *Eagle* was not indicted, but the New York postmaster was ordered by the postmaster general not to accept the paper for mailing.

The *Eagle* carried the story of the first iron-clad warship, the Monitor, being launched at Greenpoint in January , 1862. The paper was there on July 13, 1863 when the draft riots broke out in New York City and it endorsed the plan presented by John Roebling to build an expansion bridge over the East River. It announced the completion of Prospect Park and the opening of the Parade Grounds. On December 14, 1878, the *Eagle* announced the first use of an electric light in Brooklyn at Loeser's store on Fulton Street.

In a special edition which broke all circulation records, the paper proclaimed, "United! Brooklyn and New York by the Great Bridge." Brooklyn had its first great symbol, later to be added trolley cars, and the Parachute Jump in Coney Island and ultimately the Brooklyn Dodgers. In 1902 Willis Haviland Carrier invented the air conditioner in Brooklyn. That same month the *Eagle* ran a story about the complaints of Brooklyn women in regard to overcrowded street cars.

As early as July 23, 1846, the newspapers' editor, Walt Whitman, was singing the praises of the game of baseball when he wrote, "through the outer parts of Brooklyn, we have observed several parties of youngsters playing 'base', a game of ball. We wish such sights were more common among us."

Baseball really began to take hold as a prominent entry in the pages of the *Eagle* in the 1880s particularly when the American Baseball Convention met in Brooklyn in March 1888. James L. Terry in his study of early Brooklyn baseball, "Long Before the Dodgers," tells how the *Eagle* and other New York papers began to increase their coverage of local games in mid century, and how the development of the telegraph allowed reports of the games to be sent to newspapers in other areas. "When the Brooklyn Excelsiors made their first road trip to upstate New York in 1860, their reputation preceded them." (1)

The *Brooklyn Daily Eagle* reported a "Glorious Victory for Brooklyn" on June 15, 1870 when the Brooklyn Atlantics handed the Cincinnati Red Stockings their first professional loss after 92 games, at the Capitoline Grounds at Nostrand and Marcy Avenues. Thomas Rice, writing in the *Eagle*, described the first league game at Ebbets Field in April 1913, saying "our bold athletes were beaten .by the Phillies 1-0." (2)

In succeeding decades writers at the paper covered baseball and the Dodgers on a daily basis. Harold Parrott spent fifteen years at that desk before becoming the ball club's traveling secretary. It was Parrott who wrote on October 5, 1941 "Mickey Owen was pouring out his heart. He wasn't sullen or sniveling. He spoke from down deep. You knew he meant it." Owen has dropped the third strike against Tommy Henrich and the Yankees on the day before.

On October 24, 1945, under the by-line of Harold Burr, the historic signing of "Negro Ace" Jackie Robinson was announced to the world. "President Branch Rickey of the Brooklyn Dodgers has broken through the color line in signing the first Negro ball player to appear in Organized Baseball in the 70 years of its life." Dave Anderson, later a Pulitzer Prize winning sportswriter with the New York Times was a Dodgers' beat writer until the paper folded in January 1955, and Tommy Holmes, long a regular columnist for the *Eagle*, writing for the New York Herald-Tribune on October 9, 1957 made it official. Just two years after the paper went out of existence, so too did the Brooklyn Dodgers.

In the blink of an eye two of Brooklyn's stellar institutions were gone, but baseball at the Parade Grounds continued to proliferate. The *Eagle;* in 1938 changed its name to the *Brooklyn Eagle;* covered amateur sports since the turn of the twentieth century. Throughout the forties and until 1955, the sandlots had their own "beat" writer in Jimmy Murphy.

Two more ball clubs that Murphy wrote about and people came out to see were the Brooklyn Royals and the Senecas. The Senecas stellar lineup during the late forties and into the sixties included names already mentioned. Wally Edge, Richie Lupardo, and Tony Balsamo among them. Ken Avalone lived in the area that housed the Brooklyn Navy Yard. The Navy Yard, an essential part of Brooklyn history, opened in 1884. Originally a 40-acre facility, it was expanded to 300 acres during World War II when it employed 70,000 workers in a 24-hour operation. The Yard was closed in 1966.

Growing up in the pre war years, Ken played ball with the Brooklyn Senecas, a team culled by Billy Meyers and fortified by neighborhood kids like Avalone, Harry Trimmer and Jimmy Brown. Brown managed the club in the early years. Ken played his high school ball at Brooklyn Prep, a shortstop then, he later volunteered to catch in a precipitant moment and remained behind the plate for the whole of his baseball days.

By 1945 following a hitch in the military, Kenny and Harry Trimmer took over the running of the ball club and began a stretch of successful seasons that made the Senecas one of the kingpin teams at the Parade Grounds. Like all of the top teams of the era, they played in three or four leagues and spread themselves over the city's many sandlot venues including Dexter park and New Farmer's Oval.

Ken was a solid catcher, smart, a backstop who knew how to set up the hitters. Avalone calls the '50 club the best. Four professional pitchers made up the rotation and in Tony Balsamo, Tony Russo, Ronnie Heffernan, and Larry

Castalano, the Senecas held a bonanza. In addition to Edge and Lupardo, there was also Marty Somma, whom Ken calls the "best hitter on the club." Ken recalls also Tom Powers, "a terrific basketball player" at St. Francis Prep and then at St. Francis College.

Ken is now over eighty and stricken with Parkinson's disease and his voice is weak and soft, but speaking of those old baseball days seemed to strengthen him. He spoke of how he and Trimmer ran the club, attending meeting and raising money to fund the team. Like so many other teams, their equipment supplier was Friedman's Sporting Goods on Flatbush Avenue. Sam Friedman used to allow credit so that teams could get started in the spring while raising money.

Avalone laughs as he recalls going on "the cuff" for two or three thousand dollars worth of bats and balls and catchers gear. "'When can you pay?' Sam would ask us," he remembers. "Well," Ken says, "we always played money games against the Eagles with Joe Schwartz putting up most of the money." Schwartz was another Park legend with his Eagles club and a fellow who footed most of the bills for his team.

"The Eagles at that time could never beat us," Avalone recalls with a chuckle, " and by the time the season ended, we had paid off Friedman. We always said that Joe Schwartz equipped our ball club." Kenny goes over his players and pauses when he fails to remember. "Who played third? It'll come to me. Oh, yeah," he says, "Tony Nunziello was our third baseman." There was Earl McAllister and Lenny Beckoff and John Chino. Ken and John remain close friends though separated by three thousand miles. He talks of a day when the score was tied and Balsamo had the bases loaded and a big meeting on the mound ensued. After a time Chino came over from second base. "Just throw the goddamn ball over the plate," he said. Meeting adjourned . Tony pitched out of it and the Senecas scored two in extra innings to win. "With Chino," Avalone remonstrates, " you have the most fun on a ball club that you can have."

Sebi Pepi was another Seneca of the time. Kenny relates an incident involving an umpire named Bert, who, with Pepi pitching and the bases loaded and a 3-2 count on the hitter, called ball four to force in the winning run. The pitcher went berserk. "I though Pepi was going to kill him," Avalone says. After the game, he had calmed down a bit, but saw the ump outside the clubhouse and had to remonstrate about the pitch some more. "That was a good pitch, across the letters," he told the ump. In a rare admission, Bert said he'd been upset over a fight he'd had with his wife that morning and was preoccupied. "I blew it," he admitted. Kenny laughs at the recollection. "Pepi did what any of us would have done,: he said. "He went right for the throat."

Another fresh memory for the octogenarian is Wally Edge throwing from centerfield. "The accuracy of his throw would actually put me in position to make the tag," Ken says, "a great arm, and a timely hitter."

The Avalones had seven children in twelve years and Ken says now, "I don't know how my wife put up with me." They moved to Freehold, New Jersey where Ken continued to manage a baseball team, this time of senior age. And with the children grown, his wife Dorothy spread her wings by going into politics, and has served as the mayor of Freehold for several terms.

You can't see Ken Avalone smiling over the telephone, but you know he is, when he says, "I enjoyed myself so much, I would do it all over again if I could. No question about it!"

Jimmy Murphy digested the sandlots in his *Brooklyn Eagle* column and kept a running tabulation on all that was transpiring at the amateur level. He even took on the role of bird dog at times and was said to be one of the first to recognize the potential of Sandy Koufax as a pitching prospect. A synopsis of some teams could be realized by simply putting together a string of Murphy's columns over a period of years. One such ball club was the Brooklyn Royals, and their manager Gabe Verde, one of the mainstay teams to operate on the Brooklyn sandlots.

In a 1948 column, Murphy previewed the club for the coming season. "Gabby(Red) Verde, who organized the Brooklyn Royals baseball club in June of 1945 and has been managing it efficiently ever since, figures he will field his best team this season." He went on to specify the players and their particular qualities.

"The keystone combination is composed of Joe Mauriello and Chippie Aspromonte , second baseman and shortstop, respectively." Chippie is Ken , who would go on to a major league career, one of the dozen or so Royals players that Verde would send into professional ball. Of the pitching staff, Murphy mentions a couple of stellar righthanders, Carmine Mannino and Gil Olsen, the latter having won 18 games the previous season, and catcher Mike Napoli. Mannino ultimately signed with the Cardinals organization, Olsen with Cleveland and Napoli making it to triple A in the Brooklyn Dodgers system.

Gabriel Verde lived on West 11th Street in the Bensonhurst section of Brooklyn.His high school was Lafayette, and although he didn't play ball there, he teamed up with some of those stalwart players that the school produced and garnered them for his Royals roster. Verde played only in that first year, 1945, "I wasn't much of a ball player," he confesses, but managing a club turned out to be his forte'. With no one around to help the kids get started, he and some neighborhood buddies, Tony Gentile and Nick Gargone, organized the first Brooklyn Royals. They played in the Police Athletic League (PAL) for the next two seasons representing the 62nd Pct.

The 1948 season brought a Kiwanis division crown to the Royals highlighted by a couple of Lafayette high stalwarts of the 1947 city PSAL championship team. Ken Aspromonte and Bob Pasquale, a first baseman, who would ultimately sign with the New York Yankees, would power Verde's '48 ball club. Murphy reported that righthander Gil Olsen struck out 14 batters in only five innings and then repeated the achievement by fanning 14 more in six innings against the Crowns. After running down the feats of these fine young ballplayers, Murphy closes his article with a boost to Verde."Gabriel Verde is doing a swell job of managing the club." On their way to the Citywide Kiwanis playoffs, the Royals defeated the Redbirds at the Parade Grounds 10-2. Carmine Mannino , a highschool star at Alexander Hamilton, pitched the victory and Mike Napoli was the hitting star of the game.

Mannino lived on 86th street between West 10th and 11th, across from one of Brooklyn's landmark restaurants. The L & B Spamoni Gardens is still open today and Carmine, now living on Staten Island, says he never goes back to Brooklyn without stopping at the Spamoni Gardens for some pizza. Mannino was an original member of the Royals along with Verde, Joe Mauriello, Mike Napoli and Ken "Chippie" Aspromonte. Carmine was a major contributor to the team's early titles in 1946, '48, and '49.

It was a Cincinnati scout, Joe Ferro, who aided Carmine in signing his first contract with an Independent club in Kingston, Tennessee. After one season, Maninno's contract was purchased by the St. Louis Cardinals and he went to Johnson City and then to Goldsboro, North Carolina. Though having an 11-5 season, the hard throwing right hander, had a run in with his manager, Jim Herberson. "He played favorites," Carmine said, "and I didn't like that." He recalls a shortstop who "made the most errors ever by a human being," but the manager kept him in the lineup. The upshot of the story is that Maninno wound up punching his manager and was released.

But he got his revenge. Hooking up with Rocky Mount in the same league, he did so with the stipulation that he be allowed to pitch against his nemesis. He did and he won. "There was no way they were going to beat me," he says now, still seething with the memory.

The next spring though, the arm that threw fastballs in the 90 plus miles per hour range began to ache. "I don't know what happened. Maybe it was playing football in the winter," he wonders yet. But in North Dakota that year he couldn't get away from the pain and like so many of the pre "Tommy John" surgery pitchers, Maninno had to call it quits.

His memories of the Parade Grounds bring visions of the future Dodger, Tommy Brown, whom Carmine remembers "hitting balls out of Diamond 1 and onto that refreshment stand." Of all of his great performances in those sandlot years, Carmine is most vivid about a game against the Robins. A misplayed fly ball dropped in center field and scored a run. It was the only hit Maninno gave up that evening, but the game had to called on account of darkness with the score 1-1. Maninno threw a no-hit game against the Vikings in 1947, and in Gabe Verde's voluminous records, Carmine is listed as having appeared in 30 games that same year; an incredible number for a sandlotter. Further stretching the incredulous, in 1948 he struck out 186 batters.

The individual achievements of Verde's boys continued to pile up as the years went by. In 1949, pitcher Mitchell Rossano threw two consecutive no-hitters at the Parade Grounds as the Royals rode rampant over the Kiwanis Senior Division. Gabe had to do some revamping for '49 as players Bob Pasquale, Mike Napoli, Carmine Mannino and Ken Aspromonte were all in the minor leagues. But new names came to the fore, and in particular, Bobby Honor, considered by some observers to be the finest hitter ever seen at the Parade Grounds.

Bob was just 15 years old when he joined his brother Eddie and Gabe Verde on the Royals in 1949. The younger Honor was clubbing the ball from the onset. Murphy's column carried Verde's claim that two of Bob 's "circuit wallops carried 400 feet." He completed the season with a .355 batting average in 152 times at bat. Bob hit nine home runs and was awarded the Most Valuable Player trophy for the year. The Royals won their league title in both '49 and '50, and once again Bob Honor was a mainstay hitting a cool .432.

Jimmy Murphy was beside himself with praise for Honor whom he called "the 16-year-old whiz kid." At the onset of the 1951 season, Murphy hailed Honor as a lad "who has the majors interested in him and shapes up as another Mickey Mantle." This was the kind of thing that Murphy did. He bird dogged young prospects and undoubtably was responsible for a number of professional signings.

Honor, being one of them. As a member of the Journal-American All-Stars, he was courted by at least six major league organizations following his graduation from Lafayette high school. The *Eagle* called him "one of the most tremendous local prospects in years," and J-A All-Stars manager Rabbitt Maranville said of Honor, "He's one of the best hitters I've seen anywhere for a youngster."

Bobby Honor signed with the Pittsburgh Pirates and by 1956 was with the Hollywood Stars in the Pacific Coast League. His career was interrupted when he was inducted into the Army in 1957. He came home to play in the PCL where he won a batting title by hitting .352. "Bobby Honor was definitely major league stuff," Verde said. But it never happened. Following his great AAA year on the coast, the Pirates passed him over and brought up a player named Gene Freeze. Honor was hurt and angered. He gripped and the club assigned him to their Mexico City affiliate. Bobby refused to accept the punishment and quit baseball.

When Red Verde talks about Honor, he recalls how huge his hands were and makes a comparison. As an X-ray technician , Verde once did an X-ray of the Dodgers' great first baseman, Gil Hodges. "His hand was so big, I had to use an extra plate. That's how Bobby Honor's hands were also."

The Royals battled the Daytons for the division crown in '49 and in the *Eagle*, the name of my old manager, Al Fortunato, is offered as his team's leading hitter. The Daytons took the title in a best of three series at the Park. In 1950 the Royals under Red Verde chalked up a munificent record of 60 wins and only 5 losses. Pitcher, Jack Dolce won 20 of those games to hold a Royals record for most games won in a season. At one point he had thrown 26 consecutive scoreless innings. Dolce wound up the regular season with 14 straight victories. After having won three titles in the previous four years, the Royals were geared up for their best year ever, and Jimmy Murphy inaugurated their season in laudable fashion.

His spring column highlighted the usual stars, but added raves for the Honor brothers, Eddie and sixteen-year-old Bob, and added pitching strength with Jack Dalton and Frank Banach, who, according to Murphy, was "a veteran sandlotter who has been a nemesis of the Royals with rival clubs." As he did with Olsen, Verde brought over to his side a pitcher who had given his club trouble. One year prior to the onset of his professional career, catcher Mike Napoli was garnering plaudits in the *Brooklyn Eagle*. In a game against the Cadets which saw Bill DiBenedetto strike out 13, Mike had a single, triple and home run. He then poled two homers in the next game as the "league leading Brooklyn Royals chalked up four victories," and ran their record to 8 and 1. Rabbit Maranville played in the major leagues for 23 years and was elected to baseball's Hall-Of-Fame in 1954. Maranville became involved in the amateur classic games sponsored by the New York Journal-American. In 1950 Mike Napoli was a member of the JA squad and Maranville had this to say about the 18-year-old Kiwanis League star. "The best looking backstop prospect I've seen anywhere," and predicted that the kid from Bensonhurst was "only two years from the big leagues."

Mike Napoli was one of those youngsters who helped develop the reputation enjoyed by Lafayette high school as a nebular of stellar baseball prospects. Possessed of a powerful throwing arm, Mike had the opportunity while catching for the Royals, to handle some of the finest sandlot pitching around. Handling the offerings of Gil Olsen, Billy DiBenedetto, and Camine Manninio gave Napoli the kind of experience to grow on and Mike took full advantage of the chance, developing into one of the best catching prospects in the sandlot arena.

In Mike's Bensonhurst neighborhood his close friends were the Aspromontes. "We rode our trams together," Mike says indicating how far back they go. Still close today, both the Aspromonte brothers and Napoli have become Texans, even to the touch of an accent. "When I go back to Brooklyn," he said, "they tell me I sound like a Texan. Then when I go back , they call me a Yankee."

Napoli played for the Brooklyn Eagle All-Stars in the annual Brooklyn against the World classic held at Ebbets

Field on August 14, 1950. The All-Stars squared off against the Montreal All-Stars. Brooklyn defeated Montreal in two straight games by scores of 11-1 and 10-4. There were at least eight future professional players on the Brooklyn squad. Napoli hit in the .380s all season as his Brooklyn Royals won the Brooklyn Kiwanis League title. He also threw out 32 runners in steal attempts.

Napoli is appreciative of his time with the Royals. "Gabe Verde, how he kept us together was something. We owe everything to him."

Mike was courted by several major league teams including the Yankees and the Giants, but Brooklyn being closest to his heart, he signed with the Dodgers Al Campanis after the 1950 season, at the time enrolled at Long Island University. Two seasons were spent in the Dodgers farm system at Greenwood in the class C Cotton States League, and at Newport News and Miami before his induction into the Army where he spent 1953 and '54. The military at this time was a mecca for pro ballplayers and Mike entered that level of competition at Fort Dix, New Jersey and at Salsberg, Austria.

Napoli came back for the '55 season and was sent to Elmira where he utilized his exceptional speed for a catcher by stealing 24 bases, and his fine arm helped him to accumulate ninety-two assists as a catcher. He hit .269 and was third in the league in total bases. He moved up to AAA Ft. Worth in 1956 after spending spring training with the Dodgers. The Dodgers and the Cubs traded minor league franchises in order that Walter O'Malley could have dibs on Los Angeles, so Napoli was reassigned to St. Paul. Over the next three years, the catcher shuttled between the Dodgers top farms at Montreal, St. Paul and Spokane.

There are many contributing factors why careers that reach the AAA level do not go any further. Mike Napoli could sum up his career with two words; Roy Campanella. So many young Dodgers prospects wilted away in the shadows of Dodgers greats. But the years and the experiences are never to be forgotten. At Ft. Worth Mike developed a lasting friendship with Bobby Bragan, and today assists the 89 year old former player and manager with his "Bobby Bragan Foundation" in awarding academic scholarships to youngsters who cannot otherwise afford a college education.

Napoli decided it was time to quit when he married and had a child. "It's tough to go on with a family," he said. He recalls how one spring his wife and infant daughter were ill. "You have no doctor that you know so far from home," he remembers, " If it wasn't for Don Newcombe's wife; she took care of them."

He reminiscences about his baseball years all the way back to the Parade Grounds."You don't remember yesterday," he says, "but those old stories - you remember."He is in contact with Verde and old friends from the Royals He recalls Bill Dunn and the Kiwanis League. Mike worked for twenty-seven years for General Motors and played softball until he was sixty-five. He was offered a chance to manage in the minors by the Dodgers but turned it down. He was a teammate to Tom LaSorda at Montreal and caught Dodgers greats Don Newcombe, Sandy Koufax and Don Drysdale.

There was the day he was behind the plate in a spring game against the Red Sox. A lefty, Ken Lehman was pitching to Ted Williams. Lehman was throwing a floating, dancing knuckle ball. Williams stood in the box and said to Napoli. "The only way to hit this is to left field." Notorious for not going the other way in spite of the famous shift against him, this time Ted bounced one off the left field wall. As he left the batter's box, Mike says he looked over his shoulder and winked at him.

"What a hitter," Napoli said, "he could have hit .400 every year if he went to leftfield." He makes comparisons. "Maybe we're just old," he said, " but the game was better then. Now pitchers go five or six innings and they look for help."

Mike Napoli played in a better time and against Ted Williams and Mickey Mantle. "I wish I could have played in the majors," he says with a tinge of regret, but then perks up with a memory. "I had a beautiful time, I wouldn't trade my life for anything." Certainly not his three children and seven grand kids, and certainly not the memories.

Following the '50 season Red Verde was inducted into the military. Jimmy Murphy wrote "the John McGraw of the sandlots is greatly missed...." Jack Dolce was gone also, to the Navy, after compiling a five year record of 72 wins and 9 losses. "He threw a lot of junk," Verde said, "he was something."

Gabe Verde spent 17 months in Alaska, where he managed the Ft. Richmond Pioneers to a second place finish, just one game out of the top spot. With Red Verde in the army, Joe

Maida took over the running of the Royals for the '51 season and they continued their winning ways by posting a 48-9 record. Joe, as a player-manager was a mere eighteen years old when he took over the club. The *Eagle* reported Maida's success as the Royals copped both the senior and unlimited Kiwanis League crowns. Joe was a recent graduate of Lafayette high and had managed teams since he was fifteen, bossing a club called the Rovers who represented the 62nd Precinct competing in the Police Athletic League (PAL). These 1951 Royals went all the way to win the New York State Kiwanis League championship.

The Royals then took a two year hiatus as Maida also left to serve Uncle Sam in Korea and the ball club returned to competitive play in 1954 with Gabe Red Verde once more at the helm following his stint in Alaska. And once more it was the venerable columnist Jimmy Murphy who welcomed them back announcing the opening day game on Diamond # 9 at the Park against the Bosox. Since 1945 the Royals had won six titles. Murphy noted Verde's choices for his all time Royals team which included six players now in professional baseball ranks. With most of the boys either in the pros or the military, Red had to restock his club for the '54 season.

With Ken (Chippy) Aspromonte serving in the army after spending the last season with Louisville in the AAA American Association, his kid brother Bob stepped up to pace the new Royals. Following the 1957 season, Red Verde took on a new role as director of the Kiwanis League. He was able to do so knowing that he would be leaving his beloved Royals in capable hands. He chose to do so to allow more time to spendwith a growing family. Gabe and Ann Verde have three children. He considered his favorite players to be ones who put the team first. Would "do anything for the club. I had a lot like that," he says in remembering. "Mike Napoli and Nick Gargone were just two that stick out."

Joe Tomiselli joined the Royals in the middle fifties as a first baseman. A Bensonhurst boy, Joe played kid ball with a club called the Knights, and later for Lafayette high school. His high school mates included Fred Wilpon, a pretty fair left handed pitcher, and current owner of the New York Mets, and two future major leaguers in Bobby Aspromonte and Al Ferrara.

Tomiselli turned down an offer from the Kansas City Royals because he had just entered the School of Pharmacy at Long Island University (LIU) and decided not to disrupt his education for the iffy chances of a baseball career. A decision that paid dividends, as Joe earned his degree in Pharmacy, as well as degrees in Psychology and Clinical Social Work and is currently a Clinical Psychotherapist at SUNY college in Stonybrook, Long Island. But all of this was preceded by a ten-year stint as manager of the Brooklyn Royals.

In the ten seasons between 1946 and 1957, the Royals had seven first place finishes, two seconds and one fourth. They were state champs in '51 and '56. Gabe Verde has called a game played on September 3, 1956 at New Farmers Oval against the Astoria Cubs, the biggest game his team ever played. Pitchers Dick Banach of the Royals and Joe Franceshini hooked up in a scoreless tie for nine innings. With two out in the tenth, a single and a stolen base put the winning run at second. On a 3-0 count, Verde gave Ben Montalto the green light and he singled through the middle scoring John Bonkowski with the winning run. "No game since I've had this club was more exciting and thrilling and with more meaning than this one," Verde says with the same awe he experienced that day more than half a century ago.

Royals players have recalled their own thrills over the years. Pitcher Gil Olsen recalls beating the Chiefs in a play-off game at the Parade Grounds in 1948. For Bob Honor it was getting three hits against the Cardinals and making two great catches in the outfield on Diamond #1 in 1951.

Joe Saffer undoubtably speaks for all Parade Grounders when he says, "My greatest thrill was just being associated with such a swell bunch of guys." This, as it turns out was the epitome of playing baseball at Brooklyn's field of dreams.

Like so many others , Gabe "Red" Verde had a "ball down there. We had no money," he said, "so we had to make our own entertainment." He recalls with a pleasant chuckle, Bill Dunn, a Kiwanis League Director, who held court at the big palatial clubhouse, always wearing a Panama Hat. "I took him to lunch at Lundy's in Sheepshead Bay," Verde said, "every Wednesday".

It was not a good time that we had at the Parade Grounds," he says now in emphatic memory. "It was a great time!"

The *Brooklyn Eagle* folded in 1955 following a prolonged strike called by the New York Newspaper Guild. At that time the paper employed 681 people and did approximately $6 million in annual business. In 1957 the Brooklyn Public

Library gained possession of the *Eagle's* "morgue"; its collection of articles, files and records from Frank D. Schroth, the last of the paper's publishers. 1996 saw the revival of the *Brooklyn Daily Eagle and Daily Bulletin,* published Monday through Friday, from that day to the present.

The *Brooklyn Eagle* closed up shop with a final issue on January 28, 1955. The 22-page issue carried stories on Eisenhower's responsibility to defend Formosa, Mayor Wagner's moves towards economizing, Soviet warnings against rearming Germany, and a congratulations to former Dodger pitcher Dazzy Vance on his election to the Hall Of Fame. Following its demise, the *New York World-Telegram and Sun* took up the Parade Grounds reporting with some of the same writers, including Jimmy Murphy making the transition.

In an article in the *New Yorker* magazine on July 14, 1969, writer Pete Hamill listed four factors that marked the passing of Brooklyn's traditional way of life; the departure of the Dodgers, the closing of the Navy Yard, the immigration of Southern Negroes, and the folding of the *Eagle.* He could have conceivably added to that list, the termination of sandlot teams like the Royals and the Senecas.

XV.

Baseball Matters

"Nothing flatters me more than to have it assumed that I could write prose - unless it be to have it assumed that I once pitched a baseball with distinction." - Robert Frost

We completed the regular 1958 season with that stunning double victory against Sacred Heart and St. Bernadette on the final Sunday. We then prepared to meet the American Division champs, the Sabres in the first of the best of three series for the Open League championship. The crowd around Diamond One the following week would have been a sell-out had they paid.

These were baseball fans who thrilled to be out in the sun, on wooden grand-stands and watch baseball played as it was meant to be played; with desire and vigor befitting its place as America's National Pastime. Make no mistake, it was good baseball about to be seen on that Sunday. There were at least five former professional players on the field and as for the rest of us, whatever we lacked in ability, we made up for by *knowing how to play the game.*

The people in the seats carried portable radios. There was a World Series in progress between the Milwaukee Braves and the New York Yankees that year. As if that wasn't enough there was an added incentive to interest the Parade Grounds fan; the Braves first baseman was Frank Torre, Joe's older brother , who so many of these spectators , like myself, had watched play at the Park just a few years before. That explained the radios. They told us that they didn't want to miss the Series, but they preferred to be out here watching us then sitting home in front of the TV.

Most of the fans were regulars and some followed us to other venues around the city. A fellow named Sid was about as loyal to us as any fan could be. In the Saturday travel league, we'd be at Victory Field in Queens and there would be Sid; or we'd go up to the Bronx to play at Babe Ruth Stadium, which was alongside Yankee Stadium and Sid would show there too, smiling at us from behind the screen.

On one occasion several people approached Vinnie Tiani and myself and asked us for an autograph. There were folks living in the apartment houses along Caton Avenue and on Parade Place. You could see them at their windows on balmy week-ends watching the games across the street. The Sabres had been the club to beat in Senior ball when I was with the Dahills and here they were again. The core group was the same. These fellows had grown up together on Woodhull Street and began their baseball at the "Rock Fields" of Red Hook. Tom Morrissey and Pete Vicari were among that group. Also Butch

Gualberti and his brother Joey. Joey was a month older and always just missed the age limitation, so he played under the name of Joe Orsino. I remember Joe well because we would share a few words when I came to bat, but I never knew him to be Butch's brother.

The Sabres first baseman had been Sal Brocco and Vinnie Bonacure played second. By the time they got to Open ball they had added some non-neighborhood players l like Reuban Alexis, Jimmy Fanizzi, and Mike Abernathy. These fellows all played some pro ball. Also they came up with pitcher Fran Jamin. Jamin threw that heavy ball that no one seems able to explain. Pete Vicari agreed with the others that the ball was just a natural result of however the individual threw. Vicari said that Joe Orsino threw an even heavier ball than Jamin. This made it tough to handle a throw down on a steal.

It was Mike Rubino , also from Woodhull Street, who helped the boys get started. They were always playing ball and he suggested they get themselves organized and he promised to manage them. They worked out three afternoons after school and on Saturday mornings. Vicari recalls getting to the fields at seven in the morning in order to secure a spot to work out.

"Mike made us do exercises and run and run and run," Pete says. "We were running all the time. He trained us like we were going for the Olympics." But it paid off. "You'd see a guy get a triple and wind up on third base trying to catch his breath. That never happened to us."

Pete is a little guy, 5'6", and seems like a natural at shortstop, but he started out in the outfield. He remembers a kid named

JuJu who was hit in the eye on the "Rock Fields" while playing short and Vicari went over to replace him and stayed there. Peter also garnered the nickname *Rabbit*, but can't remember where it actually originated, nonetheless, he was Peter Rabbit for all the years he played.

Rubino took the team into a league in Marine Park the first couple of years before joining the Parade Grounds League at the senior level. Vicari and Butch Gualberti were with the city champs at Alexander Hamilton high school in 1958. "We almost didn't go out for the team," Pete says, "but then we figured we might get out of some classes if we played baseball."

Being a little guy sometimes fooled the opposition. Pete recalls a tournament in Zanesville, Ohio. As he stepped in to hit, the manager of the Washington club yelled out to his pitcher, "Just throw it by this little squirt." Pete doubled. The next trip the same thing happened, another double. The next time he came up, the pitcher looked to the bench, "I'll pitch him the way I want," he loudly informed his manager. Little Pete lined to the second baseman. The pitcher walked off satisfied. At least he got him out.

As it was with most of us in those days, Rubino had his boys playing sound baseball. In a game against the Brooklyn Seals on Diamond # 13, he gave Vicari the sign for a suicide squeeze bunt. With Vinnie Bunacore barreling in from third, the pitch came in high. "It must have been two feet over my head," Pete recalls. Keeping the bat level but holding it above his head, Vicari lay down a perfect bunt, ala Phil Rizzuto.

Rubino would make no bones about what he wanted. One day with a man on first base who had a propensity to steal bases, Mike hollered from the bench, "Pick this guy off". No secret to anyone. Moose on the mound looked in as if to say, "sure thing, Mike." They picked him off a few pitches later.

The core group stayed together and even a half century later, still meet periodically on Woodhull Street and have lunch at Nick's sandwich shop, now run by Nick's grand kids. Some are gone now. Mike Rubino and Vinnie Bonacore have passed on. But the others still talk over old times and revel in the company of old friends and teammates.

Playing against our Virginians club in '58 and '59, Peter Rabbit remembers a ball club much like his own. "Great defense," he says, "smart hitting; hit and run, moving the runners and good pitching." It was the way both clubs played ball. " And Hottinger," he says, remembering the Virginians pitcher, "great control, always around the knees." No wonder it promised to be a heck of a playoff series. And Pete Vicari, after all the years is still a gentleman, still a class act.

Both clubs had their pitching set. For the Sabres in game one they would send Tom Morrissey to the mound. The *Moose* was always up for the big games and this was probably one of his biggest. He was certainly up for it because the big son-of-a-gun shut us out. We hitters had to shoulder the blame because Carl Hottinger went all the way giving them just one run. The 1-0 score was typical of our battles with the Sabres and the crowd loved it. Fans of that era loved good baseball and were cognizant of the hit-and-run plays, cut-off throws and other aspects of the inside game. Someone would complement you on making a good tag or backing up a throw.

I had a rough time of it, making two errors in the first three innings. Fred sat next to me on the bench after the third inning. He saw that I was nervous, or seemed to be. I'm not sure how I felt. It was a big enough game, but after the division clinching double header against Sacred Heart and St. Bernadette, when I felt just fine and had myself a pretty good afternoon, I didn't know why this game should cause me any consternation.

Fred said to me, " you OK?" "Yeah," I told him.

"You wanna come out? You'll be in again tomorrow," he said.

"Freddie," I said. "You wanna take me out because I'm playin' like shit, go ahead. But not for any other reason."

"OK," he said, and slapped me on the knee. Maybe that helped, and maybe it was a temporary thing, but I was fine after that.

For game two we had to face the other Sabres' ace, Fran Jamin. Called *Bullet* by the newspaper, he also was a hard throwing right hander, but a different type of pitcher than the Moose. Tommy threw up and in, while Jamin kept everything below the waist. The ball he threw was so heavy that it seemed like it had been soaked in water. I'm still not sure how to describe the so-called heavy ball that some pitchers throw. Weber thinks it has something to do with the rotation of the pitched ball. Jimmy Fanizzi says it's probably just a natural consequence of the way a particular pitcher throws. Frank Chiarello concurred. He felt that it was a consequence of the rotation of the ball, but was not controlled by the pitcher, merely a natural result of his delivery.

Jamin, a student at Ithaca College had returned to the Grounds to spend the bulk of the season with the Sabres and give us headaches. But in game two we had our own headache maker, Mickey Tagliafero, another hard thrower. It's no wonder the fans enjoyed our baseball so much. Mickey Tag shut down the Sabres with only one run and we managed two off of Frannie. The Sabres had a potent attack with first baseman Reuben Alexis, center fielder Jim Fanizzi, Dom Tursellino, and Mike Abernathy suppling the muscle. And every time you looked up shortstopPeter *Rabbit* was on base. All were reasonably quiet this day and we were set up for the deciding game number three.

Over in a couple of other ball parks, the Milwaukee Braves had taken a three games to one lead in the World Series. Southpaw Warren Spahn ,on his way to becoming baseball's all-time winning left hander, had won two of the games. But the Bronx Bombers nevertheless pulled it off, taking the last three games and the Series. Bob Turley was the winning pitcher in games five and seven for the Yanks.

We went out to Diamond One determined to win it all also and had Hottinger at his best. But so was Moose Morrissey. We battled to a nine inning scoreless tie, and then the heavens opened up. The downpour was torrential and when it let up, the field was a muddy swamp. There was nothing left to do but wait for another day. There was some question about whether or not to call it. The two managers, Fred Weber and the Sabres' Mike Rubino toured the field with PGL director Cookie Lorenzo. It was even too wet for the gasoline-drying stunt. After some discussion **the** decision was made.

The final game and **League** championship went high and low for us. With Mike **Tagliafaro** pitching against Jamin, we took a one to nothing lead **into the** fifth inning. With runners at first and second and **nobody out** against us, Weber made a pitching change. Jim **Volkland had** pitched well for us all season but had been hurt **and was** sidelined for the past three weeks. While he was loosening up in the bullpen, Chick was also down there.

Chic had been injured in the previous game and was unable to play, so he hung out in the pen down the right field line. I stood on the edge of the mound during the change, not thinking too much of it. I had confidence in all our pitchers, and felt that Jimmy might get us out of this . But suddenly, that positive feeling slid right out of me. As Weber signaled for Volkland; Goletta and Stone were also down there; I saw something that scared the daylights out of me.

Chick was standing by the right field foul line and upon Fred's sign, put both hands to his head and then began waving frantically at the pitcher's mound. I didn't know what he was trying to say, but it did not bode well at all. In any case, it was too late. Tiani said to us, "he's gonna lay it down, so heads up!" Volkland took his warmup tosses and leaned in for the sign.

The way we did it, the shortstop took the sign from the catcher and flashed it to me and I then passed it on to

Putsie in right field and Marino at first base. Vinny called for a breaking ball, knowing that the hitter would be bunting. Jimmy Volkland shook him off. Tiani flashed curve again and Jimmy shook him off again. Vinny was getting mad back there , but Volkland finally got him to sign for the fastball.

The bunt was perfect, along the third base line and the runners moved up to second and third. Now with the trying and go-ahead runs in scoring position, I kept glancing over to Chick in the bullpen. He was pacing around in front of the bench, obviously agitated. Volkland threw two more fast balls for a one and one count. All the time you could see Tiani seething behind that mask.

On the next fastball, a single to left field put us one run in the hole. They scored another in the sixth and it ended 3-1. It seems that Jim, having been idle so long was afraid of throwing anything but fast balls, fearful of his control. Apparently Chick figured something was wrong by what he observed in the bullpen or maybe the way Volkland was throwing down there. Tiani was steaming after the game. He had a great deal of confidence in his pitchers and expected them to do as he indicated. He would call for a change-up from Hottinger with a three-two count because he knew that Carl could throw it. But it was over and done with.

And not a bad year at that. We'd won out in a tough division over two very good ball clubs. I had my best year to date. My hitting was up there, percentage -wise. I was in the top three on our club, along with Putsie DeBarnardo and Frank Chiarello, although I didn't match up to them as far as quality as a hitter went. But it was nonetheless satisfying to have done so well among this group of players.

In the Sunday Parade Grounds League, I didn't break into the lineup until June, but was pleased anyway to have been among the league leaders in hitting, again, in terms of batting average, since I never measured up otherwise. I was deeply indebted to Mr. Staub for all his help and encouragement and confidence throughout the season and when I tried to tell him, all that came out was "thanks", but I think he understood. I wasn't really cognizant of it then, but I'm certain that my performance must have been a source of great pride to this quiet, gentle man.

Bob Stone and I joined the Park Slope YMCA on ninth street off of sixth avenue that fall with the intention of staying in the best possible condition over the winter. We stuck to a regular regiment two or three nights each week. We loosened up by skipping rope and hitting the heavy bag, then ran five miles. After our run we donned the boxing gloves and padded head gear and knocked each other around for awhile.

We sparred for two minute rounds with a between rounds break that lasted as long as we wanted it to. We finished up with a game of handball ,the loser to pay for the banana splits we always had after the workout. Bobby lived on sixth avenue across the street from the Y in an apartment over a bar that was called Stone's and owned by his father, Bob Sr.

Big Bobby Stone had boxed professionally and was as tough as nails. He fought as a welterweight forty-three times and was particularly proud of the fact that he had never been knocked out. He began his pro career by out pointing Willie Holmat At Jamaica Arena in 1929 and ended it with a win over Al Cortez on May 23, 1941.He'd had 43 fights and won thirty, losing nine, with four draws.

Every so often Mr. Stone would join us at the Y. He would give the two of us pointers on jabbing and footwork and supervise our sparring matches. He was easy on me, just tapping me gently, but was a whole lot tougher on his son. He would yell instructions and snap a jab or a hook right on Bobby's jaw. "Why didn't you block that", he'd bellow at him. Bobby would look over at me, his face red from the blows and laugh, 'Are you kidding?" And laugh again.

Working out as a fighter was the toughest all around kind of a workout I'd ever encountered. One night we boxed seven three minute rounds with just the regulation one minute between rounds. On this night Bobby Sr. bought the banana splits. He was justly proud of us and we felt immense satisfaction at having lived up to his expectations.

This was just a part of my winter regimentation. John Keegan and I got together and talked baseball quite a bit. John had retired after the '57 season and coached with Weber this past year. It was John's idea to gather the score books from Mr. Staub, where Allen had kept such meticulous records. Our aim was to add points to my batting average.

We carefully perused each game and each and every at bat. Game situations; opposing pitchers and such. To the surprise of both of us, we found that I had hit the best pitchers we'd faced almost as well as everybody else. But as Keegan said, "You hit .315 against these guys and only .320 off of everybody else. The .320 has to get better."

We found that in blow-out games where I'd come to bat 4 or 5 times, I'd only get the same one or two hits that I'd get with three at bats. We figured that the key was concentration and I would work on that next year. Then we went out and John threw to me and I would hit. He placed a bucket of balls on the mound and when they were done, the two of us would go around and pick them up and do it all over again.

We found ourselves out there while snow flurries fell and after a while when the ground was sopping and the snow drifted against the fences. I wore gloves when I hit to keep warm. On one particularly cold day, John walked off the mound and told me that he could hurt his arm throwing in this weather. Then he thought for a moment and shrugged and said, "Ah, what the heck. I'm retired. Who cares about my arm." He went back out there and I had a winter of never having placed the bat in the closet.

We opened the 1959 season as the Riviera Virginians, by virtue of a change in sponsor ship. We also had some personnel changes. Tom Castaldo and Putsie DeBarnardo had quit, as had Eddie Mack. I was sorry to see them go. In spite of losing to the Sabres, this had been a very formidable ball club. But we picked up some pretty good replacements.

To play shortstop Freddie found Georgie Lopac, a good glove and not a bad hitter, but Georgie was wound pretty tight. He was one of those fellows who throws things and kicks things if something goes wrong. Having nine guys like that on a ball club would be chaos, but having one was an asset. He keeps you on your toes. I enjoyed playing alongside Georgie for the three years that we formed a pretty fair double play combination.

Vinnie Marino moved over to play third base and we got ourselves an excellent first baseman in Jim *Cookie* Powers. Cookie was a left handed hitter with good power and an excellent glove man. We had a good club again and were now in the same division as the Sabres so it looked to be another exciting season.

And it was. We kept pace with the Sabres early in the season and while the Moose and Fran Jamin were winning, so too were Hottinger , Taglieferro and also Jimmy Volkland. A couple of writeups had us beating the Lancers in a doubleheader with Carl hurling a three-hitter and Volkland giving up only two hits in the nightcap. In that second game, "Frank Chiarello broke it up with a grand slam home run."

On May 10, we beat the Eagles twice behind Hottinger and Taglieferro while the Sabres were taking two from the Bombers. Hitting stars for the Sabres were Mike Abernathy and Jim Fanizzi. The latter was noted as a former baseball and football star at Erasmus Hall who "had a trial in the minors" and was also a hockey star.

We lost a tough one to Sacred Heart in extra innings and it kept us from going into a first place tie with the Sabres. Chick again lead the attack in the first game with a base leaded double, but Weber was livid at the second game loss. In the clubhouse after the game , he tossed a folding chair through a window. I think he meant to just bounce it off a wall, but got a little too much lift on it and it sailed through a window.

Joe Grossman, the parkie who seldom left his perch at the desk in the office that the Parks Department had on the first floor of the clubhouse, , heard the crash and came running into our locker room. He nailed Fred and made him pay for the window. Otherwise we were doing fine. Lopac was solid at short and Cookie excellent at first. We were deep in pitchers with Georgie Hahn and Bobby Stone still with us. We had a good club capable of coming back too. Like the day we were losing to the Seals 3-0 and Lopac hit a three run home run to tie the score and Vinnie Marino singled home the winning run in the seventh.

I was having another good year, actually hitting better than in 1958 and that plus another winning team meant that I was having a ball. At one point Sacred Heart took a one-game league with us and the Sabres tied in second place with a record of 16-3. On that day it was Bobby Stone who pitched us to a win while Jimmy"Cookie" Powers "connected three times in as many trips to the plate."

In this season my old friend from the neighborhood and the Dahills, Ed Conti, joined our club. Back from college he decided he wanted to play ball again, so he called me and with the loss of some of the guys from '58, we had an opening in the outfield. Eddie wasn't a bad hitter, indeed, he won one for Hottinger with a two-run home run against Sacred Heart which dropped them to third place, but he was a heck of an outfielder and could run really well.

In high school at St. Francis Prep, Ed won about sixty or seventy track medals. He had them all in a glass front cabinet in the living room of his house on Dahill Road. I was running for Erasmus and used to wonder whenever I looked at that display, whether I would ever win a track medal. I wound up with three.

We went right down to the wire with the Sabres and on the final day of the season were tied with identical records of 22-4. It came down to one game to determine a champion. The winner would qualify for the All-American Amateur Baseball Association championship at Zanesville, Ohio. Once again, the Moose had our number. He held us to four hits, while gaining a 3-1 victory. We scored our run first in the second inning. Singles by me and Vinnie Marino and a sacrifice fly from Jim Powers got me home from third. But they came back for the second year in a row and we had to settle for number two. To add insult to injury, as champs the Sabres would play an All-Star team made up of the best of the rest of the league. I made the team once again, but we lost 5-2. A couple of our Virginians stepped up though. George Lopac singled and Vince Tiani doubled in our two runs.

On the strength of those two outstanding seasons , I had , in a sense achieved all that I could with my limited ability. Playing well with outstanding teams and teammates and against an array of some of the finest sandlot players in the country was more than I could have hoped for when I was with the Dahills.

I therefore made a decision to curtail the number of games I would play in 1960.There was, however, a method to my madness. I was to be married on May 1, and in consideration of my bride I determined to play only on Sundays. I joined Sacred Heart and began the season with them. We were married at St. Catherine of Alexandria church on Ft. Hamilton Parkway and 40 street on a Sunday. It was opening day in the Parade Grounds League. All the men in my wedding party were ballplayers. Ed Conti was one of my ushers. The other was my new brother-in-law, Jim Santore, who played the infield for the St. Catherine team.

Bobby Stone was my best man. He had left the Virginians also and gone to play with the Pollio Cubs, making Joe "Pollio", the manager, mad at me because Bobby was supposed to be his opening day pitcher.

Things didn't work out quite like I had envisioned. Although I liked the guys on Sacred Heart and got to be pretty good friends with Al Marchese, I wasn't happy playing only one day a week. My wife understood and the following year I went back with Weber.

I don't think that baseball wives get the credit they deserve. It is particularly tough in the pros. The husband is away playing all summer. The wife follows him or waits for him. When the children come it becomes even more difficult. Ted Schreiber once told me how his wife drove from New York to Seattle where he was playing, with their two children, only to find out upon arrival that he'd been sent to Johnstown in Pennsylvania. She had no choice but to turn the car around and head back across the country.

The ordeal of the sandlot wife should not be taken lightly. Here was a young woman looking to start a new life; usually working at a job all week, or raising children. Her husband would take off to the ballpark on weekends and sometimes week day evenings. There was no career opportunity or paycheck involved, just his personnel desire to play the game of baseball. On Sundays I would often drive my wife to Borough Park to visit her parents at about ten in the morning and pick her up on the way back - maybe six or six-thirty that evening. That was the week-end for a sandlot wife, her only motivation was love.

I didn't do as well in 1960 as I had the two previous years and I was sorry I had let my teammates down. In that season also was the only time I had ever been pinch hit for, before or since. I had a friend named Hippacrates Karackis; a Greek fellow we called *Hippy*. He was a flame throwing right hander whom I had knew from the army reserves and I brought him to Fred at the end of the 1959 season.

The first time we faced the Virginians in '60, Hippy was pitching. He struck me out swinging the first time up, but the next trip I lined one right at the second base-man. On my last time up in the seventh inning with us down by one and the tying run at second, they pinch-hit for me. The manager explained to me later that he thought I might be nervous against my old team and the situation, or, as he put it, overanxious. I was neither and was hungrily walking to the plate when I was called back.

Wally Edge was playing center field for the Virginians and after the game he told me how relieved he was when that happened. It wasn't my hitting prowess that Wally feared. It was the usually unforseen trajectory of my batted balls. "I didn't know whether to play in or move towards right-center or what," was the way he put it.

At the end of the season I asked Weber if I could come back and he said it would be fine. Only he'd gotten a new second baseman named Lou Mango, a fine all around ball player, but with the number of games we played, he figured I would get lots of playing time. It didn't work out quite that way.

XVI.

Remembrance Of Swings Past

"We got the setting, we got sunshine, we got the teams, so, let's play two." -Ernie Banks

My old friend Eddie Conte had an older brother that I of course knew from the neighborhood. Bob Conte had several years before put together a club called the Cardinals and built it into an organization like the Cadets, the Bonnies and the Ty Cobbs. He took them from grasshoppers to senior ball and for the 1960 season, got together with Fred Weber and formed an Unlimited division ball club.

They played Sundays in the Parade Grounds League and mid-week evenings in the Twi-Light Industrial League. On Saturdays we booked games also. Once again there was a lot of baseball to play. I came back to play with the Cardinals for the 1961 season. The only fly in the ointment was that Weber had replaced me with Lou Mango and so had sufficient infielders. I played plenty of games, but found myself on the bench sometimes also; too often to suit me, but since it was of my own doing, I lived with it.

You know the old saying, "when life hands you a lemon, you make lemonade." I made some good come out of my situation in the next two years. I didn't want to sit on the bench when I wasn't in the lineup, so I took to hanging out in the bull pen. I warmed up pitchers and developed a new perspective on the pitched ball. I think it helped to make me a better hitter. Watching the movement on a pitched ball from a catchers angle allowed me to gauge a thrown ball in a different light.

Because of the infield situation, I got to play some first base also and now had played all four infield positions. The personnel of the club had changed considerably. Fred brought over an old friend of his, John Chino. Johhny was a little guy, about 5'5", but a tough son-of-a-gun. Thinking of him brings to mind Damon Runyon's description of Dickie Kerr, the White Sox pitcher who did not throw the 1919 World Series and won two games. Runyon wrote that he was "not much taller than a walking stick....the tiniest of the baseball brood." Chino was about 33 years old then and was still playing football as well as baseball.

John was one of the nicest yet one of the toughest and most hard nosed guys I ever knew at the Park. He didn't only come to play, he came to win and he expected everyone else to share that same dedication and single-minded determination as he did. At one point there was a shortage of infielders, a coupleof the guys had gotten hurt, so Weber picked up a guy. Picked up a guy to play. He played short one day and he made two costly errors. That was bad enough, errors are, after all, part of the game, but when he failed to run out a routine ground ball, John hit the ceiling, almost literally. He tore into the clubhouse and demanded to know where the hapless shortstop was. "In the shower," he was told. "Well," Chino said," pulling off his uniform, " if he's still in the shower when I get in there, I'm gonna kick his ass all the way to Diamond 5."

The shortstop was still in the process of putting his clothes on as he exited the clubhouse. He never showed up again. But that was Johnny Chino. If someone complained on the bench about the heat, he'd better not hear it. If he did John would let loose with a verbal blast. "You're here to play ball, not bullshit about the weather. If it's too hot here, go to the beach." However, if you hustled and played the game the way it was meant to be played all the time, and most of us did, John was your good buddy and teammate.

John Chino came from the area of downtown Brooklyn near Atlantic Avenue and Fulton Street, in the shadow of the Williamsburg Bank building, the tallest structure in the borough. Born in 1927 , the 5'5" little giant started out in baseball with a club called the "Empire Reds". He played ball at Manual Training HS and with the Senecas at the Parade Grounds. John spent two years in the army and came home to baseball with a club called the " Brooklyn Windsors" throughout the mid-fifties.

A good ballplayer despite his diminutive size, Chino played in a tri-county semi-pro league with a team that called the venerable semi-pro mecca, Dexter Park, its home field. Dexter, on Jamaica Avenue in Queens, had been a hotbed of great base-ball talent for many years. Home of the famous semi-pro Brooklyn Bushwicks and scene of many Negro league games throughout the thirties and forties.

In 1947 after his army discharge, Chino was invited to a trial at Ebbets Field by the Dodgers. Limited to only twenty ballplayers, John had no great aspirations due to his size, but had a good trial anyway. It was during the post war years that Chino began to play football. Though too small for his high school football team, John played on the sandlots at Park Circle with a team called the "Gremlins" and played for years afterward. As a halfback the little guy says, he "never thoughtabout getting hurt"

A lead off man in baseball and a good one, Pete Cavallo, manager of the Virginians had thedynamo hitting fourth in the batting order at one time. John and I were teammates for two seasons with the Cardinals. Chino played second base and then moved to third when Weber had Lou Mango. At the end of the 1962 season, Chino was presented with the Parade Grounds League Hall-Of-Fame Award for ability and sportsmanship. The 1963 award went to Joe Torre.

In his early years John played with Tommy Brown on the Ty Cobbs. Brown, who would go to the Dodgers at only sixteen years of age was a terrific ballplayer but "kind of young for that level of play." Chino remembers going to Ebbets Field to see Brown's first game as a Dodger. "He picked up a ground ball and threw it over the first baseman's head. You remember Howie Schultz? He was about 6'8'"

He recalls thinking of Joe Torre as being a chubby kid who was slow as Lembo of the Dodgers' pointed out, but John told him, "he can hit the hell out of the ball."Gerry Casale was the best pitcher Chino ever saw at the Park. "A good curve ball and great control." He faced Sandy Koufax in one game. John says nobody could catch him, he was so fast. "Holy mackerel, " he remembers thinking, "where did this guy come from? What velocity!" That day John walked four times. He liked Gil Bassetti. "Even after he came back (from the minors) he was still tough to beat. A very great guy."

"The Parade Grounds was a great experience," Chino says now. He left the Park in the mid sixties and moved to Long Island where he played for a few more years. then then took up golf."Nobody throws the ball," he said, "but it's still a tough game."

Johnny Chino, my old teammate, has settled in southern California since the mid nineties and at 79 years old , sounds on the telephone as spry and as enthusiastic as he did 50 years ago, and it is that image which stays with me as we speak.

Eddie Conti was still with us and I brought a friend on board. Vic Calia and I had been friends at Erasmus Hall. Vic had his own crowd and we intermingled at times. There was Dudie Schatcher and Joe Ganz that I particularly remember. Ganz bore an amazing resemblance to the comic book drawing of Clark Kent. even down to the black horn rimmed glasses. He was a broad-shouldered kid which added to the Superman mystique. When Joe would see you coming towards him on the street, he would jump into a telephone booth; there was a couple on every block on Flatbush Avenue back then; and pull off his glasses and begin to extract himself from his clothes, sometimes even getting his shirt off.

Ganz and I were in the same graduating class of June 1956. Calia had quit high school to join the Marines. Home again, he wanted to play ball and I hooked himup with the Cardinals. Jimmy Powers and Bobby Stone were still with us and we added a pitcher named Al Tennariello. With Chino, Chic and a good catcher , Jordan Gatti, we had a pretty good ball club.

Jordan was another of those top notch ballplayers from the Park who didn't quite make the grade in the pros. Only in Gatti's case he never got the opportunity to try. Jordan Gatti came from Bay Ridge and started out in the three-B league; Bay Ridge, Bensonhurst, and Borough Park; with a team called the Spartans at the fields at Shore Road. Jordie played third base in kid ball later switching to catching. At the Parade Grounds he caught for the Bonnies , managed at the time by Joe Bonnie, on Saturdays and week-day evenings. On Sundays Gatti traveled to McCoombs Dam Park in the Bronx to play for the Billicans.

It had been said at the Park that Gatti had the mind of Maury Wills and the legsof Ernie Lombardi, but what a wonderful ball player. At Brooklyn Tech high school the husky teenager played baseball, football and basketball with a decidedly unique accomplishment. In 1959 ,his senior year, he batted .464 in baseball to erase the schoolboy record held by the former major leaguer Tommy Holmes. Another of the Parade Grounds brother acts, brother Lou also played baseball atTech and with the sandlot Ty-Cobbs.

The season of 1959 was a particularly memorable one for Gatti. Following his great high school years, he was selected to play in the Journal-American All-Star game at Yankee Stadium. It was in this game that he caught another outstanding prospect who spent some years in the Yankee chain, a lefthander named Howie Kitt. The catcher for the USA team was future major leaguer Bill Freehan.

With Freehan at bat, Gatti signaled for a curve ball and Kitt kept shaking him off. He wanted to throw the fastball. The pitcher got his way and Freehan hit a 450 foot home run. Gatti may have at that moment recalled the words of the great Dodgers catcher Roy Campanella who said, "pitchers are all dumb, that's why they have catchers."

The same year Gatti was chosen to play for the Yankee Rookies, run by former Dodger scout Arthur Dede, now working for New York. The following season the Rookies had a catcher , Frank Fernandez, who would spend six seasons in the big leagues, three of them with the Yankees. When Fernandez was injured, Dede asked Gatti to replace him, so Jordan got another go-around with the Yankee novices.

Gatti and a few others worked out every day at Ft. Hamilton high school with Dave Barrett, another of those Parade Grounds managers of legendary proportions. Jordan recalls Barrett as being the most influential of the coaches he encountered."We played baseball every freakin' day of the week," he says, "Dave was just great."

Gatti received offers to sign with the Dodgers through scout Steve Lembo and the Giants from scout Buddy Kerr, as well as from the Yankees, but chose instead to accept an athletic scholarship from Long Island University and coach

Buck Lai. His college career was a short one, he left after just a year and a half. He stayed at the Park until in 1961 he received an offer from the New York Mets. That offer came from scout Bubba Genard whom Jordan remembers as a "southern gent with a wide brimmed hat." Gatti said "yes" to the Mets and shook on it with the scout.

But there was one stumbling block. Jordan has attained a position as an apprentice in the electrical union and didn't want to lose it. When the union said that they could not provide him with a written promise that the job in local three would be there when he returned, should he not make the grade, he determined that it would be wise to keep the position. He passed on the Mets.

In the long run, it was probably the wise choice. Jordan Gatti went on to have a very successful business career, retiring as vice-president of Adco Electric company. Regrets? Perhaps some. Gatti says now that he "would like to have seen how far I could have gone in baseball." The Mets at the time had two catchers on the major league roster, Choo-Choo Coleman and Chris Cannazaro. Cannazaro was a good defensive catcher but not too much of a hitter and Coleman was just an average ballplayer. It would have been a good opportunity for Gatti to have a shot.

"The mistake I made," he said, " was not signing after high school instead of going to college." He ruminates about it nearly fifty years later. "In 1959 , I tore up the Parade Grounds."

Gatti calls Parade Grounds pitchers Sal Campisi, who had three seasons in the majors; Lou Romanuchi from Erasmus

Hall high school who signed with the Yanks; and Larry Yellon of Lafayette, also a pro who had a taste of the majors; as among the best pitchers he faced at the Park. "But I never had much of a problem with any of them," Gatti says honestly.

Rico Petrocelli and Joe Pepitone had "great wrists, just exceptional natural talent," according to Gatti. "Me and Joe Torre hit a lot to right center.' At one point someone tried to turn Gatti into a pull hitter. Jordan tried to remember who. He thinks it may have been the Dodgers. They had former major leaguer Hank Majeski work with him. But trying to change a good hitter is never a smart idea and ultimately they left him alone.

He numbers Lou Mango and Ron Solimine among the best every day players."Louie was a hell of a ballplayer," he says, "he played football also at Boys High. A weak arm held him back." Solimine got "about 100 G's from the Yankees"and had two great seasons in the minors. It was said that Joe DiMaggio called Ronnie the"next Joe D." But once more fate intervened in a young ballplayer's life. Solomine was stricken with a bout of"Colitus' and was forced to quit by the time the ailment had run its course.

We had a pitcher on that Cardinals club named Tommy Mannion. One day during a workout, Weber told Mannion to go into the outfield and run some wind sprints. Tom did as he was told. Fred got involved in the infield workout and about a half hour later, one of the guys who was shagging flies came in and told Weber,"you better tell Mannion to knock it off before he kills himself." Fred forgot to tell him to stop so Tommy obediently kept up the running. But Mannion could follow orders just as stringently when told to go out and win a game, like the day he threw a two-hitter at the Eagles and beat another pretty good pitcher, Ronnie Jankowski by a 1-0 score. On another day he threw a no-hitter at a team called the Brooklyn Gems. He fanned 12 in the process.

In the second game of that same doubleheader, Allie Tennariello beat them 5-2. In that game Chiarello had a three run home run and Ed Conte delivered three hits, one a triple with two on base. On another Sunday Carl Hottinger struck out 10 of the Brooklyn Hawks in a laughter 15-0 to put us in a first place tie with Gravesend. According to the *Telegram*, "Vic Calia clouted a round tripper with all the bases occupied and Jordan Gatti collected three for three. Andy Mele's three blows accounted for three tallies." I guess I was getting some playing time after all.

Actually Lou Mango didn't make it through the season, he'd had some physical problems which he couldn't shake. We picked up a second baseman , John Avery, who was a good lead-off hitter. He got on base and could run like the wind. Fred liked to play hit-and-run with me. After that first season I became a steady number two hitter, in part because of my opposite field hitting and the fact that I could also lay down a bunt.

The hit-and-run and the bunt were an intricate part of the inside baseball as the game was then played and I fit the bill at least adequately. With Avery we played hit- and- run a lot. One afternoon on Diamond # 1 with a pretty good crowd in attendance, we did it four times in a double header. Johnny on first, a hit through the right side , Avery on third. After the game, some folks came up to me, "you guys put on some show," they told me. The fans understood and appreciated that kind of baseball.

There was also that depth of passion that ballplayers feel for the game. Fred Weber had it and with it he had a symbol, a talisman, if you will; a fungo stick. Fred loved to hit fungoes, infield or outfield, ground balls or fly balls. Make no mistake, it is a decided talent. A good fungo hitter can graze an outfield wall or drop a fly ball on a handkerchief in centerfield. And Fred was a good one. It is therefore understandable that his interest should be piqued when he met an elderly fellow watching our club work out one day.

He was a wispy grey haired African-American gentleman who carried a long, thin case that might be housing a pool cue stick. They began to converse when the old fellow commented about the quality of play he had been observing. "Some good baseball around here," he said. It seemed the man was from the south and had only recently come to Brooklyn. Somehow they got around to talking about the case.

"What'd you have in there, a pool cue?" Weber asked him.

"Heck no. This is my fungo stick." Weber lite up. "Can I see it?" he asked.

The fellow extracted from the case a long piece of wood, the most beautiful fungo bat Fred had ever seen. The man said he'd made it himself. Having no lathe he had to whittle and shape until he'd achieved what he desired. Weber held it in his hands. "Just beautiful!" "Go ahead and use it," the old guy said.

"Oh, no, I might break it." But he insisted and Weber hit infield and you would have thought he'd discovered the fountain of youth by the elation in his demeanor. The old gent seemed equally as pleased. His precious fungo bat had a great afternoon.

In 1963 I played for the *Pollio Cubs*. They were managed by Joe Colossi, who was so linked to the team for so many years that everybody called him *Pollio Joe*. Actually, his teams were sponsored by an Italian restaurant that was on New Utrecht Avenue under the El train. Joe had run the club for about fifteen years without winning anything. He usually had two or three good ballplayers, but never enough to be champs.

Joe had a reputation of not being one of the most astute baseball men at the Park, and his teams were seldom taken seriously. At times also, Pollio Joe was known to embellish his own prowess on the diamond just a bit. Umpires Dan Liotta and Ross Quattro regal their audiences with the story of Joe playing left field in a game out on Diamond # 5. After running out from under the first fly ball that came his way, Ross says, "the next one hit him on the head." They shifted him to right field, but the hitters were on to the ruse and began slapping the ball the other way. Over all, Dan said, "it was a terrible afternoon for Pollio Joe."

As it turned out, '63 was probably the most fun I had on any ball club. Joe was never expected to win, so each time we came off the field with a victory, we'd be laughing and joking and saying, "how'd you suppose that happened?" I think he put that club together accidentally. Joe had his basic two or three good ball players. I knew Richie Broker for several years. A very good catcher and a good hitter too.

And then there was the perennial Pollio, Rudolph Valentino. Rudy was an out -fielder, short, with these long sideburns engulfing his thin face. Rudy had been with Joe Colossi from the start. They were good friends who argued incessantly. Rudy would complain about some move Joe made and Joe would tell him to mind his own business, that Joe was the manager. But Rudy wasn't a bad ball player. He hit pretty well and could run and play the outfield. In essence that was Joe's team and once again he would have gone nowhere, except for the intervention of the Baseball Gods.

After Fred Weber broke up the Cardinals, Georgie Hahn went to the Cubs. Now, Georgie was a good pitcher with a fast ball and a sharp breaking curve. With the Virginians he was always behind Hottinger or Tagliafaro or Allie Tenerello. But now he was number one. Somewhere Joe picked up a pretty good kid pitcher named Robbie Lee Simon and now he had a battery. He had also added two other good players, Barry Frazita and Nick Gennaro.

Butch Gualberti had returned to the Park from his Dodgers' minor league experience. Butch could throw as hard as any of them before he suffered a sore arm. The thing about Gualberti was that he could always hit; and not just as a pitcher, he hit just about as well as anybody at the Parade Grounds. Somehow he wound up with Pollio Joe. So Butch played third base.

Joe Colossi had been after me for a couple of seasons and after '62 I called him and said if he still wanted me, he had me. He called me a couple of days later and told me he had my uniform number. I was glad. Ballplayers often get attached to their numbers and I was wearing number seven since I went into Open ball. Then he asked me if there was anything else he could do for me. Remembering the off-again, on-again bench warming I had done over the past two seasons, I said, "Yeah, put me down at second base, in the number two slot and leave it there for every game."

I expected to play every game and felt that if I did, I would do well. When Chick asked me where I was going to play, he decided to go with me. Joe was beside himself with this unexpected shot of adrenaline.

Frank Chiarello came from 42 street and Ft. Hamilton Parkway in Borough Park. Born in 1932, his first neighborhood team was the Royals. This was also the bailiwick of the Ty Cobbs. "We hated the Ty Cobbs," Frank says, "they used to pass by going to church on Sundays and we cursed them." In those days when he was 10 or 11 years old kids played with taped up baseballs and cracked bats.

"Nobody bought us anything," Frank recalls."We got everything on our own."Frank attended New Utrecht high school and came to be known as "Chick". After four years with the neighborhood Royals, he was upgraded to Red Verde's Brooklyn Royals.

Chick played through the Senior age division and the Open division. It was in '49 that Frank went to Wellsville in the KITTY League to play in the Washington Senators organization. And it was here also that the disappointments began for him. Frank was an excellent hitter and though he was hitting well, it was decided that his roster spot should be taken by someone else; a local boy that the organization wanted to expose to the home town fans. Frank left for home.

Those men too young for World War II were just coming of age when the Korean war broke out in 1950. Chiarello was one of the many drafted for military service. He served two years in the army and came home to baseball and another chance at the pros. During this period the minor leagues proliferated. There were more than fifty leagues in the country and several hundred rosters to fill, all in anticipation of gaining a job with the select 400 - the major leagues.

It would all begin to dissipate to a degree beginning about 1953 when the major leagues started to relocate and television began to carry major league baseball to minor league venues thus destroying the fan base in those communities. But at this time a window of opportunity existed for all young ball players. Open try-outs were held in local communities and in Florida camps set up by big league clubs solely for the intent on weeding out some talent.

There was little to lose for the teams and everything to gain. Minor league salaries were minimal, bonuses were seldom paid out and when they were , they were usually negligible. A class C or D contract called for a pay of about $125 per month.

It was into this world of hopes and dreams that Frank Chiarello embarked for a second time. In 1953 he ventured to Melbourne, Florida where the New York Giants had set up shop. While there, Chick was pounding the ball at a phenomenal .400 pace when he was, incredibly, released. It staggered Frank and his friends at the camp. For the young hopeful, disappointment, discouragement and depression set in.

It was the Giants farm director, former screw balling left handed Giant pitching ace, Carl Hubbell who made the call on Frank. His words echoed with a virulent persistence over the years. "Kid," Hubbell said, "you're *a hell of a ballplayer*, but you're too small." Frank was 5' 9" and weighed about 160 pounds at the time and a better hitter would be difficult to find, but "you're *a hell of a ballplayer....*"

Chick Genovese, New York native and a Giant scout was there. Obviously not part of the decision making process in Frank's case, Genovese advised the young player to go to see a friend of his , who was managing a B club in South Carolina.

"Go see him," Genovese told Chiarello, " I'll call him and he'll sign you."

In addition to being discouraged, he was out of funds, so the dejected young man just wanted to go home. "I screwed up," he commented many years later. "I should have gone." But he didn't and life played out in a different direction. He made his way home and to that mecca in Flatbush, the Parade Grounds.

Frank Chiarello , at 75, has not yet stopped playing baseball. Over the years as he aged he put on weight and hit home runs and doubles with alarming regularity. He faced some outstanding pitching. He remembers facing Sandy Koufax on two occasions, "he walked me about eight times."

He found Tony Balsamo, whose overhand curve ball got him to the Cubs in 1962, the toughest to hit. Butch Gualberti was tough too, "he threw hard and had a sharp break on his curve." Gil Bassetti went as high as AAA and lamented to Chick. "I can't get you out!" Not many could. *A hell of a ballplayer....*

Joe Colossi had himself a pretty good lineup. With Barry and me at the top of it getting on base, and Chick, Gualberti and Richie Broker through the middle, and the bottom not bad at all, we knew we would score some runs.

And so we did. A photo in the *World-Telegram* showed Nick Gennaro sliding into third "on a long triple in a PGL game against the Brownsville Boys Club." A game we won 7-3. In an extra inning game we defeated the Ty Cobbs 2-1; the clipping read, "Andy Mele's single in the ninth won the thrilling tilt."

I was having my best year since 1958, actually better, in terms of batting average. We were winning games and having a lot of fun, especially with two certified characters on the team in Rudy Valentino and Georgie Hahn. Rudy and Joe were still arguing all the time and all of us got a big kick out of it, as we pretty much stayed in first or second place all year. I got my print even in a losing cause. A fellow named Don Puretz shut us out 4-0 and struck out eleven. He threw real hard. The quote in the *World-Telegram* said, " Andy Mele's lead off single in the first inning spoiled Don's bid for the hall of fame." He had thrown a one-hitter at us.

But games like that were unusual that season. We were drawing some pretty good crowds, even on the outer diamonds as the word got around that we had a pretty good club.

Against the Brooklyn Lancers we won 8-2 with Butch Gualberti getting a home run, a triple and a single and driving in five runs. In another game I scored from first when Frank Chiarello hit a grand-slam home run over the right field fence on Diamond # 1. And so it went. We won our division championship and faced the Eagles in the play-offs. For some reason, it was only one game and they shut us out, 4-0.

We were beaten by a left hander named Jerry Boxer. At this time Boxer had already been in the minors and returned to play at the Park. Jerry was a hard thrower who had a curve that broke down and hard and he tempered it with terrific control. His fast ball rose, the kind of a pitch that jumps up at you, all of this made him a tough guy to hit.

He had been highly rated in the minors; at one point being considered the number one pitching prospect in the organization of the Kansas City Athletics. But some of the stories about Boxer indicated that the right hander marched to his own drummer. One such episode involved a time when the pitcher did not show up for work on a day that he was scheduled to pitch. His manager, Frank Novacile, went searching for him. He found his starting pitcher in his apartment sitting in front of an easel about to tickle a pallet of oils.

Novacile starting yelling at him and the errant ball player explained, "I woke up this morning and had a vision of a scene and I just had to put it on canvas." The manager, sans any appreciation for the arts, roared, "If you're not at the ball park in twenty minutes, I'll put *you* on canvas." If these kind of stories are true, then Boxer was undoubtably his own worst enemy. But this day at the Parade Grounds, he showed up for work and in the process struck out twelve of us Pollio Cubs.

Delighted at the Cubs winning a division title, the owners at the Pollio restaurant threw us a party. At the party someone suggested we go crabbing at Sheepshead Bay. Richie Broker had a boat that was moored there. Four or five of us went and we got ourselves a bucket of crabs. On the car ride back the bucket somehow overturned and the crabs got loose in the back seat. One of them was crawling on one of the guys' legs. He was yelling, "get it offa me!"

Chick was in the front passenger seat. Chiarello was a fellow who kind of went with his emotions, whatever he felt like doing or saying, he did. He also was a member of the NYPD. He drew his service revolver and turned to the back. "Hold still," he said, pointing the weapon, " I'll get him." Overall though, It was a good evening and we enjoyed each other's company all year, so it was a fitting way to end the season.

The Pollio owner pointed out to me a shelf he'd had placed behind the bar. "He told me," he said, referring to Joe Colossi, "that he would fill up that shelf with trophies. That was fifteen years ago." We looked at the trophy we'd just won, sitting there alone like a piece of driftwood on an ocean. I don't think there were any more after that either. The story has a sad ending.

Joe Colossi passed away some years ago. Dan Liotta visited him at a nursing home in Coney Island where Joe implored him to "get me out of here. Tell these bums who I am," he said. "Tell them about the great players that I had. Tell them, Danny." For so many of us, like Joe Colossi, those years at the Parade Grounds were very nearly the epitome of life itself.

It was my last full season of playing baseball. The next year, I did some umpiring and played a dozen or so games. While umpiring a softball game in Brooklyn, I met an old friend from the Virginians, Vinnie Marino, had retired a couple of years before. "Hey," I said, "I thought you retired." "From baseball," he told me."This softball is something else. You can play this game until you're ninety!"

Apparently he meant it. Some friends were in Florida a couple of years ago and they saw Marino; playing in an over 75 softball league.

Meeting Vinnie introduced me to softball. I never thought much about it until that day. The upshot is that for the next thirty years I played softball. All in all, I can't complain about my baseball career. When you consider that I had little natural ability, the fact that I played on the same field with nine or ten future major leaguers and fifty or sixty or so who played in the pros, meant that I at least held my own in some pretty good competition. In the six plus seasons that I played Open ball, I wound up with a collective batting average of .370. It may have been a soft .370, but in that time I watched a ball off of my bat drop safely about 300 times.

The USSR launched the first artificial satellite in October, 1957, although we hadn't a clue that in a mere twelve years men from Earth would walk on the moon. The *Peking Man*, the so-called missing link in the anthropological timetable, was exposed as a hoax, and the first open heart surgery was performed by Dr. John H. Gibbons Jr. who is credited with developing the first clinically successful heart-lung pump.

While not being a prospect myself, I was able to conjure up those boyhood fantasies. Not expectations, but dreams, even if no one else shared them; except maybe Louie Shalaba, God bless him!

But after the 1965 season, I didn't set foot on the Parade Grounds for another forty years.

XVII.

"Hey! Blue"

"Umpiring is the most fun you can have without laughing"
-Irving Piatek

In the 1950 Columbia film, "Kill the Umpire", actor William Bendix is cast as a diehard baseball fan who detests umpires as much as any man can detest anything. His character, Bill Johnson, whose devotion to baseball and loathing of the men in blue has cost him job after job, is persuaded by his wife and father-in-law, who happens to be a former umpire, to enroll in umpire school.

Johnson intentionally gets himself expelled from the school . After witnessing a kids' baseball game played without an umpire and the ensuing chaos, he learns to respect the position and begs himself back into school. The rest of the film is worth seeing for Bendix and co-star, Tom D'Andrea's slapstick comedy, climaxed by a zany chase sequence.

The *Men In Blue* are probably the most vilified species on Earth and have been for as long as the game has been played. I recall years ago at a vacation resort in the Catskills, an umpire being pelted with ripe tomatoes following a softball game. At Ebbets Field the Brooklyn Dodgers Sym- Phony band would go into their tinny version of "Three Blind Mice" whenever the umpires made their entrance.

In his book, "The Umpire Strikes Back, American League umpire Ron Luciano says that "it took me a year of arguments and yelling and cursing to get used to the idea that my blue suit set me apart from human beings....." He also wrote that umpiring is best described as the "profession of standing between two seven year olds with one ice cream cone," so it is not at all easy. (1) Consider also that a player who succeeds thirty percent of the time is considered at the top of his game, but if an umpire is not perfect 100 % of the time he is cause for vilification.

Over the years however, umpires have forged ways to battle back. Bob Ferguson once attacked a player with a bat during an argument. But that was in the 1880sand it has become difficult, if not impossible , to get away with such action today. Nevertheless, umpires have figured out new ways to get even with troublesome ballplayers.

Jocko Conlon, who umpired in the National League for twenty years has a duffle bag full of stories that he related in his autobiography, *Jocko,* one involving his nemesis Frankie Frisch. The old *Fordham Flash* was managing the lowly Pittsburgh Pirates on a steaming New York day against the Giants. Frisch came storming out of the dugout for no apparent reason waving his arms and screaming. Nose to nose with Conlon, he said, "Jock, old boy, I want you to do me a favor." "What are you talking about?" The umpire queried.

" I can't stand watching these .220 hitters anymore. And it's hot. It's too hot. I got a nice keg of Schlutz all iced up at my house in New Rochelle. Do me a favor, will you, Jock, throw me out of this game. Let me go home."

"Frank," Jock told him. "You're right. It's hot. But I'm standing out here in a dark blue suit, in a mask and shin guards and a chest protector. I'm dying out here and you're going to die with me. If you think I'm going to throw you out, you're crazy. Go back and suffer."(2)

On October 1, 2005 during a game between the Houston Astros and the Chicago Cubs, umpire C.B. Buckner took some menacing abuse from pitcher Roger Clemens in a dispute regarding the whereabouts of the strike zone. He then had to listen to Astros manager Phil Garner as he furthered the discussion. Buckner should have been used to it by this time, since he had been subjected to verbal bashing from players and managers all the way back to his days at the Parade Grounds.

C.B. started out by playing centerfield for the Bonnies as an eleven year old. He later went on to manage the ball club and then most likely caught in a weak moment, turned to umpiring. After being an umpire at the Parade Grounds for three years, Buckner determined to enroll in umpire school with an eye towards the pros. As a member of the Parade Grounds Umpires Association, he had been dutifully brought along by Dan Liotta and Ross Quattro until he was ready to move on.

Adhering to the PGUA's number one adage, "umpire every game like it is game seven of the World Series," Buckner was selected as the top umpire out of 465 student umpires and was selected for the pros. C.B. Buckner reached the major league level in 1999 and is still active as a major league umpire. Dan Liotta calls C.B. "One of the nicest kids I ever met.

At the sandlot level it was a lot easier to criticize umpires. Often their training was limited and knowledge of the rules elementary. But so was, in many cases , the comprehension of the rules by the players and managers. In my own limited career as an umpire , I was working the bases once when I came upon the most incomprehensible call by an umpire I had ever encountered. What made it more startling was that he got away with it.

Artie was working the plate that day. With a runner on first, the hitter lined a single to center field. The runner headed for third where there was a play. Artie came up the line to call the runner safe. As is their habit, a runner will immediately call for a time-out, this one while still on the ground. The umpire should not give a time out until *no further play is possible,* but Artie blew it.

In an automatic reaction, he signaled for time out. As it happened the batter was around first base attempting to go to second on the throw. The third baseman threw the ball to second where I called the sliding runner safe. The second baseman immediately tore in after Artie, whose back was turned as he meandered towards home plate. "You called time out!" he was yelling. "You called time out!"

Artie whirled around on his heels and pointed at third base. With a flourish and great authority he bellowed, "I called time out over here, there was no time out over there," and he waved at second base.

"Oh-oh," was all I could think of. I eyed my car on the street in anticipation of making a dash across the infield. To my delight and utter surprise, the second baseman said nothing, but turned and went back to his position. At the end of the inning he approached me. I figured that he knew what had happened and wanted to get a gripe in while he had the chance.

I was dumbfounded at his question. "I understand that he called time out at third base," he said. "But if the throw to second had been wild, how could the runner go to third since there was a time out over there." I couldn't think of anything to say except the truth. He took it philosophically, apparently wisely chalking it up to knowledge gained.

One umpire from the Park figured a way around the rules question. His name was Irving Piatek. Everybody called him *Pie.* One of his eyes was squinted nearly shut and he sort of growled when he talked, which was out of the side of his mouth, a bit like the cartoon character Popeye. Pie was a big fan of the ponies. One day a team called him on a play involving a rule. Pie whipped a publication out of his back pocket. "I got a rule book right here," he said, "let's see who's right about this."

The other team backed off, figuring that he wouldn't pull a rule book out if hecouldn't back up his call. After the game someone commented how great an idea it was to have had that rule book in his pocket.

"What rule book," he growled, and displayed a racing form. "I always have one on me."

A bone of contention for all umpires is that one pesky player or manager who always somehow manages to be a briar on their butt. Ron Luciano had his Earl Weaver, all National League umps had Leo Durocher. In 1953 the Dodgers Carl Furillo climaxed an ongoing feud that he'd had with *The Lip* for years , by charging into the Giants dugout at the Polo Grounds and wrestling Durocher to the ground. The home plate umpire that day was Babe Pinelli, who ran over to the bench at the outbreak of the melee. When he got there he saw Furillo with a stranglehold on someone. "Who's he got down there?" the umpire demanded. Someone said, "it's Durocher." Pinelli leaned into the dugout and apparently speaking for all of his fellow National League arbiters said, "Kill him, Carl! Kill him!"

At the Park during my days , my manager filled that bill for a number of Parade Grounds umps. Fred Weber was an umpire baiter. He never hesitated to argue ball and strike calls, fair balls or foul or safe or out decisions. As a result Freddie was bounced a number of times. Of course it was at times difficult to get the offending individual to retreat all the way to the clubhouse, especially when you were playing on one of the outer fields. On Diamond Five one day, he was bounced by Petey Larkin. Weber retreated all the way to Diamond number Four, where he stood and began waving signals to John Keegan to pass on to us. Larkin saw him and stopped the game, and pointed towards the clubhouse. Fred retreated a bit further, to Diamond Three where he stopped and pulled the same exercise. Larkin held up the game again this time jumping up and down and gesturing wildly. "Get outta here," he was screaming. "Get him outta here!" Eventually Weber made it to the clubhouse.

But he found a way on Diamond One. We were playing before a large crowd and the stands were full. This time when he got the heave-ho, Weber went to the club house without so much as a whimper. When the game resumed he doubled back and crawled under the bleachers and laying flat on his belly, proceeded to manage the game from there. He wasn't seen by the umpires and the crowd covering him wouldn't give him away.

There were good umps at the Parade Grounds and some not so good, but no one questioned their dedication. Some were quiet and some gregarious, but none were like Irving Piatek. Pie was in a class by his lonesome. He never worked the plate,only the bases or one man jobs where he would call balls and strikes from the pitchers' mound. Inevitably, when someone disagreed with a call, the obvious comments would be, "Hey, Pie, open both eyes next time," or "use the other eye, too." His comeback was a growling, " I can call the photo finishes at Aquaduct, so I can call a ball and a strike here."

He was not adverse to giving the pitcher advice. "Throw this guy a curve," he'd say. "He'll never hit a good curve." Dutifully, a young pitcher would take his advice and watch as his curve ball would be lined into a double. The kid would look at Pie with a frown, "I thought you said he couldn't hit a curve ." and Pie would come back with, "I said a good curve, not that piece 'a crap you threw." On a good fastball when Pie called a strike and got a rebuke from the hitter, he'd often come back with, "it sounded like a strike and that's good enough for me."

Pie also had his own set of ethics. If an infielder made a good play, say, the shortstop dove , rolled over and came up throwing, but just missed nipping the runner at first, Pie would bang him out, loudly and emphatically. "Are you kidding?" the coach or the hitter would start screaming. "Hey," was Pie's response, "You expect me to call him safe after a play like that?"

Everyone who knew Pie has a story to tell. Frank Chiarello recalls that the only time he was ever ejected from a ball game, it was Pie who gave him the thumb. "It was a 3-2 pitch," Frank said. The next pitch was across the letters. "Yeah, the letters of my hat," Chiarello swears. "I spread my hands and shrugged and Pie threw me out of the game."

Eddie Mack had him down pat. He knew you had limited vision from the mound. On a play at second when covering for a steal, Mack would sweep the tag and turn to the mound, knowing Pie could never see the tag that he missed. "Half the time I missed the tag," Mack recalls, "and Pie always called 'em out. They'd be yelling, 'he never tagged me', but Pie didn't care. He made the call and that was the end of it."

But no one accused him of not having guts. Once he was hit with a line drive through the box. The ball bounced over to the shortstop who threw the runner out. Pie was on his back writhing in pain. His arms and legs extended into the air like an inverted insect, but he feebly punched the air and shouted,"You're out!"

Herbert Johnson remembers a good umpire he used to see officiating games on Diamond # 1 in the thirties. Mr. Johnson says that "he was colorful to watch," in part because he was a mute and his arm and thumb signals were frantically applied, in particular when tossing argumentative players out of a game. He also carried a whistle which he used to call the game. "One blow on the whistle meant 'foul' , two meant 'fair'.

It was in 1976 that Cookie Lorenzo asked Dan Liotta to step in and take charge of the umpires in the PGL. It was Lorenzo who got Dan started as an umpire in the first place. Dan was a player-coach with a team and a go-between as far as any gripes the players had with the manager. After seeing Dan get hassled by a problem, Cookie said to him, "If you're gonna take abuse, why don't you become an umpire and get paid for it." Dan and Ross Quattro agreed to take on the umpires for the PGL with the stipulation that they could form an umpires association and handle all of the assignments. Lorenzo okayed the plan and thus was born the *Parade Grounds Umpires Association* (PGUA). Their aim was to form a more orderly program than existed, with an emphasis on appearance, attitude and knowledge of the rules.

They began their association with eleven umpires and one league. As they developed a reputation the association began to proliferate. Tony Curcio, chairman of Kings County American Legion Baseball requested that they take over the officiating in the American Legion sandlot program. Ultimately they were to expand to include some Little League programs as well as the Public School Athletic League(PSAL) which meant that they now handled the umpiring for NYC high schools.

Two of their officials, Stu Hershkerwitz and Allan Tupper had attended Bill Kinneman's umpire school. Each spring the association conducted clinics that were presided over by the two professional students. There is of course, a concentration to updating rules and complete clarification of the rule book. Attention is paid to positioning on the field and even how to communicate with players and managers.

The established credo of the PGUA contains two adages; Umpire every game like it was the seventh game of the World Series, and never let sportsmanship become secondary to winning. The dedication of Liotta and Quattro and their staff of umpires has resulted in an organization of more than 70 members.

The aim of the two founders is to recruit dedicated men and Ross recalls the fellow who followed him around with a pad and a pen jotting down every word the senior umpire told him. He was so serious about learning that his questions began to be just a little bit academic. One day when he asked Quattro how far from the line he should stand when working at first base, Quattro impatiently remarked, "about as far as a chicken bone flies when you do a Heimlick maneuver." He realized that the stream of queries would not end when he saw the novice ump entering the answer into his notebook, word for word.

When Dan Liotta worked his first game behind the plate, his base partner was Irving Piatek, the one and only Pie. "Don't worry, kid," the older ump assured Dan, "I'll help you out." He then proceeded to signal from his position on the bases to Liotta on every pitch. He'd stick his right hand out for a strike and the left hand for balls. Liotta was trying to watch the pitch and was so distracted by the hand motions, that he barely got through the game without his sanity being questioned by both teams. "See," the venerate Mr. Piatek said after the game, "I told you I'd get you through this."

Mention Irving to anyone who knew him and you will get a "Pie" story. Nick Defendis recalls a day that Pie was working behind the pitcher's mound with runners at first and second bases. The runners attempted a double steal. While Pie was turned towards the base preparing to make the call at second, the catcher's throw caught him flush in the seat of his paints. The ball bounded towards the first base foul line where the pitcher picked it up and threw home to get the runner trying to score from second. The greatest wonders in these stories is that no one who knows him ever doubts that incidents like this really happened. It is simply part of the lore of Irving "Pie" Piatek.

It was the team of Liotta and Quattro who on one occasion went far beyond the umpire's call of duty when they actually saved a human life. It was on the cinder road that led from Coney Island Avenue to the parking area in the Parade Grounds. The two umps had worked a game at Marine Park and had parked their car for a scheduled game at Park Circle. A car pulled in along side of them and the driver started to get out of the vehicle when he began gasping for breath and started to collapse.

The two umps ran to him and gently laid him on the ground. Ross had a balloon chest protector on the back seat. They had left it blown up rather than taking the air out and blowing it up all over again. While Ross used the protector as a pillow, Dan ran to the police precinct house on the premises for help. It took the ambulance a long time and Dan kept running in and asking the cops, "where the hell is the ambulance, this guy is dying out here."

There was a happy ending. The man was suffering a heart attack and the quick work of the umpires did help to save him. Thanks to the partners, the man recovered.

Ross and Danny make a great team. Quattro is an affectionato of Jackie Gleason's "Honeymooners" and often is heard quoting lines from the show. Once when working a game together, Liotta ordered a man who was ambling across the outfield to get off the field. The man refused to step up his pace and threw some choice words at Dan. Soon there were threatening sounds and gestures . At this point Ross pointed a finger at the trespasser and in his best Ed Norton voice said, "my friend will fight you anytime, anyplace...."

Dan Liotta has been accosted on occasion because of calls he made. One day he was getting the bird about his ball and strike calls from the pitcher's father, who stood behind the home plate screen. "Hey," the father said, "you keep making calls like that, I got something for you." He lifted his shirt and Danny saw what he says was or resembled a revolver. "What is this? Hunting season?" He thought to himself. "Come to think of it," he says now, "a lotta guys wanted to kill me."

Liotta and Quattro teamed up for a number of memorable moments and one of them involved the soon-to-be major league star hurler for the New York Mets, John Franco. It was a day that the two arbiters would just as soon forget except that it was one of the best games that they ever officiated .

It was at the Parade Grounds in 1979. Franco was pitching for the Gil Hodges team against the Ty Cobbs. The game went ten innings and young John lost it in the tenth on a walk, a steal and a opposite field bloop single. But it was in the seventh inning that the boys in blue had an embarrassing moment. Ross Quattro was on the bases and Liotta behind the plate. A Texas League pop up into short left field brought the two of them on the run to be in the best position to see the catch or the trap.

In their zeal, each determined to make the call; the result being Liotta banging the hitter out on a catch, with Quattro signing safe at *the same time.* Having made the mistake, the boys recovered quickly. They held back the rampaging ballplayers and assured them that they will rectify their error. They huddled, just the two of them.

"How sure are you,?" Ross asked. Liotta responded, "95% sure."

"Well, I'm 99% sure ," Quattro said. They went with the numbers and ruled no catch. "But thank God they didn't score," Dan sighed in remembered relief.

Dan Liotta recalls working the plate for Franco's last game before signing his professional contract. "It was in '81," he says, "and Johnny threw an 8-0 shutout." Shortly after, on June 8, Franco was drafted in the 5th round of the free-agent draft and signed by the Los Angeles Dodgers.

Benny Distefano also played in that game. Benny was drafted by the Dodgers and played his first pro year at Greenwood in the South Atlantic League. Benny, a first baseman, was selected by the Pittsburgh Pirates in the secondary phrase of the free-agent draft in January of 1982. He got to the majors in '84 where he spent five seasons , four with the Pirates and one with the Houston Astros.

On occasion I found myself balking at an umpires decision , but I only recall being thrown out once. As usual I was standing next to Fred Weber when he went ballistic on a tag play. I was mad also but the ump waved everybody within the immediate area out of the game, actually Weber , me and John Keegan. In any case, I consider it "tossing by association", since I probably would not have been thrown out otherwise.

One indication of a good umpire is positioning. If an ump is close to the play he can see it better than anyone else, and a player on the other side of the diamond can hardly squawk at a call. One of the best in my time at the Parade Grounds was Steve Albanese. Steve was a hustler who was on top of plays and was a good ball and strike man as well. His ability as an arbiter had to have some genesis in his ability asa ballplayer. Albanese grew up on Fourth Avenue and Fourteenth street in the Sunset Park section of Brooklyn. He was the only one of four boys in the family who played the game; and did he play it. A shortstop with the Mohawks at the Park, Steve played quite a bit of semi-pro ball during the thirties.

Companies would hire ball players to work, but actually to play ball on those company teams. Albanese was hired by the Hotel New Yorker. When he reported for work, he asked what they wanted him to do. "Oh, just walk around," was the reply. On that club he played with future major league player and manager, Sam Mele. At 89 years old, Steve's memory has begun to wane, but some things seem to be entrenched. He recalls Mele and says they were friends, "Sam was a good ballplayer," he says. He also is very clear on the methods used by companies to use the players on the team.

At that semi-pro level he was offered a chance to play with the famous bearded House Of David team. He describes being told that he would have to "cover his face." He grew a full beard for that experience. As a member of the House Of David he got to play in many ball parks in the area including Dexter Park in Queens where Steve played against teams in the Negro Professional leagues.

It was in 1942 that Steve was scouted by the Brooklyn Dodgers and made a contract offer. It was in 1942 also that the United States had gone to war. Albanese was drafted into the navy and by the time he was discharged at the war's end, he was just to old to embark on a pro career. But Steve's naval stint involved baseball playing primarily. With so many outstanding players in the military, the service branches were always trying to field the best teams. When it was learned that he was a ballplayer, Albanese was told to "go sick" and instead of reporting to the hospital, played ball. He repeats the story with a smile these sixty years later, almost in disbelief. He played a lot of service ball with some of the best competition around and when he came home his great love for the game took him to umpiring.

For more than thirty years he worked games at a great many ballparks in the metropolitan area, but home was the Parade Grounds. His son Steve recalls going with dad to the Park and the impressive clubhouse. "There were always card games in the back room," he recalls, "and when they opened the door, there would be a huge cloud of cigar smoke. You wondered how they could even see the cards."

Steve Jr. Is now a detective working at Fire Island in the Firearms and Tactics division. He has two brothers. Robert is a fire department Battalion Chief and the youngest of the Albanese brothers earned his degree in engineering. There are two granddaughters in the Albanese clan, with the fifteen year old playing baseball. The boys didn't play much ball after a Little League stint, their mother Vita relates, "Steve was too tough on them." A keen competitor and perfectionist, Albanese tried to instill his knowledge into his boys. They found it more desirable to seek other pursuits.

Even today, living near Marine Park in Brooklyn, Vita says, "we had to stop taking Steve to see games. He would criticize and argue with the players and umps." But baseball remains a part of the life of the Albanese family to this day because of fond memories. Steve became a NYC firefighter. Working at a fire house just a few blocks from the Parade Grounds, Steve would work an overnight tour on a Friday, go straight to the Parade Grounds to umpire three games, then back to the firehouse for a Saturday night tour and three games on Sunday morning without going home.

Vita would pack the boys and a picnic lunch and walk to the Park from their home at Vanderbilt Avenue and 20th street to meet husband and dad. "People told me what a great wife I was," Vita laughs, "but I said that it was the only way the kids would get to see their father." Memories of the Park are deeply ingrained. Steve recalls Diamond #1 and 13 before the fences were built. "The crowds around the outfield had to be waved back off the playing field. In center field they came right up behind the outfielders."

Steve Albanese had an excellent baseball career and umpiring career to remember. He umpired games when Chuck Connors played and worked the plate when Sandy Koufax pitched. He has a wonderful wife and family, but there is one other thing worth thinking about.

In June 1961 while on the job Steve Albanese and Lt Joseph Boeri responded to a fire at Coney island Avenue and Cortelyou Road and saved the life of two children. Being a great umpire was only a part of Steve's accomplishments in life, albeit a major part for him.

The group of umps from that period were close and nurtured friendships that lasted a lifetime. Steve and Tommy Corrodo and Pat D'Angelo remained particularly close.

D'Angelo was known to all of us as *Pitsie*. He was a little guy at 5'5", and in Italian the word *Pit-sa-de-geel* means small and so the shortened version , *Pitsie*. Pitsie also walked with a noticeable limp, the result of a hip injury he suffered as a kid whenstruck by a hit and run driver while playing stickball in the street.

Yet, despite the accident, Pat became a good pitcher. He developed excellent control, a good curve ball along with a sinker, change-up and a pretty good fast ball. In 1937 he went 5-0 at Brooklyn Tech high school. From that season through 1939 in high school and at the Parade Grounds, Pitsie won 32 games without suffering a loss. He played for teams out of Park Slope and South Brooklyn. In 1940 his team, the Hilford Club won the championship of the Intercommunity League, the forerunner of the Parade Grounds League. In that year he threw a no-hitter striking out 18 batters in a seven inning game.

Pat also played shortstop and caught along the way winding up his playing days as a semi-pro with the Springfield Greys. Playing against legendary semi-pro clubs like the Brooklyn Bushwicks, Pat was teammates with future major leaguers Sam Mele, Saul Ragovin and Buddy Kerr. By 1938 Pitsie gradually segued into umpiring, beginning another career that would last more than 40 years.

He garnered a well-deserved reputation not only for his ability and judgement on the field, but for his qualities as a human being off of it. As an umpire he controlled the game. One of the Park's veteran players Eddie Mack recalls that Pitsie "was a good umpire. We always wanted him when we played money games, but he was a tough bastard. He took nothing from no one."

Pitcher Bill Litras of Sacred Heart remembered Pitsie as an ump who "keeps the game going with no dissension. Pits never wavers when making a decision." A familiar sight to Parade Grounds regulars was Pitsie lying flat on his belly at home plate getting the best possible view of the tag. A recommendation was once made for Pat to umpire in the minors but was sidetracked because of his injury.

Once asked if he had any advice for ballplayers, Pitsie said, "Never argue with an umpire." Also asked what was the greatest satisfaction he got from umpiring, the littledynamo responded, "when a game is over and a player on a losing team pats me on the back and says, '*Nice game, Pits*'!"

All things considered it may be that *Pitsie* was the wrong name for this big little man. Perhaps for all those years he should have been called *Grande*.

One of the few who umpired in the major leagues after spending their youth at the Parade Grounds was Andy Olsen. Olsen spent thirteen seasons in the National League but preceded it with a minor league playing career. Andy grew up in Flatbush, at 606 Flatbush Avenue, to be precise, and played for the "Redbirds" at the Parade Grounds. His high school was Westinghouse Vocational and after graduation, Andy headed south to take a shot at pro ball. A left handed pitched, Olsen caught on with Andaloosia, an independent team in the Alabama State League. He won 18 games in 1950 and was drafted by the Pittsburgh Pirates.

Olsen went as far as Hollywood in the AAA Pacific Coast League and played for manager Bobby Bragan, before suffering a sore arm. Andy explains that it was a rotator cuff injury but in those days they called a tendon spasm. "I used to throw everyday between starts," he said. "I don't know, maybe It was overwork." Not willing to give in to it, the pitcher struggled through two more seasons, at Lincoln in the Western League and Waco in the Big State League where he still managed a record of 12-6. Olsen went to spring training in 1957 but the pain by this time had become too great to ignore and Andy got his release.

Like so many others in his position, he hated to get away from the game, but not like so many he chose umpiring as a way to remain in baseball. Olsen went to Montana and played some semi-pro ball to build up enough money to attend Al Sommers Florida umpire school. He was picked up by the Sophomore League in West Texas, New Mexico, and then spent three years in the Northern League. From there he went to the Eastern League where Andy was a part of an unusual occurrence, an umpires trade.

The trade took Olsen to the Pacific Coast League where a recommendation prompted the National League to take an option on his services. Two years later Andy Olsen was in the big time. Hitters remember their first hit in the majors; umpires recall their first ejection. For Olsen it was Leo Durocher. Andy's dad had been the catalyst for the youngster's dedication to the Brooklyn Dodgers and in the forties, Leo was the Dodgers skipper, and a popular one in Brooklyn.

Coming in contact with an old hero brought back memories for an old Brooklyn boy. He remembers being at Ebbets Field the day that super fan Hilda Chester gave center fielder Pete Reiser a note to give to Durocher. The note advised Leo to get relieverHugh Casey up in the bullpen because starting pitcher "Wyatt was losing it." Thinking that the note came from owner Larry McPhail, Durocher followed orders and almost lost the game. Olsen laughs at the memory. "When Leo found out, he went crazy," Andy said. And here was Durocher in the Cubs dugout, and here was Andy Olsen working behind home plate. "Randy Hundley was the catcher," he recalls, "and he was beefing about balls and strikes."

Olsen heard the unmistakable voice from the Cubs bench, "Don't mess with him, Randy, he's horseshit." And Leo was gone. "I got him three times," Olsen said. But he remembered another lesser known Durocher. The day Leo retired he came to the umpire's dressing room and said goodbye to umps Olsen and Tom Gorman and wished them well. "It was a nice thing for him to do," Andy said.

Olsen worked the plate in game 5 of the 1974 World Series between the Los Angeles Dodgers and the Oakland A's. Oakland won the series with that game 5 victory behind Blue Moon Odom with a save by Hall-Of-Fame closer Rollie Fingers. Olsen recalls with pride getting letters from umps Gorman and Shag Crawford commenting on calling a good game. Andy remembers his days at the Park as clearly as those major league years and recalls Joe Torre as "one of the best right handed hitters in the National League" during Olsen's time there. At 75 Andy Olsen is in retirement in St.

Petersburg,Florida; twelve hundred miles from the Park, but a whole lot closer in memory.

At the tail end of each season there would be an exhibition game in the Parade Grounds League between the managers and the umpires. The umpires were referred to in print as the "Ten Blind Mice" allowing for a short center fielder. Begun in 1950, the league tried to make this fun day an annual event.

In the 1958 game the umpires were beaten 8-7 to suffer their first defeat. Nat Maslin, a part-time coach with the Holy Innocents club had taken on the thankless task of umpiring the game. The umps good-naturedly stormed the beleagured Mr.Maslin at every opportunity. The *World-Telegram* reported Tom Corrada bellowing,"Get some new glasses, ump," at the bespectacled Maslin, and Pete Bellone's snarling, "Y'er blind - he never broke his wrists."

The managers victory was sparked by the pitching of Fred Weber and Joel Schwartz and the hitting of Chuck Robinson and Mike Rubino. The umpires' Steve Albanese cracked out a pair of hits and was "picked off base on both occasions." Diamond #1 had seen better baseball but never as much fun. The respite would be broken barely a week later when the natural order of things would be restored.

As we learn from the opening you cannot play baseball without an umpire. You sometimes hear it said that major league baseball considers using machines or radarto replace the umpire. No doubt it will someday be a probability, but to dehumanize the game would be to destroy it. The umpire is as much a part of the game as the leather glove and the Louisville

Slugger bat. Anything short of a Petey Larkin dusting off home plate on Diamond #1 and turning to bellow to the crowd in the bleachers, "PLAY BALL", would not be baseball at all.

XVIII.

On And On

"The jollity of aged men has much in common   with the mirth of children." -Hawthorne

It is the 1990s and a few of us *Old Boys of Summer* have gathered at Willowrook Park on Staten Island to toss a baseball around and relive some old times and to laugh. Harry Trimmer is here and so is "Irish" Eddie Jordan, the old fighter. Sibi Pepi, who played with the Bisons and the Senacas, is there , along with Tom Siracusa and Chick Chiarello of the Virginians.

While loosening up, Harry is regaling us with tales of a bygone era. "We booked this game," he says, "out in Bayside, Long Island and we need a couple a more guys so Kenny gets Chick to come along. They got this lefthander, about 35years old who's been in the minors for 10 years and he's got this slow curve that breaks about *this* wide." Smack! The ball hits the glove and echoes over the park."So Chick Ks three times and he don't talk to Kenny for five years. He says,'You brought me all the way out here for this?'"

Siracusa tells us how lucky we are that he makes the time for us since he is so occupied playing paddleball. "Al Marchese was playing golf today and so is Peter Rabbit." Pepi loves to play golf. " I've been playing golf since I stopped playing baseball." He tells us that for the first three years "I hit nothing but infield flies." Chick hates golf, "Yeah," he says, "Pepi's had it, he's done."

Jim McElroy of the Cadets comes over and Siracusa greets him with a hug and everyone waves or calls out a hello.

There is a snappy pepper game in progress. "Way ta go, Chicky baby," says Tom Siracusa. McElroy calls out some advice, "I hope you guys all got your cups on." "I don't go noplace without it," Sebi Pepi tells him.

Siracusa starts in on me. "Andy was the biggest banjo hitter we ever had. He would hit a blooper to right, a bouncer up the middle and another bloop over third...." "Oh, no" Chick interrupts, "he never hit anything over third." "That's right," Tom agrees, "everything was up the middle or to the right side. But he could run," he adds. "I'll give him that."

"Hey, look," somebody says, "it's the Moose." Tom joins Jim McElroy on the bench and a few of the boys go over to say hello. Tom has a noticeable limp. A voice says, "I hear Billy had a stroke." The reminders of aging men are in evidence. Harry starts another story. "Remember when we played in the Luis Olmo League with Manalapan Shipping...."

I had left the Parade Grounds in 1965 and had little contact after that. I played two years of softball on Randall's Island with my company, Burlington Industries, and then moved to Staten Island. Frank Chiarello and Carl Hottenger hooked me up with a club they were playing with and I spent the next twenty-eight years in Staten Island softball. At 56 years old I figured that it was time to quit. I mentioned it to a friend, Pat Granowski, and he suggested we toss around a baseball one morning a week. Pat was a retired police officer and worked as a court officer with Mondays off. I was employed at the Brooklyn Public Library and did not have to report to work until 12 noon on Mondays.

Pat had a friend. He and Frank Fellicetti and myself began workouts. What a thrill to hit a baseball again. We would drop a dozen balls on the mound and with only one fielder would go around collecting the batted balls after each turn. Granowski was also from Brooklyn and like me lived on Staten Island. We gradually built up our little group and the ritual still goes on today.

Pat Granowski was from South Brooklyn, 20 Street and 5 Avenue. He was at the Parade Grounds as early as Grasshopper ball with a team called the "Sparks", and then the "Bluejays." They played in Cookie Lorenzo's Parade Grounds League in the middle fifties. Then Pat took a turn most of us hadn't followed. For his first high school year, he entered the seminary of the Graymoor Friars near Watkins Glen in upstate New York. But there were difficulties. With an ailing father and a large family, money was not readily available, and so the youngster returned to Brooklyn and began attending Manual training high school.

It was a far different experience. Granowski recalls that on his first day at the new school, he witnessed some kids toss a ladder out of a seven story window. "I just came from a seminary," he says with astonishment even after nearly a half century has passed. " I couldn't believe what I saw." But somehow Pat settled in and played football and sandlot baseball at the Park.

He traveled by Fifth Avenue bus to 39 street and took a trolley car to Park Circle. Pat recalls a historical moment. It was on one of those trips that the trolley car conductor informed him that this was the very last trip that this mode of city transportation, the very one that had given Brooklyn's *trolley* Dodgers their name, would make. All of Brooklyn's trolleys would be replaced by buses.

Like most of the Brooklyn kids during the fifties, Granowski spent a good deal of his youth in and around Ebbets Field, ofttimes more around than in. The youngsters would congregate where baseballs were prone to travel. Foul balls over the first and third base roofs and beyond the right field fence on Bedford Avenue. These used balls had more value than merely as a souvenir or a plaything. They were often used as a medium of exchange. At times it meant free entry into the ballpark, or a sale of 50 cents or a dollar, or as a payoff to an usher who'd let you sit in a box seat, with the admonition, "If somebody comes, you gotta give up the seat."

"Do I get my ball back?" Pat remembers only sneerful looks in answer to his question.

He recalls the thrill of actually parking Roy Campanella's Cadillac in the lot on Bedford Avenue. "I never drove before," he says , "the guy just said, 'this pedal is the gas, that one is the brake.' " When his older brother Joe signed with the Giants and went to play in the Midwest League, he would see to it that his kid brother was supplied with used baseballs.

Already the entrepreneur, the younger Granowski devised a way to make a profit from the old balls. He would run to a spot where a ball landed, often inside the park, and pretend to have snagged the prize. Having rubbed away the Midwest League identity, he would sell the ball to a fan happy to get a souvenir off the bat of Gil Hodges, Duke Snider or Roy Campanella.

"Sometimes," he said, "I would make four or five dollars in one day. Not a bad take for a 13-year-old kid with no money."

After an army tour from '62 to '64 , he came back to Brooklyn and baseball. On a memorable day on Diamond #1, Pat belted one over the refreshment stand beyond the left field fence. In a later at bat he drove a ball to the deepest reaches of center field where it was caught. Approached by a scout from the Baltimore Orioles after the game, Granowski was invited to a try-out at Midwood Field. Taking some swings against pitchers doing their best to impress, Pat remembers hard throwers. "This guy was throwing inside and I'm ducking," he says, "and it's supposed to be batting practice." but he managed to get good wood on a few. Told they would hear from the club

THE BOYS OF BROOKLYN

by mail, it was two months and late in the season when he received a postcard asking him to come back for another look. Once more a young Parade Grounder had to face a decision . Married with a child on the way, Granowski had just gotten notice of acceptance by the New York City Police Department. It seemed a more secure employment at the time and so Pat turned in his dreams.

I had no further contact with the Parade Grounds after 1965. On days when I had to report to the Library's Main Branch at Grand Army Plaza, I would drive past the Park. I saw the clubhouse razed in the mid-sixties and was saddened by it. Sometimes you identify decrepit old buildings as having *character* , and that was how I always felt about that huge old edifice. The gaping space where it once stood left me with memories and I often told myself that I had left the old Park just at the right time, knowing also that no more quality ballplayers would emerge from there, that our generation represented the last and the best.

I was totally ignorant of the decaying conditions through the seventies and eighties, engrossed only in the smug satisfaction that I had been a part of the last golden age of the fabled Parade Grounds. It was only in the last few years that I learned with some shock that future major leaguers like Willie Randolph, Shawon Dunston and John Candelaria had been spawned at my old ball grounds.

Lee Mazilli had played there as had Manny Ramirez. And so had the New York Mets star closer, John Franco. Franco grew up at the Park at a difficult time as the fields were in disrepair and the Parade Grounds was a shambles prior to the

2004 renovation. But John developed nonetheless and played at Lafayette high school and St. John's University before being drafted by the Los Angeles Dodgers in June of 1981. At St. John's University he teamed up with future major league star Frank Viola. A bird-dog scout had this to say about Franco while at college:"Great control, nothing above the knees. Good pitching selection, far ahead of his peers in setting up hitters and changing speeds. Fastball moves away from right handed hitters."

From sandlot ball and throughout his minor league career, John was a starting pitcher, winning ten games at San Antonio in the Texas League in '82. Traded to Cincinnati in 1982, Franco came to the Reds in 1984 as a relief pitcher and did not start another game in professional baseball. He was traded to the Mets in 1989 and began a memorable period playing in his home town, developing into one the of baseball's outstanding closers. He pitched in two playoff series and won a game in the 2000 World Series against the Yankees. Franco completed his career with 424 major league saves, in the top five on the all time list. John Franco is one more Parade Grounder who is a possible candidate for the Hall-Of-Fame in Cooperstown.

Former Yankee star infielder and current New York Mets manager Willie Randolph signed his first professional contract at the Parade Grounds. "I signed at field 7," Randolph said. "The scout from the Pirates was nickel-and-diming me....and I signed for $5,000. Little did he know I would have signed for nothing.

A memory of Willie from the Parade Grounds is very clear with Marty Glickman when he played against Randolph in the American Legion League. Glickman was with the "Rams", and Willie with "Cummings Post." Marty remembers him as "very quiet and classy....he hit line drives up the middle and was always on base. He was called 'little Willie' by some."

At a Legion All-Star team tryout, Glickman found himself at second base and Randolph at shortstop in an infield workout. Prospects like Randolph were known to the rest of us as they were Park celebrities on their way into the pros. "I was so nervous," Marty recalls, "that I kept fumbling the toss from Willie on the pivot throw to first. I was visibly upset and he came over to me and quietly said, 'relax, man.' It helped and I never forgot that."

Possibly an early revelation of the managerial qualities that Willie Randolph later showed that he possessed. In the fall of 2006, Jay Price in the *Staten Island Advance* wrote, "one of the things that made the season more fun at Shea - at a time when so many professional athletes act like a day at the park is like a sentence, instead of a gift - is that so many of Willie Randolph's guys look like they're having fun."

During the play-offs that year, Willie made some moves that seemed unorthodox.He left a right-handed pitcher in to face a left-handed pinch hitter, and in game seven did just the opposite, allowing a left hander to pitch to a tough right handed hitter in Albert Poulhols. Both moves worked out in the Mets favor. "I've always managed by my gut, my instinct," Randolph was quoted as saying. "I go by what I see, and I don't second-guess myself." Instincts that may, perhaps, had begun festering at the Coney Island avenue facility thirty or so years before.

In a 2007 game he pulled his star shortstop, Jose Reyes, from the game because he failed to run out a ground ball. This was Parade Grounds style of ball and although Willie gathered his great experience from all his years in the majors as a player and coach, there may be some subliminal Parade Grounds murmurings lingering there also.

The Bonnies' Boys Club was established in 1949 and built a history over more than 57 years. Al Bonnie Sr. owned and operated a company called the "Bonnie Movers." With a desire to give back to the community that helped to make him a success, Al established an organization dedicated to youth baseball, the "Bonnie Boys Club." With his sons Al Jr. and Joe managing, the Bonnies began to proliferate throughout the fifties.

Jerry Katzke was a player for the Bonnies in the early sixties and by 1966 had become one of the coaches. Devoted to the organization, Katzke ultimately reached his current status as manager of the senior entry in the Parade Grounds League, a director of the PGL and President and Athletic Director of the entire Bonnies' organization. Now with 19 teams ranging in age from five to college age, they compete in several leagues and take part in regional and national tournaments annually.

While not affiliated with Little League, the Bonnies conduct instructional leagues for 5-7 year olds. From there they are elevated through the system to college level. There are now more than 400 youngsters taking part in the activities. The primary aim of the organization is, as Jerry Katzke points out, "to develop the skills and a sense of sportsmanship among the youth." Proudly he notes that there are 60 Bonnies' in colleges with more than half on academic or athletic scholarships. The Bonnies have over the years been one of the most dominant organizations at the Parade Grounds and in Brooklyn youth development.

Mike and Richie Hartley played with the Bonnies in the 1970s and '80s. Mike played shortstop and second base with the Bonnie Cubs at the Parade Grounds and in high school for Bishop Ford who used the Park as their home field. Richie, seven years his senior went to Tilden high and both brothers ultimately played ball for Youth Services.

While playing short with Youth Services, Richie Hartley played alongside Shawon Dunston at third base. Both boys were scouted by the Chicago Cubs while at the Parade Grounds, with Dunston getting the call in 1982.

The Parade Grounds has not been without its benefactors over the years, some more notable than others. The *New York Post* reported that after reading about the financial plight of a local Ty Cobb Freshman Division Team in 1982, an anonymous donation of $2,000 was sent to the ball club. This generosity allowed the boys to travel to Memphis, Tennessee to compete in a national tournament. It was screen tough guy, James Cagney, who made the generous gesture after reading about the Bay Ridge teens' problem in the *Post*. "He's just a softie," said a Cagney spokesman, "he just loves to do things without anyone knowing it." (1)

Nick Defendis came from Bensonhurst, at Avenue U and West 9 Street and was one of a long list of outstanding ball players to attend Lafayette high school. Born in 1956, Nick was part of the Little League generation and played in the Gil Hodges League along with teammate Lee Mazzilli. He recalls that a 5 lb salami was given to any kid hitting a home run. "It was the greatest thrill," he says, " when the concession guy handed you the salami, it wasn't even wrapped, and everybody knew you had hit a home run."

Playing with the Little League All-Stars , the team played in different parks around Brooklyn and in Long Island. After high school, Defendis played for the Chiefs at the Parade Grounds. Having an extremely strong throwing arm, Nick turned to catching and was good enough to be offered a contract with the Detroit Tigers. But by this time , 1979, he had married and started a business and felt tha the had to pass on the uncertainty of professional baseball.

Nick is the middle rung of three generations of athletes. His dad was a Golden Gloves fighter and dedicated to his son's welfare. One day he stood behind home plate at the Parade Grounds watching his son take a called third strike that both father and son agreed was "way outside." The plate umpire was Dan Liotta. Defendis Sr. informed Liotta, "I'll see *you* later." As Dan tells it, "Nicky had to put his arm over my shoulder and tell his dad, 'it's okay, he's a friend of mine. Leave him alone.'"

Nick's son , a center fielder from Xavarian high school was signed to a pro contract by scout Joe Nigro and has played in the organization of the Chicago Cubs.

As a strong armed catcher, Nick was asked why catchers threw so few runners out stealing today, he said that "years ago, the players had more savvy, more attention to detail and a better approach to the game." Pitchers worked on such fundamentals as holding runners on, giving catchers a better chance to prevent steals. Defendis is engrossed in these kind of fundamentals as he monitors the baseball organization he founded in 2003.

The Richmond County Baseball Corp. conducts instructional fall leagues and winter clinics to instill in these youngsters the proper way to play the game of baseball. Nick says that the mission of the organization is to prepare young boys for college recruitment. The aim is to aid players in obtaining scholarships by achieving the utmost in academics and athletics. To this end they have succeeded brilliantly. Last year alone the RCBBC has helped several players to succeed in being the recipients of over $600,000 in scholarship awards. These scholarships came from Seten Hall , St. Joseph University, Concordia college and Malloy.

"Perfect Game Baseball" is a recruitment program for colleges. They conduct workouts in various parts of the country and transmit the films on web-sites. In today's technological world, a college coach can tune into his computer and scout players without leaving his chair at home. Richmond County Baseball has teamed up with Perfect Game to run try-outs on Staten Island.

Defendis has recruited some strong coaching for his ball clubs including fathers who have sons in the program, like John Franco. Another dad with a thirteen year old son playing is Phil Venturino. Phil grew up in Bay Ridge in Brooklyn and after his first years with a team called the Rams, went on to one of the borough's classic clubs, the Ty Cobbs. Phil's most formative years were from 1977-'81, the latter season he was chosen as "pitcher of the year" in the senior division.

Venturino pitched a complete nine inning win over a New Jersey aggregation at Johnstown, Pennsylvania in the National Tournament in '81 and then attended St. Francis College where he was listed in the amateur draft the following year. He signed with the California Angels two years later and began the climb through the minor leagues. On the strength of an 11-6 season and then a 15-3 in AA, Phil reached Edmundton in the class AAA Pacific Coast league.

It was here that the organization effected a change; Venturino would become a relief pitcher, a right handed set-up man. There was a glut of starters at the top and it was determined that Phil's sinker and slider would qualify him for the role. But the "no room at the top" specter evolved into the sore arm syndrom that has cut so many careers down too soon. In this case Venturino thought he knew the cause. That spring he began doing some weight training which he believes was responsible for a tear in a bicep tendon. He took a year off, but his velosity was so reduced that the end came shortly after.

Phil's Parade Grounds years were studded with memories. Playing there at a time when the conditions were severely deteriorating, he recalls how the pitching mounds were protruding so far above the ground, that you had to step down into a hole when delivering a pitch. But Venturino calls his experience with the Ty Cobbs in the Parade Grounds League "tremendous." He said that "all the Ty Cobbs went onto

Division I colleges or signed professional contracts." He shakes his head at the memory. "I loved it," he says with emotion. "I still miss it."

The program that Nick Defendis started is growing in other ways also. A complex of baseball diamonds have been constructed in the Travis section of StatenIsland. They will be " well cared for with excellent facilities for boys to play baseball," according to Defendis. And he should know what it takes. Nick was at the Parade Grounds in the late seventies and eighties when the playing areas had degenerated to torn up patches of dirt and sod. Cricket games were being played at the same time as baseball and overlapped so much so that players were crowding into each other. There was no authority at the Park and virtually no maintenance. These are the conditions that greeted those young players who developed their skills in this environment.

A boy born in 1972 in the Dominican Republic would find his way to the Parade Grounds and to an outstanding career in the Major Leagues. Manual Aristides Ramirez grew up playing baseball every day in that now legendary lode of raw baseball talent. "I remember that my mother would get upset, because I never came home in time to eat at the table with the rest of the family," Manny would later say, "I was always at the field playing."

Then in 1985 when Manny was 13 years old, his young life would take a new turn. He and his family moved to New York and settled in Washington Heights. He continued to play baseball at 170th street and Amsterdam avenue and then at George Washington High School where his developing talents led his school to three straight Manhattan Division championships. It was during these years while Manny was receiving All-City honors , that he played his summer ball with Youth Services and his travels around the city brought the very promising youth to Brooklyn's Parade Grounds.

Ramirez was selected in the first round of the Major League Amateur Draft in1991 by the Cleveland Indians and signed by scout Joe Delucca. His road to Big-League stardom began in Burlington in the Appalachian League and took him to the Majors in 1993. On December 12, 2000, he signed an eight year $160 million contract with the Boston Red Sox and was a part of that phenomenal playoff in 2004 when Boston won eight straight games to defeat the Yankees and then sweep the Cardinals in the World Series. Manny's performance earned him the World Series Most Valuable Player Award. John Harper in the *New York Daily News* in 2006 called Ramirez "the most feared right handed hitter in the game." For Manny it has been a dream come true. "I think God is blessing me with a lot of stuff," Ramirez says, "there's nothing I can complain about."

Pete Falcone Sr. , a right handed pitcher, played semi-pro ball with the "Cyclones" in Brooklyn as well as in the rest of the metropolitan area. It remained, however, for his son, Pete Jr. , a pitcher throwing from the port side to take the family name all the way to the major leagues.

The younger Falcone grew up in the Bensonhurst section on Avenue Z. He playedhis Little League ball with Gravesend where he teamed up with Lee Mazilli, another future big timer. Pete was an alumni of Lafayette high school as was Mazzilli, just two more names added to that distinguished list. Falcone played with the Gil Hodges team, named, of course for the Dodger star, an icon in Brooklyn, and recalls a heated rivalry with the Ty-Cobbs.

The Parade Grounds of the seventies was deteriorating badly and Pete says that the "conditions were horrible." Even so , "all thirteen diamond were filled all day each Saturday and Sunday." So much so, he remembers , that balls hit in the gaps might get picked up by a fielder playing on another diamond. Young Pete began to draw scouts in high school when Lafayette won the city championship in 1972, his senior year.

Scouted by Herb Stein of the Minnesota Twins and Steve Lembo of the Los Angeles Dodgers, Falcone was ultimately drafted by the San Francisco Giants, and signed by scout Sal Margaglio. Pete reported to Great Falls, Montana for the 1973 season. The left hander got off to a great start going 8-1 in the Pioneer League. He won ten while losing only four with Fresno in the class C California League in 1974 and was in San Francisco by 1975.

Traded to the Cardinals, Pete spent three seasons in St. Louis before coming home to the New York Mets for the '79 season. Though happy to be in New York, Falcone said that it was "difficult because the Mets had bad teams." He teamed up with a second cousin, Joe Pignatano, then a Mets coach; the man responsible for the tomato garden in the left field bullpen at Shea stadium. "I was a part of that." Pete says with the pride of an Italian gardener.

The Mets manager was Joe Torre. The same "laid back , easy going" manager and as well respected by his Met players as the later Yankees. As a starter, Falcone would take about 15 minutes to get loose before a start, "a little longer if it was cold." Pete ended his career with the Atlanta Braves in 1984. Traded three times in his career, the ten-year major league veteran said that trades never bothered him. "Who cares. We were just happy to be there. You didn't care who you played for."

He acknowledges how different today's game is, however. With weight training, players are stronger, "but not better equipped," he said. Middle relievers are now specialists. Falcone echoes the sentiments of so many others when he says that "money drives baseball today. We had more passion. Take the money away," he says ,"and how many would play for nothing?" He is emphatic. "We would have played for nothing," he says, probably remembering fondly when he did.

John Candelaria was the "Candy Man", all 6'7" and 218 pounds of him. Born in1953, John couldn't avoid the Parade Grounds even if he wanted to. His family lived in an apartment at the corner of Caton and Coney Island Avenues, across the street from Park Circle and directly opposite the Bocci court. As a youngster John would head over to the Park on summer and week-end mornings and play until supper time. His sister Maria, a Staten Island attorney, remembers how "my mom would look out the window and pick out the biggest kid and call him home for dinner."

John started his baseball career with his school team, "Holy Innocents", and later with the Brooklyn Mets. Parade Grounders of the time like Dan Liotta, have said that at age 14 and 15 John was throwing bullets. "I was blessed with a strong arm," Candelaria acknowledges. Scouts began to mark their territory early in John's boyhood career with the Pittsburgh Pirates in the vanguard.

Former Yankee Hector Lopez, scouting for the Pirates visited the Candelaria home when John was still in high school. Candelaria did not play baseball for two years and in that time the towering youngster went to Puerto Rico and played basketball for the Quebradillas Pirates. He was visited there by the Pirates Danny Murtaugh and scout Dutch Deutch and drafted by Pittsburgh in the second round. Then came the negotiation stage.

The Pirates flew John and his parents to Pittsburgh to work out for Murtaugh and general manager Joe Brown. The club also brought in a baseball , and Puerto Rican icon, Roberto Clemente. Teams often used idols to help them to sign a prospect, as when the Dodgers had Jackie Robinson make a phone call to Tommy Davis. At the meeting the Pirates offered Candelaria a bonus of $25,000 to sign. Clemente told Brown that he would speak to the parents in Spanish. He proceeded to advise them not to accept the offer. "It's not enough," he explained in their native language, "he can get forty thousand." They did as he said and John got his $40,000 bonus and was a Pirate.

Playing winter ball in Puerto Rico, the Brooklynite was joined by two other kids who spent those early days at the Parade Grounds, Lee Mazilli and Willie Randolph. It was in 1973 that the twenty year old went to Charleston in the Western Carolina League and posted a record of 10-2. He won 11 games in '74 and after starting the next season in the AAA International League came to the majors. That season, 1975, he combined for a 15 -7 record and John Candelaria was on his way to a eighteen year big league career.

That year Pittsburgh went to the play-offs where they were swept by the Cincinnati Reds, though on October 7, Candelaria struck out 14 Reds before being beaten by a Pete Rose home run in the eighth inning. In 1979 John was a member of the Pirates World Championship team after extracting their revenge on the Reds in the LCS. In the Series Candelaria combined with relief pitcher Kent Tekulve on a 4-0 shutout victory in game six, setting up the game seven triumph for the Pirates.

His best season was 1977 when he went 20-5 with a 2.34 ERA and pitched 230.2 innings. The flame throwing left handed finished with a career record of 177-122, but that was still not the whole story.

On August 9, 1976, twenty-two year-old John Candelaria achieved a pitcher's Valhalla when he threw a no-hit, no-run game in the major leagues. He did it against the Los Angeles Dodgers. He survived a third inning situation after a walk and two errors had loaded the bases and continued to a 2-0 victory. But things weren't always so tough for the young pitcher. On September 16, 1975, he eased to a 22-0 massacre win over the Cubs in a game that set a major league record for the biggest score in a shut-out game in the twentieth century.

Plagued by injuries to his back, knee and elbow over his career, Candelaria wonders today "what I could have done with no injuries." But John has no regrets about his fine career and exhibits a trait that seems to be rare among today's major leaguers; Pride. The pitch-count mentality of today, "I don't like them," or the current attitude of five innings and out, has no place in the Candelaria mentality.

Speaking of the 2006 post season performance of the Tigers Kenny Rogers' 23 consecutive scoreless innings, John is incredulous over Rogers' removal from the game after 8 shut-out innings. "Eight shut-out innings in the World Series," he says, "and a 5-0 lead. I don't care about the 23 innings, I want a shut-out in the World Series." But closers are a way of life in the big leagues today. "Well," the major league veteran concedes " I'll take a Rivera behind me."

Later in his career, Candelaria did a stint with both New York teams , the Mets and the Yankees, putting up a 13-7 record with the latter club in 1988. The trek from Caton Avenue to the top of the pile was a triumph for the kid from Brooklyn and one more gold star for those alumni of the skinned diamonds of Park Circle.

Names like "Candy" evoke a flood of memories from Parade Grounders. Marty Glickman played against Willie Randolph, and Lee Mazzilli as well as John Candelaria, when he played second base and shortstop for St. Bernadette in the CYO League. His mind serves up a championship game at the Park in which his club faced Candelaria. The already hard throwing young pitcher pitched a 2-0 shutout in which he struck out 17 batters and gave up only two hits. The memory glistens for Marty because he got both hits and was the only hitter in the lineup not to strike out. He calls Candelaria the most talented player he ever faced. "He exuded an air of superiority and confidence," Glickman remembers, " but," he adds, " it was obviously deserved."

An integral part of the Park experience was being on the same field with players who distinguished themselves in later years. To have seen them and played with and against them at the sandlot level allowed each of us a subliminal brush with the glory that would become a part of them.

XIX.

Rise Of The Phoenix

"A mythical bird that never dies, the phoenix represents our capacity for vision....It creates intense excitement and deathless inspiration." - The Feng Shui Handbook

The Parade Grounds fell into disrepair in the seventies and eighties, then like the mythical Phoenix rising from the ashes, it was reborn at the turn of the new century. Amid the labyrinth of financial appropriations and city politics, the reincarnation was nothing short of miraculous. Bobby Moore, playing second base for Mary, Queen of Heaven in the CYO League at the Park in and around 1980 recalls horrendous playing conditions. "It was a disaster to play there," he said, "the whole place was covered with rocks and bottles."

By the late fifties, although in constant use, the open fields had become dust bowls, they were scarcely maintained; mounds were flattened out and the holes in the batter's boxes had become abysses; so that a hitter lost precious time climbing out of the deep pits to begin his journey to first base. The surrounding neighbors in the apartment dwellings on Caton Avenue and Parade Place began to complain that they could not raise their windows on Saturdays and Sundays for fear that the dust would settle on their furniture. In an attempt to alleviate this problem, a layer of oil was spread on the infield dirt in order to keep the dust down and that created offensive odors, not to mention the sliding players carrying remnants of the smelly lubricant on their person. Nothing less than an overhaul was the only possible prescription .

In March 1958 it was announced , once again, that money would be appropriated for the reconstruction of the Parade Grounds. Parks Commissioner Robert Moses said that $1,648,000 will be requested in the 1959 budget and work will commence next year. Although this plan had apparently been talked about for years, the one ray of hope this time was that $41,000 has been included in the '58budget for preparation of the redevelopment plans. The planned first phrase called for a new field house, 10 clay tennis courts, four baseball diamonds and bleachers, two football fields and horseshoe courts.

The *Daily News* on March 24 quoted a local fan who said, "I've been carrying on a one-man campaign for years to get the backstops fixed, it's been unsuccessful. The whole playing area is run-down." In June of 1959 it was reported that the Board of Estimate will be asked to "launch the Parade Ground rehabilitation program by approving the first phase of the $1,500,000 project." (1) The idea was to transform the Park into a diversified recreation center to now include a playground. The 53-year-old clubhouse would be replaced by a new structure, the funds of which were expected to be provided by the 1960 and 1961 Capital Budgets. By 1965 when I left the Park, work had not yet begun.

Progress can often be disheartening. I didn't see it happening, but one day I drove by and the old clubhouse was gone. The big, broken down, peeling, warped old clubhouse was committed to memory. I never entered the Grounds again until the ribbon cutting ceremony on June 26, 2004. As a result I was not aware of the transfiguration of the diamonds themselves. There were now ten instead of thirteen. Our beloved Diamond #1 was gone. The numbers had changed so that they were unrecognizable to those of us who preceded the altering. On the Caton Avenue side there was now diamonds number seven, eight nine and ten, in place of one through five. On Parade Place there were two fields, numbers five and six and one through four ran along Parkside Avenue. The sixties renovation also brought indoor tennis courts at the corner of Park Circle and Parkside Avenue.

But there was now more space for soccer, a sport that was beginning to grow among the kids and in the schools. In part changes in the sixties and later were motivated by the changing demographics of the neighborhood. There was also ,over the next two decades a graduating deterioration of the facilities. Tightening city budgets limited the number and hours of maintenance allowed for the Park. Always in the past , teams themselves would lend a hand. The *Parkies* would let them use shovels and other tools and the players and managers cared for the fields, particularly after inclement weather.

Dan Liotta was there during those years. "We couldn't get shovels or wheel-barrels to do the work ourselves," he said.

The area was not cleared of debris. Broken glass and rubbish permeated the Grounds. Vandalism was rampant and no personnel was provided for maintenance . Roberta Newman, an educator from New York University still resides in the Park area. "Unfortunately," she says, most of her memories are of "down-trodden, litter filled fields of weeds in a decidedly bad part of the neighborhood. Sad to say, I saw more junkies than ballplayers."

Yet in spite of the deteriorating conditions , the kids came out to play and struggled through it all. In those years from th 1970s on, players continued to make their way to the pros. A random look at a copy of *The Sporting News* in the spring of 1971 reveals a dozen former Parade Grounds players in the lineups of major league teams. That class of '71 also brought a plethora of first year players from the Park debuting in the major leagues; among them Rusty Torres with the Yankees, and Richie Zisk wearing the uniform of the Pittsburgh Pirates.

Rosendo Torres was born in Aquadilla, Puerto Rico in 1948. A switch-hitting outfielder who got some valuable playing time at the Parade Grounds, Rusty signed with the Yankees and went to Greensboro, North Carolina in the Carolina League in 1967. By 1971 Torres was in AAA ball where he hit .290 in 133 games for Syracuse, earning him a promotion to the big club at seasons end. He appeared in nine games for the Yankees and hit .385. Altogether Torres spent nine years in the majors and had over 1300 major league at-bats.

Frank Tepedino was a member of the Youth Service League on a club managed by his uncle, a former minor league infielder, also named Frank Tepedino. Young Frank was a left handed first baseman/outfielder, signed by the Baltimore Orioles and drafted from that organization by the New York Yankees in November , 1966. Tepedino appeared in nine games with New York in '67 and split the seasons of 1969 and '70 between the majors and the minors.

After hitting .355 with five home runs at Syracuse in the AAA International League, Frank was expected to have a good long look in 1971,but in June he was traded to the Milwaukee Brewers. Tepedino stayed in the major leagues for eight seasons finishing up with Atlanta in 1975, batting .304 in 1973 while appearing in 74 games.

Shawon Dunston played in the Youth Service League in the late seventies before signing with the Cubs. He reached the majors in 1985 and stayed there for18 seasons. The shortstop played in the post season with the 1989 Cubs and again with the St. Louis Cardinals in 2000 and the Giants in 2002. He spent part of one season in his home town in 1999 when the Mets went to the play-offs.

In the nineties Luis Lopez , Rafael Novoa and Rey Palacios all got a whiff of the big time. Kevin Baez played some shortstop for the New York Mets between1990 and '93, and Nelson Figueroa had 33 big league starts at the turn of the newcentury.

The Mets' John Franco got his start at the Parade Grounds and played there prior to signing with the LA Dodgers in 1981.

"I have a lot of fond memories of the place," he said. "But to be honest, the conditions weren't that great. I remember having to share the field with a soccer team and a lot of rocks." An alliance of sorts was struck between the baseball and soccer leagues to help alleviate some of the conflicts that persisted between the two sports, but budget cuts regularly reduced funding for the city's parks and recreational facilities.

Things came to a head in the mid-nineties. Debbie Romano , an organizer with the Prospect Park Alliance witnessed her 14-year-old son, Thomas, chase a fly ball at the Park, step on a can and pull a groin muscle. Mrs. Romano decided that it was time for action on a possible renovation plan for the entire facility. Jerry Katzke of the Bonnies Boys Club allied in the course and by 1998 a master plan was close to consummation.

By the spring of 2000 another thorn appeared in the thicket. The New York Mets and the New York Yankees had agreed to enter teams in the New York-Penn League, a short season class A minor league. The joint agreement superceded the need for each major league club to approve the others actions. The idea of two teams in the adjoining boroughs would, it was hoped, stimulate an Interboro rivalry dedicated to selling tickets. Plans were laid to build new stadiums in the boroughs of Brooklyn and Staten Island. But temporary homes were needed to be found for the 2001 season while construction was taking place. Staten Island solved its problem by the use of the field belonging to SI Community College in Willowbrook, but in Brooklyn there were additional ruts in the road posed by a conflict between Mayor Rudy Giuliani and Borough President Howard Golden over the idea of constructing a temporary facility for the Brooklyn team at the Parade Grounds.

There were two sides to the growing conflict. One, who thought that allowing the minor league field to be built and retained would guarantee a rehabilitation of the Park. The opposing view thought it detrimental to give up their facility even for the short time required and some balked about private admissions being charged at a public facility.

Confusion arose because of the varying views and organizations that were becoming involved. The Economic Development Corporation - the EDC, a quasi-public development agency that is a "conduit for most of the city's spending on economic development" was in support of the minor league park proposal. Community Board 14 has responsibility to oversee the Parade Grounds, and groups like the American Youth Soccer Organization (AYSO), who utilize the Grounds , were deeply concerned about the outcome. A march across the Brooklyn Bridge to City Hall was organized by soccer families and community residents. An organization leading the effort was ACORN the Association of Community Organization for Reform. The kids chanted all the way, "We like soccer a whole lot! We don't need a parking lot!"

A public meeting brought all the factions together. Borough President Howard Golden reiterated his position against the Mets' affiliation plans. Golden had been holding out for a higher level minor league or independent team. Mark Naison, of the Bonnies youth baseball league bemoaned "elected officials so willing to sell out the Bonnies." Councilman Stephen DiBrienza accused the EDC of setting part of the community against part of the community. And he stated that the plan for renovation by Prospect Park administrator Tupper Thomas "can be done without this temporary ballpark!"

The president of the Prospect Park Alliance is Tupper Thomas. Ms Thomas moved to New York from Minneapolis, Minnesota in 1969 and settled in the Crown Heights section of Brooklyn. She became administrator of the Alliance in 1980. It was in the late eighties that the Alliance under Ms. Thomas began a campaign to raise private funds for the care of Prospect Park, and, by extension, the Parade Grounds.

Forced to operate within the quandary of city politics; albeit par for the course; the unraveling of which would constitute a minor municipal miracle, the Alliance plunged ahead. Debbie Romano said at the time," to get a few ballfields fixed, we had to go to war - and boy, did we get caught in the political crossfire."

Now the opposing factions mounted the parapets. The Brooklyn Cyclones loomed as a force in the political battle that raged between Mayor Giuliani and Brooklyn Borough President Howard Golden. New York Mets owner Fred Wilpon suggested building a temporary home for the projected Cyclones on the Park site. There would be a parking area in addition to the stadium , which would later be turned into soccer fields. The ballpark would remain for the use of the sandlot teams. The brass ring here was that the city would foot the bill 100 %. Mayor Guiliani was in full support of the plan.

It was at this juncture that the terrible tangled web of city politics and conflicts arose. Brooklyn Borough President Howard Golden opposed the plan. It was his idea that the borough deserved a stronger representative minor league presence. At least an AA or a triple A franchise. The battle was on. The Alliance would have been happy to accept the plan that allowed the Cyclones at the Park for one year, in exchange for which they would have no financial obligation and would enjoy the use of the entire facilities once the Cyclones moved into their permanent home in Coney Island.

Golden fought the plan on whatever grounds he could muster. He brought a lawsuit against the Mayor to block the plan, charging that it had not gone through the mandated public review for the stadium construction. He claimed the city needed to file an "Environmental Impact Statement." The city and the Mets' promise to overhaul the Parade Grounds was made contingent on lawsuits being dropped. This from Economic Development Corp. President Michael Carey. While a portion of the community activists agreed, Community Board 14 and Borough President Golden refused.

City Hall dropped the plan in January 2001 and the Mets looked to St. Johns University in Queens where the city agreed to upgrade the school's field for the Cyclone's use. The *Daily News* reported in March, 2001,that it was "a sweet moment for Golden, whose feud with Giuliani has reached an intensity and vitriol rare even in this city's bare-knuckled politics." Not wanting to have egg on his face following his political in-fighting victory, Golden then announced that he would put up $10.3 million of capital money he controled to which will be added $1.5 million already committed city money.

Henry Christensen, Chairman of the Prospect Park Alliance praised Golden, "the result is what the community wanted, which is a first class set of fields." The Alliance, spearheaded by Director Tupper Thomas had at this point raised $450,000 aimed at maintaining the renovation project. A timetable was established calling for completion in 2004. After four years of renovation, the Park was ready to reopen and an official ribbon cutting ceremony took place on June 26, 2004.

To the old-timers of the mid-century Parade Grounds, it was sad to see the 13 baseball diamonds reduced to 4 with an additional two for softball. But otherwise the changes are awesome. There are now eleven fields. Field number 3 boasts major league dimensions, with dugouts, lights and a scoreboard. There are bleachers reminiscent of the old Diamonds # 1 and 13. There is included a state-of-the-art football field with artificial turf as well as a soccer field   Five of the fields are covered with the artificial turf and a new irrigation system will keep the natural grass fields maintained.

One of the innovative features of the new Parade Grounds is this artificial grass, called *Field Turf.* A new mixture that makes the ground softer than dirt. Made from a composite of sand, rubber, and *Nike Grind;* something made of ground-up recycled sneakers. When the Monsanto corporation introduced Astroturf for the Houston Astrodome in 1966, it was hailed as the future for all baseball stadiums; chiefly due to the lack of expense to maintain.

Over the years the mounting injuries because of the slick hard surface caused a number of ballparks to revert to real grass. Domed stadiums were stuck with it, however, and their solution was to demand new fields with retractable domes or no roof at all. And then along came *Field Turf*, a good deal more expensive to install than natural sod, but only half as costly to maintain. The company will even spray the field with the aroma of fresh grass for $2,000 extra.

New basketball and volleyball courts are part of the new Parade Grounds and in addition will facilitate "Net Ball", a women's sport brought from the Caribbean. "The change is dramatic, " said Thomas. "Before the renovations began, the Parade Grounds was in horrible, horrible condition." Picnic areas and a snack bar and horseshoe courts are to be included.

The Prospect Park Alliance has made an agreement with the City of New York to manage and maintain the Parade Grounds. Alliance fund raising efforts and private donations are necessary to raise the $500,000 per year needed to keep the facility as good as new. Responsibility for the Prospect Park Tennis Center and the Youth Resource Center located on the grounds also rests with the Alliance.

Among others , support comes from Fred Wilpon and the New York Mets and Cyclones. Wilpon, having pitched at the Parade Grounds has not lost touch with his roots.

The Youth Service League under Director Mel Zitter has developed into one of the more productive organizations for youth baseball in Brooklyn and the City of New York. The

League was founded in 1954, but it was in the late fifties that Mel played for his dad with the league's Sheepshead Bay Little League aggregation.

Both of Mel's parents, Herb and Frances, were prominently active in the early development of Youth Services and maintained that dedication for more than forty years. Zitter followed his playing days as a scout with the Cleveland Indians and the Tampa Bay Devil Rays from 1993 through 2001. The Youth Service League maintains ten teams ranging in age from 8 to 20 years old, sending their senior division teams to national tournaments.

The aims and directions of the organizations through the mid-century years to today have been vastly altered, in a way that has seen the demographics of the 40 acre tract change as well. At one time the thirteen diamonds were filled with young ball players who often performed in front of big league scouts, men who flocked to the hallowed Grounds in the hope of seeing some new prospect light up their eyes. The players played and the scouts showed up at their door with a piece of paper. "Sign this and you can go to Peoria or Danville or Oshkosh and pick up $100 or $200 a month playing professional baseball." And who knows, if you stand out and don't get hurt and somebody on the big club drops dead , you may get your chance.

There is still a dream to be had and in the process , today one can become a millionaire, but the approach and the methods have changed drastically. The colleges have become major stepping stones to the pros and the amateur draft initiated in the mid sixties has rendered the old system virtually obsolete. The Youth Service League is but one of the sandlot organizations that has dedicated itself to preparing youngsters for college as well as for life. Zitter says to his charges, "Use baseball as a means- don't let it use you." To this end they work to help their kids enter colleges where their skills, geographic preferences, and academic standings can best be utilized.

In addition to scholarships, Youth Services has sent 18 players to the major leagues and another 80 into pro ball at the minor league level. It is the result of discipline, and education that is the hallmark of the organization. They run a program from January through October, beginning at Ditmas Junior high school where the kids make use of the facilities to run and throw a ball and have meetings with coaches.

But another major difference has taken place over the years. Once, utilized primarily as a local park by kids basically from Brooklyn neighborhoods, it now has more far reaching effects. There are a large number of players who travel from other boroughs to play at the Park. As Zitter says, "if they travel by train for an hour and a half, you know they want to play." A preponderance of African-Americans and Latinos make up Youth Services today and many do not have the means to attend a college except with the aid of the league.

Following their success in 2006, the New York Mets looked to improve in an effort to reach the World Series in 2007. One area of concern was at second base where they felt a younger player should be sought. Of the few names mentioned , two, Rich Aurilia and Julio Lugo had both played ball at Brooklyn's Parade Grounds. Aurilia was born in Brooklyn in 1971 and attended Xaverian high school and St. John's University. A shortstop, his first pro year was in 1992 at Butte, Montana in the Pioneer League where he hit .337 in 59 games. Aurilia reached San Francisco in '95 where he appeared in 9 games and hit at a .474 clip.

Julio Lugo was born in the Dominican Republic in 1975, and grew up in Brooklyn. He played shortstop at Grady high school and for Youth Service at the Parade Grounds. Lugo was drafted in the 43rd round by the Houston Astros in the 1994 amateur draft. In his last two minor league seasons, the infielder hit .303 with Kissimee in the Florida State League, and then hit .319 in the Texas League. Joining Houston in 2000, he has been in the major league since. In seven big league seasons, Julio has compiled a .277 batting average playing both the infield and the outfield. It is in reaching out to the entire city that brought future major league stars like Manny Rameriz, and Alex Aries to the Parade Grounds. Helping these youngsters to be in a position to be offered pro contracts has led to most recent signings of Pedro Beato from Queens, by way of Xavarien high school, to a 32 round draft pick by the Baltimore Orioles. Dellin Betances comes from lower Manhattan and signed with the Yankees. Both boys are right handed pitchers and both received bonuses of $1 million.

Dan Liotta's Parade Grounds League, the legacy of Vincent "Cookie" Lorenzo, has 80 teams active in and around the Park. One problem that has arisen for the local leagues is the reduced number of diamonds available to them. As a result they have had to seek other venues in Brooklyn.

Youth Services utilizes American Legion fields at Seaview Avenue and E. 102 Street. The Kiwanis League plays most of its games at the Ben Vitale fields at Bay 8 Street in Bensonhurst, and the Parade Grounds League has had to use Shore Road Diamonds for their overflow. None of this has dimmed any enthusiasm, however, the Kiwanis League has 600 boys participating, the PGL played over 2000 games at Park Circle in 2006, their boys ranging in age from seven years old to the Open division which has no age limit.

In spite of the marvelous improvements, there is nonetheless, a hint of melancholy for those of us who were baseball players fifty years ago. Baseball has lost its prerogative of being the "only game in town." In 2006 the "Brooklyn Crescents " announced a program for boys and girls youth teams in Lacrosse. The "Brooklyn Patriots" Soccer Club are an organization established in 1994 who use the Parade Grounds as their home field. Baseball, though, at the Parade Grounds, is still a popular entity now as it was a century ago. The Gauchos wiped out the Bonnies 16-7 and then defeated the Richmond County Cardinals from Staten Island 7-2 at Park Circle in the 2006 baseball finals.

The new Parade Grounds offers something for all of the areas' young people. Teens can find out how they can get involved in team sports and other opportunities at the new Youth Resource Center, located at the restored Bowling Green cottage. The Parade Grounds has persevered through decades of change and with the continued efforts of Tupper Thomas and the Prospect Park Alliance, the facility will continue to honor its tradition of the best in baseball, offering in addition, football, soccer, volleyball, basketball and netball. The joy and opportunity provided to so many thousands over the years will continue to be available to New York City's most populous borough, the future of the fabled fields being brighter than ever before.

There were drastic changes in the last decades of the twentieth century, and most were a great deal more far reaching than the Parade Grounds. In May of 1961 Astronaut Alan Shepard spent 15 minutes 115 miles in space. On December 3, 1967 at the Groote Schuur Hospital in Cape Town, South Africa, Dr. Christian Barnard performed the world's first heart transplant on a human being. And miracle of miracles, on July 21, 1969, men from the planet Earth visited the moon. By 1973 the average income had grown to $12,965.00 and life expectancy to 71.4 years. The minimum wage had ascended to a whopping $2 an hour and "The Sting" won the Academy Award for Best Picture. The Twin Towers in lower Manhattan were completed at a cost of $750 million dollars. Introduced was the "home appliance that answers your phone," the new Phone- Mate.

In 1988 when George H W Bush was elected president, the United States had the highest birth rate since 1964. The Pontiac Grand Prix was the 1988 Motor Trend car of the Year, and the average income in America had nearly doubled from '73, to just under $25,000. Life expectancy was now 75.2 years.

Extremely proud of the efforts of the Alliance, administrator Tupper Thomas says that watching the kids play , "makes you want to cry." Brooklyn has always been a place of immigrants and it was the goal of the designers of Prospect Park to teach democracy through the Parks.

"After a long time of it being such a disaster, I take a lot of pride in seeing it now," says Thomas. "This is a place that Brooklyn can really be proud of."

XX.

It Ends With A Memory

"The older I get, the more things I gotta leave behind."
-Rocky Balboa

"Just because they're old enough to remember riding the trolley to baseball games at the Parade Grounds doesn't mean they can't still hit line drives. *"The Old Boys of Summer,"* a group of former baseball players who get together regularly to practice and play ball, are coming back to the historic ball fields where many first fell in love with the game." These words were written by Eugene Patron of the Prospect Park Alliance in August of 2006. And return we did. On that August summer morning we were joined by many from that bygone era in addition to the young men only beginning to dream. Jim McElroy and Fred Weber and Butch Gualberti were there. Jim brought some of his senior division Cadets and they took the field with our *Old Boys.* Gil Bassetti showed his 1988 World Series ring. As a scout for the LA Dodgers, he earned two of them. The fellows were in awe, not just at the size and magnitude of the gem, but of what it represents.

The other Jim McElroy, *Mac,* the old Yankee bird dog brought along the catcher's mitt that had been designed by scout Arthur Dede. The mitt is round like a pillow with an indentation only a shade larger than a baseball, in the center. A good fastball when caught in that spot would sound like a cannon going off. There was method to the madness here. Mac recalls an episode that had a pitcher named Jack Dalton, "who could really bring it," warming up before a game. "We're getting BOOMS in the bullpen," Mac says laughing. By the time Dalton got on the mound the other team was "so intimidated they were back on their heels, afraid to stand in there against Dalton." Of course, Jack was no slouch, and ultimately played in the pros.

Clarence Irving arrived and was greeted by Gil, who played for him, and old friends Jimmy McElroy and Fred Weber. Clarence has the qualities of a sage and the old guys gathered around him on the bleachers.

Eddie Mack looked over the 40-acre expanse and saw it as it once was. "They're gonna spread my ashes here," he said, only half in jest. "I always enjoyed myself here, there were a lotta good times. We'd play an American Legion game in the morning and then go running across the field to play in the Kiwanis League in the afternoon." He laughed. "We had some good fights here too. And always there was Freddie at the bottom of the pile." Somebody jabbed Weber in the ribs good- naturedly. "You'd get hurt and wrap some tape around it and keep playing."Eddie continued, " nobody went to the doctor or had x-rays. We didn't want to miss the next game. No worries," Mack went on, "just played baseball....then life got serious."

The *Old* and *Young* Boys of Summer were united by the common bond nurtured over more than two centuries by the mystical aura of the game of baseball. Dan Liotta, president of the Parade Grounds League and founder of the Parade Grounds Umpires Association , and an umpire himself is his usual entertaining story-telling self. Jerry Katzke is the Director of the Bonnie Boys Club, another storied Parade Grounds organization of sandlot teams.

We were a different group than we were only ten years before. Harry Trimmer was gone, the first of us to join the *Boys of Eternal Summer.* Others had moved south to spend their retirement. Sebi Pepi is in Florida close to the golf links he has come to enjoy so much. Tommy Siracusa followed his children to Atlanta, Georgia. Ted Schrieber was headed for Florida but found a comfortable spot just outside of Atlanta and settled in there. Sixto Morales left for Puerto Rico. Chick and Freddie Weber and myself are the only ones left, but our ranks have further swelled with new, though, aging blood. Norman Root does most of the batting practice pitching, at 73 years old, he prides himself on being able to toss more than200 pitches in a session.

There are no more Diamonds #1 or 13. The entire transfiguration of the Park had changed. There are but four baseball fields now as opposed to the 13 we knew. There are a couple of softball fields and lots of soccer room. A tennis center lay across the Park Circle end and the site contains a playground. The main baseball field is now Diamond #3, on the Parkside Avenue side, covering an area once allocated to the diamonds 6 through 10.

We took our workout on this field and it was a beaut. Completely fenced in with signs announcing dimensions. The right field line is 300 feet; down the line in left, 320 feet; and dead center is 397 feet. There is a scoreboard above that397 foot sign and the infield manicured so that the bad hops are minimized. I took some hot grounders at third and only one went awry on me.

There are enclosed dugouts, not the old-fashioned kind, that are below the levelof the ground like bunkers. These are huge and comfortable with a water fountain. And shade; you can cool off a bit between innings, unheard of at the old Parade Grounds, where you baked in the sun awaiting your turn at bat. Something completely new has been added this time around. Diamond #3 is lighted. There are seven towers which engulf the field, each looking like a tall, angular pitcher about to kick and throw.

Our old nemisis', the Sabres, had brought a along a contingent to *Old Boys of Summer Day*. The little shortstop, Peter *Rabbit* Vicari grabbed a glove and went out onto the field. "I got some knee problems," he told us. "I can't do much." Butch and Joey Gualberti were there also. I recognized Joe from 48 years ago. I saw the same face that looked up at me from behind the mask each time I came up to hit. The same face, just a little grayer, older, with a few wrinkles. Sonny Panico and Frank Mazza were there also. Sonny joined us on the field for the workout. In his late sixties, he is still playing up to 100 softball games a season.

Occasionally there are mishaps on the field. Tony Famular is hit on the head by a pitch from Norman Root. "It didn't hurt," Tony says. "What bothered me was that I ducked and got hit when I was on the way up." I felt good to come up with a hot grounder to my left and hear Jimmy McElroy call from the bleachers, "Attaway to go, Andy!"

Several of the teen-age Cadets stood behind the screen as we hit. One of them could be heard exclaiming, "boy, these guys can hit; but they look like they're about 80 years old!"

"Hey," someone on the field shouts back, "you shoulda seen us 48 years ago." The kids all laugh.

The intricacies between man and boy are played out to the extreme on the baseball diamond. The boy reaches manhood but clings irreparably to his youth. If we were to elicit a term for this it might be the *Peter Pan Syndrom*. It would necessarily follow that the Parade Grounds would be *Neverland*, "the enchanting world where childhood lasts forever," and we would all be those wide-eyed youths, who, try as we might, can simply never grow old.

Here, at the rejuvenated Parade Grounds with the "Old Boys" and the teen "Young Boys" and the Brooklyn Cyclones, that world is played out. The older ones remember the Rock Fields of Red Hook and the old lot on MacDonald Avenue and the weeded meadows at Marine park before the WPA came in. This place on this August morning is the link between young and old, boy and man and we all remember. It is as the father of the Darling children in *Peter Pan* comments, "I have the strangest feeling that I saw that ship before, a long time ago when I was very young."

Once, late on a summer Saturday afternoon, in a game being played on Diamond #3, a woman strode onto the playing field between the pitcher and the catcher and pointed to the fellow on the mound. "Don't you dare throw that ball," she ordered. He didn't. She stopped near second base and began gesturing to Frank Chiarello in center field. It seems that Chick was late for a wedding and his wife had come to summon him to fulfill this obligation. But the game had run long and first things first, he finished playing the game.

As the fifties wound down much of the perceived tranquility of the decade would fester in the tumultuous sixties. In 1954 at the siege at Dien Bien Phu in southeast Asia 13,000 French troops were trapped by the forces of Ho Chi Minh. President Eisenhower refused to commit American forces to the fray saying, "I never want to see this country bogged down in a land war in Asia."

In the presidential election of 1964 in which the Democrats were able to depict Republican candidate Barry Goldwater as a warmonger and a threat to the peace of this nation, President Lyndon Johnson ran away with a landslide victory and preceded to increase the number of American troops and our involvement in the war. Thus prompting the comment from Republicans, "they told me if I voted for Goldwater, there would be war. I voted for Goldwater and sure enough there was war." The war or the handling of it would divide the country throughout the sixties and into the seventies.

In 1960 the average income was $5,199, a new car could be bought for $2,610 and a house for $12,675. A loaf of bread could be had for .20. The minimum wage was $1.00 and life expectancy was at 69.7 years, which meant that most of our *Old Boys of Summer* would be playing in a heavenly league.

The civil rights movement would take hold nearly twenty years after Jackie Robinson broke the color line with the Dodgers and ten or more years since the landmark Supreme Court decision in *Brown v Topeka Board of Education* would outlaw school segregation. There were three political assassinations in the United States in the sixties. These events would polarize the country and bring chaos to the streets of America. The world and the country would begin to change in the next decade and the fifties would be gone for good but for the memories. The memories come from all over Brooklyn. Tony Socluizzo recalls that one of the greatest sounds "of my youthful ballplayin' days was listening to the clack clack of our spikes as we walked down the concrete steps of the old clubhouse on the way to the diamonds." Tony was there in the 50s and saw Joe Torre as a "pudgy catcher wallop a shot over the fence on Diamond One," and the greatest pitching performance "was turned in by Howie Kitt of Nathan's."

John Patterson lived on Woodruff Avenue during the forties and fifties and "practically lived on the Parade Grounds." As a 12 year old in 1955, Bill Stanley played for the *NY World Telegram & Sun* "I remember riding my bike past Gil Hodges' house on the way to the Parade Grounds, hoping to get a glance," Stanley recalls.

Herbert Johnson lived adjacent to the Park and when he was about eight or nine in the late twenties, he was fascinated with a Parade Grounds team. "The *Argyles* were one of the best around in those days. " Johnson remembers going to Ebbets Field to see the Dodgers play. "Although the action was stimulating and the noisy fans made it all exciting, I felt that the players were miles away from me."

In contrast, it was easier to be a part of the excitement at the Parade Grounds. "I was able not only to see the faces of the players but even talk to them," Mr. Johnson remembers fondly. When he was fifteen, Herbert played with a team called the *Centrals,* not one of the better teams, according to Johnson, but "I learned my base-ball fundamentals at Diamond # 1, eagle-eyeing the Argyles."

For Herbert Johnson, there were magical moments at the Parade Grounds, a different world, "one that I can remember with great pleasure." But over the years there were a number of strange sightings reported in and around the Parade Grounds, like the black billowing smoke of one of the bon fires meant to dry off a muddy field.

But there was none so strange as the report filed with HBCC UFO Research in August 1965. A ten-year old boy and his mother were walking their dog at about 8:30 PM. As they strolled along the Parkside Avenue perimeter of the Parade Grounds , they saw above them a huge, grey, submarine shaped cylinder. They reported "no lights, no sound, no windows." They observed it heading westuntil it "faded from sight about a half mile west of the Parade Grounds."

An episode of a recent TV program "The X - Files", titled "The Unnatural" was about an alien who came to Earth to infiltrate but saw a game and fell in love with baseball. Disregarding his assignment , he became a baseball player. One can only wonder if on that August summer night, a similar metamorphosis didn't take place. If you spent time at the Parade Grounds, you have undoubtably witnessed some very out-of-this-world personalities.

Memories. Mike Montesano is eighty years old and remembers his kid days on Bergen Street off Underhill Avenue. Stickball was Mike's game and they played it on Dean Street. Although a short distance from Ebbets Field Mike was a Yankees' fan. The Dodgers of the thirties were the *Daffiness Boys* and Mike and his family found it hard to accept them as lovable losers. Montesano spent a good deal of time at the Parade Grounds, though played very little himself. He went there in support of his cousin, Mike Sofia. Sofia played a lot of baseball in the late thirties including some semi-pro ball in the metropolitan area. It was here that he came in contact with as teammate and opponent the fathers of future major leaguers Joe Pepitone and Carl Yastrzemski.

When the war broke out Sofia wound up with the Eighth Army and played short-stop along with major leaguers Ken Silvestri, the Cardinals Irv Dusak, Dale Long and Phillies pitcher Hugh Mulcahy. Mulcahy was the first major leaguer to enter the military following Pearl Harbor.

When the war ended Sofia was already twenty-three years old and past the age that most scouts would consider signing a prospect. But Sofia, at 5' 8" and about 140 pounds was able to lie about his age and pull it off. He signed with Pittsburgh and went to the Florida State League. He hit well in the early part of the season , but as cousin Mike relates, " he would lose weight in the summer and drop to about 120 pounds, and his hitting usually fell off." He is quick to add, "he was a good glove man and could run." After two seasons, like so many others, Mike was married and decided it was time to plan a life without baseball.

Montesano is a throwback, remembering not only his cousin but has fond recollections of the DiMaggio brothers and players of that ilk. "Today's players are selfish", he says in no uncertain terms, and pauses to reflect on another time. There were some whose connections to the Park were not voluntary. Fran Goetz Koenig had a box seat. "My family lived in the building at the corner of Argyle Road and Caton Avenue in the early 50s," she recalls. "On mild spring Saturdays and Sundays I'd wake to the sounds of bats cracking, balls thwacking and 'pitch it right in here, baby boy.'"

Memories. Alan Zarrow used to watch several games at once from "the roof of my apartment house on 17th street between Church and Caton Avenues." Another who lived on Westminster Road and walked to the Parade Grounds when he was eight or nine years old, realized his dream of catching a foul ball. But he says, "there's this guy with a pot belly, but in uniform, with his fingers grasping the wire fence and telling me to throw it back."

Memories. Billy Polcari has been living in East Brunswick, New Jersey for more than forty years, but there is Brooklyn in his heart. "You don't think I was once a shortstop?" he challenges as he caresses an oversized mid-section. "I played short for the Blue Jays and we won championships." Polcari played for St. Francis de Chantel and New Utrecht high school. "I played short and Jackie Elias was at third," he recalls. "Elias played nine years in the minors." Polcari sits back in the chair on his deck on this hot summer Sunday and reflects, "I loved that place," he says with emotion, " that was the greatest time anybody could have!"

Frank Cunningham pitched in the Industrial League for teams like IBM and New York Telephone, but recalls in particular a game his cousin pitched on a Sunday in 1942. His battery mate was Steve Lembo and the first baseman Chuck Connors. "Oh, " Cunningham laments, "for the days when the ball fields were full from 9 AM to 8 PM 7 days a week."

Frankie "Bo" Taylor was the cousin who was pitching in an All-Star game that included Lembo and Connors. At 5'10" and a mere 145 pounds, Taylor nonetheless threw a 90+ fastball and a devastating curve. "It would start at your belt and finish at your feet," Cunningham said as he fondly recalled days as a 12 -year-old watching his cousin master the Parade Grounds pitching mounds. Taylor was signed by the Dodgers and sent to Zanesville, Ohio for his first pro season. With a war raging, Frank, as well as Steve Lembo and Chuck Connors all went into the service.

After the war ended, Taylor was picked up by the Pirates and played at Rehoboth, Delaware, but a war injury curtailed his activity and his opportunity ended there.

Mike Pisano from Hart Street couldn't make his high school team at St. Leonard's in Ridgewood, so he volunteered to manage and "spent a lot of time at the Parade Grounds. Our star player was our catcher Tony Mangieri who hit many line drive home runs into the endless gaps at the Parade Grounds."

There are those major league memories of the *Boys of Brooklyn*. A day in 1961when Sandy Koufax defeated Bob Gibson 1-0, the one run, a home run by TommyDavis. The '63 day when Teddy Schreiber stepped into the batter's box at the Polo Grounds and greeted catcher Joe Torre. And in '62 when Davis stood in left field with his hands on his hips and a voice from the Chicago Cubs bullpen hollered out,"Hey, where do you think you are? Diamond 13?" "I hear you," Tommy said, but I don't see you." And Tony Balsamo waved to his old compadre . And when Rico Petrocelli and Chuck Schilling were teammates on the '65 Red Sox.

And in 1967 on their way to an American League pennant, the Boston Red Sox had Petrocelli playing short, and when they played the Yankees and Rico was on first, he and Joe Pepitone might exchange a word or two. Petrocelli recalls a humorous incident in his book, *"Tales from the Impossible Dream Red Sox."*

During the 1967 season, the Red Sox and Yankees got into a brawl in New York. It was on June 21 and the Sox ultimately won the game 8-1, but it was in the second inning after Red Sox Joe Foy was hit by Yankee pitcher Thad Tillotson following a dusting of a Yankee hitter by Boston pitcher Jim Lonborg that "both benches and bullpens emptied, and the brawl was on."

According to Petrocelli, "Yankee first baseman Joe Pepitone and I sought each other out. We had both grown up in Brooklyn and knew each other, and we started playfully throwing grass and dirt at each other, waiting for things to settle down." Caught up in the excitement they started throwing punches and "ended up at the bottom of the pile."

Pepitone later complained that there were "twenty guys were on top of me, and one guy kept pulling on my hair. That ticked me off more than anything." Pepitone by that time had become renown for the use of a portable hair dryer in the clubhouse and the vain concern he had for his hair. (1)

Still listed as director of the Parade Grounds Leagues after more than sixty years, Cookie Lorenzo adamantly applauded the Park personnel with a vigorous appraisal. Over the past thirty years os so, whenever engaged in conversation, hewould sooner or later glare at the other and growl defiantly, "Gimme an all-star team from the Park and I'll beat any of these so-called big league clubs today."

An exaggeration ? Of course. The ravings of an old man? Possibly. But in deference to his age and his contributions to the youth of Brooklyn baseball, perhaps we could humor the old director and examine the quality of a Parade Grounds Major League All-Star team just for fun.

Our first choice will be a catcher. *The Ole Professor,* Casey Stengel, when making his choices for the expansion New York Mets chose a catcher, Hobie Landrith, number one, with the explanation. " If I don't take a catcher first, a lotta balls are gonna roll all the way to the backstop." So we'll follow Case and chose Joe Torre to be our catcher. Praised as the successful manager of the New York Yankees, Joe had an 18 year big league career in with he hit a combined .297.Joe Pignatano and Steve Lembo will back him up. *Piggy* played in the majors for six seasons and had a long career as a coach, including the 1969 Mets miracle year.

At first base a couple of good left handed hitters in Joe Pepitone and Frank Torre, both slick fielding around the bag. The rest of the infield can be made up of Willie Randolph, Rico Petrocelli and Shawon Dunston. Willie is well known for his fine career in New York with the Yankees. Rico hit 40 home runs as shortstop for the 1969 Boston Red Sox and appeared in two World Series. In 12 full season Petrocelli hit 210 home runs.

Shawon Dunston completes our starting infield. Dunston came up with the Cubs and spent 18 seasons in the big-time. A pretty solid infield but with some decent back-ups. The Aspromonte brother combined for 20 seasons in the majors, both having seasons hitting in the .290s. Teddy Schreiber had one year with the Mets in 1963, but is ready to fill in at second, third or short. Chuck schilling is a back-up to randolph

Our outfield consists of Tommy Holmes, .302 in 11 National League seasons. Holmes also set a modern National league record in 1945 when hitting safely in 37consecutive games; Willie Keeler had hit in 44 in 1897; a record that lasted until broken by Pete Rose in 1978. Tommy Davis had won two batting titles and garnered 230 hits in 1962, finishing an 18 year career with a .294 batting average. To round out the outfield we have one of today's top sluggers, the Boston Red Sox' Manny Ramirez. Ramirez has led the American League in hitting, home runs and in 1999 drove in 165 runs to lead in that category also.

Reserve outfielder Cal Abrams will back up our three starters and Joe Judge will get an honorable mention. There's a good possibility that Judge played at the Parade Grounds but it is difficult to make that determination beyond a doubt. Another bench sitter is Tommy Brown; major leaguer at 16 years old, "Buckshot" spent nine years in the majors.

Not a bad ball club at that, likely to score some runs, but as anyone knows you can't win without pitching. For one-two starters, the Parade Grounds have a lefty righty combination of Hall-Of-Famers in Sandy Koufax and Waite Hoyt. To complete a staff there is John Candelaria, Saul Ragovin, Bill Lohrman ,Marius Russo and Jerry Casale. In relief we can go to Don McMahon and Tony Balsamo. If we want to play today's game we'll need a closer, and who better than John Franco who closed out a brilliant career with 424 major league saves.

This is the club Cookie Lorenzo would have loved to manage, but if he should need a break , both Joe Torre and Willie Randolph are available to take over.

Here is the cream of the Parade Grounds crop, but if you suck away the icing on the cake you'll find a very tasty top layer. With fellows like Matty Galente, Georgie Fallon, Butch Gualberti, Gil Bissetti, Richie Lupardo and Jerry Boxer, to name just a few. It is , however, that bottom layer that is the footing and the foundation of the dreams and trials of the Park.

It is here that we stumble over Wally Edge and Billy Gates; Al Fortunato, Pee Wee Parasgondola, Georgie Lopac and Jim *Cookie* Powers. It is at this level that the nearly 140 year history of Brooklyn's Parade Grounds is truly leavened into the mixture that blossoms as the final product. And these young Cadets are a part of the new order. Mathew Wulff hits while "Old Boy "Bill Langsdorf dons the catchers' gear and rails at the young hitter. "Hey," the kid says, "somebody shut this old guy up."

The old and the new, the tired and the fresh. There is the passing of knowledge and experience and I think of how fortunate I was to garner such lore from Ed Mathieson, Al Fortunato, Fred Weber and Milton Staub, my own citadel of baseball wisdom.

Cadets Anthony LaFauci, Nolan Smalls and Steve Candela were on the field, covering the bases and taking lofting one-hop throws from the old timers.

The Brooklyn Cyclones arrived. Fred Wilpon has been generous to the community of his youth and his Class A Short - Season New York-Penn League affiliate has sent over three players and Sandy the Sea Gull, the clubs mascot. Sandy is in full bird regalia and takes the field with the rest of the boys.

Josh Appell is a left handed pitcher from Valley Stream, Long Island. Josh played for the Valley Stream Cadets in McElroy's organization and visits with Jim in the dugout. Appell signed with the Mets out of the University of Pennsylvania and pitched last season in the Gulf Coast league.

Joe Holden roams center field for the Cyclones. The twenty-two year old is a left handed hitter who throws righty. Joe is from Wantaugh, Long Island and is a graduate of Malloy College in Rockville Centre, N.Y.. Holden was signed by scout Scott Hunter, who is currently the Cyclones' hitting coach. I asked Joe how the transition from aluminum to wood bat was for him. "Not a real problem," he said, "even though the sweet spot got so small." Joe played in a wood bat summer league, the ACBL, and got an initiation which helped him considerably.

The aluminum bat situation is a sticky one though there seems to be more wood bat opportunities available. The Cadet players said there would be a wood bat tour-nament for them this season.

Jeremy Mizell is a right handed pitcher, the only one of the three from outside the New York area. "Baton Rouge, Louisiana," he announced proudly when asked where he was from. Jeremy is in his first year of pro ball out of Southeast Louisiana University. When they heard his name a couple of the old timers immediately spoke of "Vinegar Bend" Mizell, the old Cardinals pitcher of the fifties. Jeremy knew of him, but the other Cyclones said, "Who?"

Jeremy is 23 years old, Anthony Scafaci is 16, and Frank Chiarello is 75. The history of the Parade Grounds is a mosaic laid out across the " playing fields of Brooklyn" and displayed by the Prospect Park Alliance on an August morning in2006.

The young Cadets commented about how great it was to have the chance to connect with and thank some of the players who came before them. One said that it was a good experience to see what the game used to be like and that he was "amazed to see the elders out on the field. It gave me a greater appreciation of the sport."

Bill Langsdorf said, "who you callin' *Elder?*"

Early on a summer's evening in 1949 or '50, three men parked their car on Parkside Avenue and went to watch a game in progress on Diamond 13. They watched for about two innings before they were recognized, and then the other spectators came over to ask for autographs. The three smiled and signed and then left. Fred Weber was pitching in the game and from the mound he picked out the Dodgers' Pee Wee Reese. He thought another was Carl Erskine. The players were on their way from Ebbits Field to their homes in Bay Ridge and stopped to take in a sandlot game. It was Brooklyn and baseball at mid-century.

There is a story in the New York Times in late summer of 2006. Shawon Dunston , now living in California, was visiting his native borough and showing his young son some of his old haunts; the old neighborhood, his high school, andthey stopped at the Parade Grounds. Shawon Jr. noticed a bunch of middle-aged men in uniform taking batting practice. "Why are those guys out there?" He asked. "They're so old." It was the Parade Grounds at the dawn of the new century.

Judge Aldon R. Waldon used to play for Clarence Irving's Bisons in the fifties. He recalls hitting a home run. His Honor says now, "I touched heaven with that wallop."

Shakespeare called memory, "The warder of the brain," and we've all taken away some wonderful retention of days at the Parade Grounds. And not just winning and losing. There were rainy days and sunny days, there were friends and comrades. There were those whose devotion to helping and teaching gave others the chances they would otherwise have missed. I could not have become a Park Circle veteran of so many years if not for the help of guys like Louie Schalaba and Chick Chiarello.

As we cavort about the new Parade Grounds in old Brooklyn at the turn of a new century, our old bones reaching back allowing us one more swing of the bat, a scoop of a ground ball, or guiding a lazy fly ball into a well worn mitt, there is a continuance with that other time.

There is also a mind full of memories that recall things as they once were and have long since gone. The *Brooklyn Eagle* folded in 1955. Trolley cars were gone from the Brooklyn streets by 1956 and one year later there went the Dodgers. Stickball became a less viable game as the years passed , what with traffic getting heavier and cars traveling faster. And the last egg cream I had commercially was at a throw-back candy store on 15 Avenue and 62 street about 1990 - gone now.

At the Parade Grounds at mid-century there were a group we called the *Old -Timers*. They appeared Saturday mornings and evenings through the seasons of baseball; slamming the ball in a pepper game and driving line drive after line drive in batting practice. We watched in awe at these *ancient* septuagenarians in knickers and sanitary hose and marveled that they could even stand up at their age. We, who were robust and fit, in our teens and twenties. And now we bridge a gap, a legacy had been passed on. We are the wonders of *our* age, ancient, as we thought we never could be. Josh Appell of the Brooklyn Cyclones said upon observing us that August morning, "It's pretty cool to see what they had to go through and what we get to play with today."

But the greatest wonder of it all is the friendships that endure after forty, fifty, and sixty years. There are fellows who are aging and some are ill, but old teammates drive them to functions or to do errands. Others pick up an infirm friend and take him to breakfast or lunch each week. They call and correspond regularly; they meet at reunions and laugh and talk over old times; great times. They went from camaraderie to friendship to devotion, and this, after all is the real legacy of the Parade Grounds.

There is a time when age begins to take control of the athlete's body. For some ballplayers it might come at thirty or perhaps forty years old. For some of us who do not want to quit, the aches and pains are fought off. The idea that sitting on the front porch might be a bit more comfortable is disdained. We reach back and continue to throw the ball and swing the bat.

But each fall when we contemplate that another year has dissipated and we've grown older, we consider that it might be time to relegate it all to memory at long last. But then the words of that venerable old Negro Leaguer, major league coach, scout, and sage, John "Buck" O'Neil hits against our brain like Pete Reiser slamming against a padded-less outfield wall:

"But next spring, when the birds started singing; when they started throwing the ball, I was ready to go again."

****

"I once hit a home run at the Parade Grounds; I touched heaven with that wallop." -Judge Aldon R. Waldon
Brooklyn Bisons

433

APPENDIX:

Following is a partial list of ball players who signed professional contracts and played at the Parade Grounds in Brooklyn. NOTE: There are more than forty World Series rings won by Parade Grounds players. * indicates player played in the major leagues** indicates players who umpired in the major leagues

Sal Apria

Rich Aurilia*

Cal Abrams*

Sonny Amodio

Bill Antonello *

Reuben Alexis

Alex Arias

Ken Aspromonte*

Bob Aspromonte*

Charlie Aspromonte

Mike Arsenik

Ralph Addonizio

Bob Applebaum

Gil Bissetti

Tony Balsamo*

Tommy Brown*

Frank Boembeman

Shelly Brodsky

Ed Banach

Jerry Boxer

Joe Behlcastro

Fritzie Brickell

Lenny Beckoff

Chris Bruno

Dave Barrett

C.B. Buckner**

Jeff Bittenger

Kevin Baez*

Dick Banach

Keith Bodie

Larry Barnarth*

Dave Cardwell

Charlie Costello

Chuck Connors*

Nick Costello

Vince Carlesi

George Caldwell

Bob Cocadrilli

Jerry Casale*

Frank Chiarello

Charles Cummings

Ed Cahill

Herman Cohen

Frank Colosi

John Crimi

Jack Conway

Sal Campisi *

John Candalaria*

Bob Carroll*
Al Cuccinello
Mike Coster
Manford Chandler
Dan Cooper
Mario Cuomo
Ben Castillo
Joel Chimelis
Al Cardwood
Larry Ciffone
Tom DeCiglia
Bob DiLombardo
Al Davis
Jack Dalton
Fred DeFalco
Tommy Davis*
Larry DiVita
Angelo DeBarnardo
Larry DiPippo
Billy DiBenedetto
Art Dede *
Babe Daskalaksis
Norman Diamond
Shawon Dunston*
Larry Dunn
Benny DiStefano*
Dan D'Oca
Rob Esposito
Barry Ertos
Harry Eisenstat*
Ruben Feliciano
Chuck Feinstein

Jose Flores
Cornel Foggie Jr.
Frank Fernandez*
George Fallon*
Al Ferrara*Chad
Fontera
Bill Frankenhauser
Jerry Falkman
Jim Fanizzi
Pete Falcone*
Nelson Figueroa*
JohnFranco*
Willie Francis
Andy Fronduto
Billy Farrello
Len Farrello
Jose Flores
Mike Fermaint
Phil Festa
Mike Fiore
Paul Gargone
Joe Granowski
Ben Galante
Matt Galante
Irving Glaser
Butch Gualberti
Bob Giallombardo
Steve Gardella
Bob Grim*
Marty Grossman
Sonny Giordano
Ray Gilbert

Waite Hoyt*
Tommy Holmes*
Roberto Hernandez
Ken Handler
Bob Honor
John Holmlund
John Halama*
Ron Heffernan
Charles Isles
Bill Hill
Tom Johnson
Mike Jorgensen
Howie Kitt
Sandy Koufax*
George Kalafatis
Jason Katz
Steve Klein
Dan Kopec
Willie Lozado
Dennis Leonard
Julio Lugo*
Rudy Lugo*
Steve Lembo*
Vic Liriano
John Lepik
Wally Laurie
Tommy LaPinto
Santo LoBerto
Bobby LaneLuis
Lopez Sr*
Luis Lopez Jr *
Anthony Lembo

Bill Lohrman*
Rich Lupardo
Kelsey Moffett
John McLean
Alan Marr
Don McMahon*
Tom Mirabito
Joe Modiea
Tony Maglio
Ralph Manriello
Joe Musachio
John Malone
Tony Mele
Lee Mazilli*
Ralph Manriello
Larry Morello
Sal Mirra
Mike Munsinger
Carmine Mannino
Joe Messina
Ron Marietta
Dick Miller
Rafael Novoa*
Sonny Navarro
Larry Napp***
Mike Napoli
Tony Nunziello
Gerry Orlemac
Gil Olsen
Andy Olsen***
Emilio Palazzo
Rico Petrocelli*

Sonny Pace
Irv Piatek
Mario Picone*
Bill Pepitone
Bill Pierro
Rey Palacios*
Bob Pasquale
Joe Pigatano*
Hank Pascone
Willie Palumbo
Joe Pepitone *
Johnny Powers
Dave Parouse
Mike Papa
Burke Probitsky
Stan Rosenzweig
Andy Russo
Frank Rodriguez*
Jerry Rosenthal
Frank Romano
Jim Romano*
Charles Riccio
Charley Ready
Herb Rossman
John Rucker
Mickey Rutner
George Ryan
Marius Russo*
Willie Randolph*
Pat Russell
Jerry Rosenthal
Saul Rogavin*

Manny Ramirez*
Pedro Rabassa
Andy Rubilotta
Lou Romanochi
John Rodriguez*
Gil Roman
Norman Roman
Wayne Rosenthal
Rosendo Roman
Jose Rubiera
George Schneidmuller
John Seneca
Eddie StankoTony
Russo
Luis de los Santos
Rich Stankavish
Carmine Sperto
Mike Silber
Chuck Schilling*
Smokey Joe Salmon
Pete Scarpati
Rich Simons
Archie Schwartz
Paul Speckenbach
Ron Solomini
Len Sasso
Marty Somma
Rex Shanahan
Joe Sauralin
Len Scott Frank
Scarney Bob Sundstrom
Bob Spier

Frank Seminara*
Jim Stagnato
Ted Schreiber*
Freddie Smith
Mike Sofia
Bob Schultz
Carmine Sperto
Joe Sambito
Nick Testa
Frankie "Bo" Taylor
Mike Tagliafero
Pat Tennerella
Frank Torre*
Dom Tursellino
Claude Tinsley
Joe Torre*
George Thomasino
Frank Tepedino*
Rusty Torres*
Ray Tully
John Tepedino
Frank Tepedino Jr
Tony Tjera
Vince Tiani
Jim Ursillo
Trovin Valdez
Bill Van Arden
Frank Viola*
Bob Vaz
Phil Venturino
David Wallace
Fred Weber

Art West
Dallas Williams
Sonny Williams
John Weiss
Mike Weltman
Ken Wirell
Frank Yurman
Larry Yellen*
Richie Zisk*
Bill Zonner
Alexis Zapata

ACKNOWLEDGMENTS:

The idea of writing a book about the Parade Grounds never entered my mind until it was suggested by Bob McGee, who is the author of an exceptional history of the Brooklyn Dodgers, *The Greatest ballpark Ever*. Bob and I spoke at the Grand Army Plaza Main Branch of the Brooklyn Public Library in October, 2005. After I did my talk about my experiences playing ball at *Park Circle*, Bob commented about the things I had said. "I would have loved to have had those experiences," he said, You ought to write about it."

After pouring over old scrapbooks and clippings I began to realize just how extensive the material was. I called some friends from my days there and discovered the first of many pleasant surprises. The dozen or so fellows with whom I had stayed in touch were in turn in touch with a dozen or so more and so on. The network extended to what seemed like an infinity, much like the foul lines on the diamond , which are more far-reaching the further they go.

My thanks to writers Donald Honig and Tom Knight who are so generous with their advice and memories.

Dave Anderson is a Pulitzer Prize winning columnist for the *New York Times*,and I am indebted to Dave for writing the forward for this work. I have yet to meet a finer gentleman in and around sports.

Brooklyn Borough President Marty Markowitz kindly consented to add his sense of the value of the Parade

Grounds to the community over the years and I appreciate his contribution.

I am grateful to everyone who provided photographs for use in this volume for as Jim McElroy said when he handed me an envelope, "take good care of these, they are gold!"

Richie "Rebo" Lupardo did some editing and added his thoughts and memories. "I just want to be a part of this," he told me. He has my gratitude. Old friend and manager Fred Weber was a constant source. His stories and ties with countless old Parade Grounders provided invaluable information. As a manager, Fred always made me feel like a ball player.

Legendary managers Clarence Irving of the Bisons, Jim McElroy of the Cadets and Gabe "Red" Verde of the Brooklyn Royals are each worthy of a book themselves. They provided me with indispensable material and memories.

One of the great pleasures was reuniting with my first manager Al Fortunato after 53 years. What a joy to recall the treasure trove of baseball knowledge that this man imparted, the genesis of my baseball journey for the next half century.

There is no way of calculating the contribution of my wife Mildred. Forty-seven years of marriage, and a relationship of more than 50 years all told, and baseball, baseball, baseball. Without her this book would not have been written, this life not led.

A special thanks to Michelle Hascup, without whose assistance the computer age would surely have done me in.

And to all the rest as follows, this book, such as it is, belongs to them. Ken Avalon, Bob Aspromonte, Steve Albanese, Larry Anderson, Tony Balsamo, Gil Bassetti, Forte' Bellino, John Candelaria, Maria Candelaria Frank Chiarello, John Chino, Frank Cunningham, Mario Cuomo, Nick Costello, Mike Chiappetta, Tommy Davis, Larry Di Vita, Nick Defendis, Helen D'Angelo, Wally Edge, Manny Fernandez, Pete Falcone, Jim Fanizzi, Anthony Ferrante, Leslie-Anne Fallon, Matt Galante, Butch Gualberti, Joe Gualberti, Lou Grant, Jordan Gatti, Lou Gatti, Peter Goyco, Gene Hermanski, Carl Hottinger, Bob Johnson, Ed Jordan, Jerry Katzke, Mark Levine, Anthony Lembo, Vincent Lorenzo, Dan Liotta, Al Marchese, Dick Miller, Carmine Mannino, Jim "Mac" McElroy, Jim Mosley, Nick Maglio, Tom Miskel, Sal Marchiano, Tom Morrisey, Ed McDonough, Ray Nash , Larry Napp Jr., Mike Napoli, , Bill Nigro, Andy Olsen, Joe Pignatano, Jay Price, Sebi Pepi, Ray Pecorara, Ross Quartto, Paul Rotter, Tony Rubilotta, Andy Rubilotta, Norman Root, Tony Russo, Chuck Schilling, Ted Schreiber, Arthur Schwartz, Jack Tracy, Tupper Thomas, Bobby Thomson, Tony Sogluizzo, Jim Ursillo, Pete Vicari, Phil Venturino, Fred Wilpon, Larry Yaffa, Larry Yellen, Bill Zonner.

THE SCOREBOARD (NOTES):

SOURCES:

Newspapers

Brooklyn Eagle - Brooklyn, New York
    World Telegram and Sun - New York, NY

Chapter III - The Best of Times

1. Sandy Koufax: A Lefty's Legacy - Jane Leavy - Perennial - 2002

2. Sporting News - Bob Broeg - August 14, 1971

3. Tales From the Dodgers Dugout - Tommy Davis/ Paul Gutierrez -Sports Pub-2005

Chapter IV - The Sparkle in Brooklyn's "Jewel"

1. The Battle of Brooklyn - John J. Gallagher - Castle Books - 1995

2. Brooklyn Daily Eagle - June 8, 1867

3. Brooklyn Daily Eagle - May 29, 1896

4. Long Before the Dodgers - James L. Terry - McFarland Publishers - 2002

5. Brooklyn Daily Eagle - May 10, 1883

6. Brooklyn Daily Eagle - October 12, 1901

7. Brooklyn Daily Eagle - April 25,1883

8. Brooklyn Daily Eagle - May 27, 1883

9. Brooklyn Daily Eagle - April   , 1894.

10. Chasing the Dream - Joe Torre/ Tom Verducci - Bantam Books - 1997

11. Where They Ain't - Burt Solomon - Free Press - 1999

12. The Big Bam - Leigh Montville - Doubleday - 2006

13. Terwilliger Bunts One - Wayne Terwilliger - Insiders Guide - 2006

14. Sporting News - Pat Frizell -1971

Chapter VII - Brooklyn Against the World

1. Baseball Before We Knew It - David Block - Univ of Neb Press - 2005

2. Ibid

3. Ibid

4. Ibid

5. Long Before the Dodgers - James L. Terry - McFarland Publishers - 2002

6. Triumph and Tragedy in Mudville - Stephen jay Gould - Norton - 2003

7. The Rocky Road of Pistol Pete - W.C. Heinz -A Brooklyn Dodgers Reader -Andrew Paul Mele - McFarland Publishers - 2005

8. Chasing the Dream - Joe Torre / Tom Verducci - Bantam Books - 1997

Chapter VIII - The Race That Counts

1. Into My Own - Roger Kahn - St. Thomas Press - 2006

2.   John McGraw - Charles Alexander - Bison Books - 1988

3.   Bums - Peter Golenboch - Putnam - 1984

4.   The Brooklyn Dodgers-The Bums, The Borough, and the Best of Baseball--Carl E. Prince - Oxford Univ Press - 1996

Chapter IX - Warts and All

1. Sporting News - 5/7/71

Chapter XI - Did Anybody Here Play In Brooklyn?

1.   Mario Cuomo: A Biography - Robert S. McElvaine-Scribners-1988

2.   Ibid

3.   Ibid

4.   Ibid

5.   The Greatest Ballpark Ever - Bob McGee - Rutgers Univ. Press - 2005

6.   Eight Men Out - Eliot Asinof - Henry Holt & Co. - 1963

7.   Red Legs and Black Sox - Susan Dellinger - Emmis Books - 2006

8.   The 1937 Newark Bears - Ronald A. Mayer - Rutgers University Press - 1980

9.   Ibid

10.   Superstars and Screwballs - Richard Goldstein - Plume - 1992

11.   Ibid

12.   "Hooks" - Robert Leuci from Reaching For The Stars - Larry Freundlich Ballantine Books - 2003

Chapter XII - The Dream
1. The Impossible Dream Red Sox - Rico Petrocelli / Chaz Scoggins-Sports Publications - 2007

Chapter XIII - Legends in Their Spare Time
1.   Joe, You Coulda Made Us Proud - Joe Pepitone/ Barry Stainbach-Playboy Press- 1975
2.   Ibid
3.   Sporting News - April 1971 - Jerome Holtzman
4.   Chasing the Dream -Joe Torre/ Tom Verducci - Bantom Books -1997

Chapter XIV - Wings of the Eagle
1.   Long Before the Dodgers - James L. Terry - McFarland Publishers - 2002
2.   Brooklyn Daily Eagle - April 10,1913

Chapter XVII-Hey, Blue!
1.   The Umpire Strikes Back - Ron Luciano/ David Fisher - 1982
2.   Jocko - Jocko Conlon / Robert Creamer - J.B. Lippincott -1967

Chapter XVIII - On and On
1. New York Post - April 2, 1986

Index

Printed in the United States
204874BV00003B/31-36/P

9 781434 340405